D0387269

Federal State, National Economy

As the free trade talks continue uncertainly, as Ottawa and Washington toss protective tariffs at each other's goods, and as the provinces continue to disagree among themselves and with the federal government, the search for a national economic policy goes on. A critical element in that search is the balance between regional needs and federal priorities.

Peter Leslie's interpretive essay provides a context in which to view the political and economic forces that make up that delicate balance, including those highlighted in the report of the Macdonald Commission. He discusses the nature of Canada's federal system and its relevance to policy, especially in the economic sphere, where differential effects among regions are often difficult to avoid.

Leslie offers a thoughtful appraisal of a historically complex set of relationships and suggests the ways in which it will determine strategy in an area that will continue to occupy political centre-stage in Canada for some time to come.

PETER LESLIE is director of the Institute for Intergovernmental Relations at Queen's University.

PETER M. LESLIE

Federal state, national economy

UNIVERSITY LIBRARY

UNIVERSITY OF TORONTO PRESS

Toronto Buffalo London

© University of Toronto Press 1987
Toronto Buffalo London
Printed in Canada

ISBN 0-8020-5677-6 (cloth)
ISBN 0-8020-6611-9 (paper)

Canadian Cataloguing in Publication Data

Leslie, Peter M.
Federal state, national economy

Includes index.
ISBN 0-8020-5677-6 (bound). – ISBN 0-8020-6611-9 (pbk.)

1. Federal government – Canada. 2. Political planning – Canada.
3. Canada – Economic policy. I. Title.

JL27.L48 1987   320.971   C87-093313-2

UNIVERSITY LIBRARY
181327 Lethbridge, Alberta

This book has been published with the help of a grant from the
Social Science Federation of Canada, using funds provided by
the Social Sciences and Humanities Research Council of Canada.

To my dear friends J.M. and M.M.

Contents

Preface

Federalism appears to have far greater significance in Canada than it does in other federal countries such as the United States, Australia, or West Germany. To an outsider, at least, federalism in those countries appears to be just one feature among many that characterize the system of governance. This makes it a concern of political scientists, a matter inviting study and critical inquiry, about on a par with topics such as the structure of formal-legal institutions (e.g. whether the regime is presidential or parliamentary), the characteristics of political parties and the party system, or processes of political socialization (induction into political roles such as voter, judge, or bureaucrat). These are all subjects deserving investigation because they affect society's capacity to organize itself to achieve common goals, the sorts of claims that the individual can successfully make against the collectivity or that the collectivity routinely lays upon the individual, the extent of privilege, who enjoys privilege, and the effectiveness of devices to reinforce or diminish it.

Federalism, where it exists, is a significant feature of a society's political arrangements and as such warrants the attention of those who concern themselves with public affairs and the welfare of the citizen. Indeed, it has frequently engaged the interest of Canadian political scientists; but it has also, for a rather obvious reason, become an object of widespread political controversy. In Canada, the most fundamental political relationships, defining the character of Canadian society, are bound up in the structure of the federal system. It shapes them, and they shape it.

Among the relationships in question three are especially important in this context: relations between cultural communities (anglophone majority and francophone minority, or francophone majority in Quebec and anglophone majority in Canada as a whole), among the regions, and between Canada and the United States. (Mention of the last of these may occasion surprise, in the context of a discussion of federalism; but the policy roles falling to the federal government and the provinces respectively are a major determinant of Canada's economic ties with its southern neighbour and can certainly also affect the extent of Canada's cultural independence.) The importance of these relationships to Canadians, and the threat to the very existence of Canada posed by attempts to redefine or reshape them, placed the issue of constitutional reform high on the political agenda for several years, especially from 1976 to 1982. Priorities obviously varied from time to time, from one part of the country to another, and from group to group. Sometimes the focus was on Quebec and its place in Canada as a whole, and sometimes on economic ties between central Canada and the regions dissatisfied with – and trying to escape – traditional hinterland status. These two major issues were, in my opinion, more closely linked than most people appear to have recognized. Neither has been fully resolved, although the salience of the constitutional reform issue has now clearly receded. The dominant issue now – though I think it also is inseparable in practice from the other two – is Canada's economic, political, and cultural relationship to the United States. This is no less a constitutional issue than the others, if for no other reason than that Canada's capacity to implement and therefore to negotiate a bilateral trade agreement depends upon the powers of the federal government and the provinces respectively, and upon the policy roles to which they aspire. Indeed, even if Canada's ability to enter into a trade agreement were not itself a constitutional issue, the constitutional implications of doing so are vast.

These substantive issues are closely tied to the structural and procedural ones that have been prominent in Canadian constitutional debate. Federalism affects policy decisions and policy outcomes. To the extent that it does so, it affects also the capacity of certain interests or groups to prevail over others. How significant or pervasive are these effects? How have they been perceived by various segments of the Canadian population in recent years? To what grievances and demands have they given rise? When policy is discriminatory or appears to be so, to what extent does it make sense to blame the decision-makers – and to what extent should the institutions and processes through which decisions are made come under review?

These are the questions that prompted me to write this book. I have not found it possible to deal comprehensively with all of them; but I have focused on policies for economic development and the extent to which decisions on these matters have been and will continue to be conditioned by federalism. This is an area where it has proved difficult to devise policies without regionally discriminatory effect, calling into question not only the capacity of the federal government to devise and implement overall development strategy but also the desirability of its attempting to do so.

The matter of industrial policy was squarely addressed by the Macdonald Commission (the Royal Commission on the Economic Union and Development Prospects for Canada), which delivered its report in September 1985, after the first draft of this book had been completed. Its comments on this complex issue spurred me to rewrite the final chapter and to turn the book, contrary to my original intentions, into a work of advocacy. It retains its original character as an interpretive essay on the Canadian federal system and that system's bearing on the orientation or main features of public policy, particularly in the economic sphere; but it concludes by endorsing a far more active role for the federal government in shaping economic development than the Macdonald Commission was prepared to countenance.

Chapter 1 sets the context for the argument presented in the rest of the book. It interprets the constitutional preferences of the provinces other than Quebec as a reflection of their economic interests. The chapter identifies alternative orientations of federal economic policy, or two economic development strategies which may be pursued within a 'third national policy' and notes some regional implications of the choices now facing federal policy-makers. It suggests that those provinces that rely heavily on resource production and seek economic diversification around their resource base began to get interested in constitutional issues because they felt threatened by federal economic policies during the 1970s. This attitude largely determined their position on the constitutional initiatives of the federal government in 1980-81 and resulted in the formation of a provincialist coalition that included Quebec. But the coalition was dissolved, isolating Quebec, when the federal government, in November 1981, made important concessions giving the provinces assurance that their economic powers could not be infringed upon without their consent.

Chapter 2 expounds in a more systematic and abstract way a point already illustrated in chapter 1: that constitutional issues may have major implications for the ability of governments to achieve certain policy objectives and that the kinds of interest implicated in constitutional questions are correspondingly varied and extensive. It is noted that much public discussion and some of the scholarly literature on the constitution tended to focus on somewhat trivial issues, or on important but still relatively narrow ones, apparently failing to perceive what ultimately may be at stake in the way that a political community structures its collective decision-making processes. To elucidate the matter, I construct a six-point 'impact scale,' identifying the types of issue and, beyond them, the range of political interests that in principle are bound up in debates over a constitution.

Chapter 3 continues, still in a fairly abstract vein, the discussion of the policy relevance of a federal constitution; but it does so from a different angle. Rather than trying to identify the interests at stake, as in chapter 2, this chapter surveys various explanations of policy and tries to see how federalism fits in with them. Some writers have urged that federalism imparts a conservative bias to government, or has the effect of expanding the scope of government activity, or correlates in some other way with certain characteristics of public policy. My own conclusion is that such generalizations are very shaky. It is wiser, I argue, not to focus on 'federalism' as one factor among several that influence policy (as if each had some identifiable weight as an explanatory variable). Rather, I argue that one should attempt to assess the impact of federalism through, or in combination with, other factors influencing policy in federal and non-federal states alike. This approach takes account, as one logically must, of the uniqueness of each federal country and of the particular historical context in which it is being examined.

Chapter 4 returns to a more concrete style of inquiry. It is the first of three chapters dealing with the structure of the federal system in Canada and the changing relationship between orders of government as they work with, and against, each other to implement policy in areas of shared responsibility. Chapter 4 distinguishes the concept of jurisdiction from that of responsibility and argues that a constitution cannot usefully allocate powers according to the categories normally employed in thinking about policy responsibilities. If it did so, either the courts would have to accept an overtly political role in interpreting the constitution, or they would have to disqualify themselves as constitutional arbiters (this too would be a political decision). Do Canadians wish to rely upon a written constitution, judicially enforced, to protect the autonomy of the provinces? Then it will be necessary to accept the conferral of governmental powers largely in terms of policy instruments, acknowledging that they may be used for diverse purposes and that they sometimes will be employed at cross-purposes by the two orders of government.

Chapter 5 distinguishes various types of interaction between orders of government when both assume policy responsibilities in the same field. Special attention is paid to what happens when policy goals are incompatible: interaction may be characterized by aggressive unilateralism, resulting in continuing conflict, or the reaching of a modus vivendi that expresses existing power relations between orders of government. Changes in the structure of central institutions might reduce governments' capacity for aggressive unilateralism or might reduce their inclination to resort to it. The 'federalization' of central political institutions would alter power relationships between orders of government, either in a centralizing or a decentralizing direction. This in turn would alter the relative political strength of some of the major political interests in Canada, especially regional ones.

Chapter 6 discusses the phenomenon of (de)centralization and its implications for the capacity of governments at both levels to realize their policy goals. Opinions differ, apparently genuinely, about whether the trend in Canada has recently been centralizing or decentralizing. The divergence of opinion is understandable when one realizes that different criteria are being used. Public finance and other indicators suggest a considerable expansion of the role of the provinces over the past quarter-century. However, use of the federal spending power and assertion of federal jurisdiction in certain regulatory areas have limited the provinces' capacity to exercise their powers as they see fit. An examination of the western premiers' complaints (1979) about federal intrusions into areas of provincial policy responsibility shows that the complaints were as much about the way in which federal powers have been exercised as about the range of matters with which federal policy dealt. This suggests that squabbles about '(de)central-ization' are really a sign that both orders of government are worried about their own capacity to deal effectively with what appear, in the present context, to be the most pressing public issues. Behind a terminological or conceptual dispute lie a number of substantive policy questions and the twin concerns that in a decentralized state the residents of the wealthier regions may enjoy the benefits of political union without sharing fully in its costs, and that in a centralized state regional interests may have slight protection against national majorities which may overrule ('dominate,' 'exploit') them.

Chapter 7 traces out an argument that applies to federal states in general, though it is supported with examples drawn from Canadian experience. The concept of 'regional' interests is subjected to scrutiny, and it is shown that scarcely ever do issues engage a purely regional interest. This undoubtedly weakens the moral force of the allegations, made (at least in Canada) with considerable frequency, that some regions are treated unfairly relative to others. The main purpose of this chapter, however, is not to facilitate ethical judgments about the character of a federal system in which some regions enjoy an allegedly privileged position. Rather, the intent is to scrutinize and question a major proposition in federal theory, a proposition that has figured largely in Canadian political debate. Federal theory tends to associate decentralization with diminished levels of conflict within the political system, especially diminished interregional conflict. The validity of propositions of this sort is investigated, drawing on a distinction made by Jack Mintz and Richard Simeon between 'conflict of taste' and 'conflict of claim,' as well as on the distinction between 'regional' and 'non-regional' issues. The conclusion, following from a complex argument (which takes account of the fact that political leadership may considerably affect how people perceive or define the issues), is that in some circumstances centralization, rather than decentraliza-tion, may reduce interregional conflict. But this will depend upon the policies followed – for example, the economic strategy embodied in a third national policy for Canada – and upon the ultimate compatibility of regionally defined and/or regionally concentrated interests making up the political community.

Chapter 8 explores the economic rationale for integration, political and economic, and shows that the case for integration cannot be made abstractly or a priori but depends upon historical circumstances. The rationale for creating a central government with extensive economic powers rests upon presumed or hoped-for advantages flowing from state intervention in the economy. With these two facts in mind, the chapter reviews and comments on various assessments of the National Policy put into place by Sir John A. Macdonald, which, implicitly, provided the economic rationale for Confederation. It identifies various reasons for thinking that state interventionism may, depending on the circumstances, contribute to economic welfare. The question whether those circumstances obtain now, in the late twentieth century, is left open.

This possibility richly deserves investigation, for it is highly pertinent to an evaluation of the merits (and of course the disadvantages) of protectionism. Unfortunately, no one that I know of has rigorously pursued the matter; the contemporary critics of protectionism, including (as noted in chapter 9) the Macdonald Commission, seem to have contented themselves with the assertion that the long-term effects of liberalizing trade are not necessarily employment-reducing. They have not followed up Dales' argument about the employment effects of the tariff, examining it in the context of the late twentieth century; and their rejection of the labour movement's fears about a net loss of jobs from free trade thus lacks persuasiveness.

Finally, Chapter 9 identifies three major options for economic policy or for the policy roles to be assumed by the federal and the provincial governments respectively: liberal-continentalist, interventionist-provincialist, and interventionist-nationalist. The chapter explores the political and constitutional preconditions for each of these options and also tries to identify, in each case, their political and constitutional consequences. This is done in large measure by referring to their anticipated economic consequences; in this way the chapter extends and builds upon the argument presented in chapter 8. The analysis and recommendations of the Macdonald Commission are a foil to the argument presented in this chapter, which carries on a running dialogue with its report and challenges some of its most fundamental presuppositions.

Kingston, August 1986

Acknowledgments

Parts of this book have their origin in conference papers presented over a span of several years. Many intellectual debts have been incurred in the process of restructuring and adapting these papers, both to weed out error and to fit the fragments into what I hope is an integrated argument. It would be impossible to trace and acknowledge all these debts, but I should like in particular to express my gratitude to Keith Banting, Ed Black, André Blais, Alan Cairns, Roger Gibbins, David Hawkes, Michael Jenkin, Réjean Landry, Jim Mallory, Jack Mintz, Richard Simeon, and Ian Stewart, as well as to anonymous reviewers of an earlier version of the manuscript.

I wish also to thank Patti Candido for word-processing – no simple job, as it involved putting up with my endless fiddling with the manuscript. In this, as in so many other ways, she has been a godsend.

Rik Davidson, Social Sciences Editor at the University of Toronto Press, offered me valuable advice and gave me encouragement at a time it was badly needed. John Parry was a most skilful and helpful copy-editor. I am glad to acknowledge their vital contribution.

Chapter 3 is based on a chapter I contributed to *Introduction à l'analyse des politiques*, edited by Réjean Landry and published in 1980 by les Presses de l'université Laval, which I should like to thank for its permission to reprint parts of that article.

Finally – and in reserving this remark to the end I hope to give it special emphasis – I gratefully acknowledge two sources of financial support. This volume was originally planned and partly written as a contribution to a research project of the Institute of Intergovernmental Relations, entitled Queen's Studies on the Future of the Canadian Communities, which was funded by the Donner Canadian Foundation. This book outgrew my earlier intention, and much of it is the fruit of my labours when I was supported by a research grant and leave fellowship from the Social Sciences and Humanities Research Council of Canada. Without the financial assistance of the Donner Canadian Foundation and SSHRCC this book would not have been written.

Federal state, national economy

1

Provincial alliances
and a third national policy

The interplay of economic policy and the politics of constitutional change has been prominent throughout Canadian history, but never more so than in the 1970s and the first half of the 1980s. During the 1970s what may be called 'a third national policy'[1] began to take shape, successor to the national policy of the late nineteenth century and to the 'new national policy' initiated during the inter-war years. The steps toward a third national policy were tentative; one version of it, responding primarily to the needs of central Canada, was at best a patchwork of measures haltingly and inconsistently applied, while a version aiming to underline the complementarity of the regions, although more explicitly formulated, was never translated into action. Both were later shelved or abandoned; by 1983 or certainly by 1984 the thrust of policy had become continentalist. In one respect, however, the third national policy (in either version) and the continentalism of the mid-1980s were alike. In all cases the objectives aimed for and the strategies employed required support from provincial governments, or implied the necessity of curbing provincial powers over the economy, or both. In other words, economic policy either would bring about de facto redefinition of the respective roles of the federal and provincial governments or would demand some measure of formal constitutional change as a prerequisite for its implementation. As policies shifted, alliances among the provincial governments − formed to support or challenge federal constitutional initiatives − were created, dissolved, and formed anew.

The impetus for formal constitutional change did not originally come, of course, from anybody's desire to chart a new course for economic policy. Indeed among journalists and 'the public' it was until recently a commonly voiced complaint that political leaders (especially former prime minister Pierre Trudeau) were concerned too much with the constitution and not enough with the health of the economy. It has been rightly perceived that the salience of constitutional issues stemmed from the growth of a Quebec-centred nationalism and, after November 1976, from the election of the Parti québécois. What has been less well understood is the extent to which the aspirations that gave rise to the electoral successes of the PQ were economic as well as cultural, and the extent to which the formation and eventual disruption of provincial alliances on the constitutional issue stemmed from economic considerations.

The present strength of continentalism may be lasting or short-lived; that one cannot know. Observe, however: the political-economic considerations that induced the Trudeau government to piece together elements of a third national policy have not disappeared. The options now before the country are the same as those that faced it prior to the federal election of September 1984. The Liberals were, as we shall see, anything but single-minded in their selection among them, and there is no reason to suppose that the Conservatives will opt for consistency and clarity – along the lines, say, proposed by the Macdonald Commission[2] – where their predecessors showed ambivalence. What can be said with some confidence is that economic policy and constitutional affairs will continue to impinge upon one another, that provincial aspirations and alliances among the provinces in relation to them will be an important factor in determining outcomes, and that this complex situation may usefully be analysed in relation to two versions of a national policy for Canada and a policy of minimum interference in the workings of the market economy, implying continentalism.

THE FIRST AND SECOND NATIONAL POLICIES

Canadians like to think of their country as one created by an act of will, 'in defiance of geography,' as W.A. Mackintosh once wrote.[3] Thus, an enduring theme of our history is the continentalist embrace and the resistance to it offered by nation-building policies such as those implemented by the Macdonald and Laurier governments. The original post-1867 set of national policies consisted of recruitment of immigrants, imposition of a protective tariff (the 'National Policy' of 1879), and an aggressive program of railway-building. Through these policies Canada had, by the First World War, successfully affirmed its claim to the western plains north of the 49th parallel, established an east-west pattern of communications, and created a rudimentary manufacturing industry in Ontario and Quebec. During the war, the financial community was to come of age, freeing itself from the tutelage of the London money market. Thus, by the 1920s the first national policy (as it is sometimes called, implying a coherence that its formulators perhaps did not perceive) had achieved its purposes. In 1930 the era of the first national policy was symbolically closed when ownership of 'ungranted or waste lands' in Manitoba, Saskatchewan, and Alberta – originally retained by the federal government to be administered 'for the purposes of the Dominion' – was transferred to the respective provincial governments.

After the First World War the goal of building a new nation no longer preoccupied Canada's governing elites: the external challenge to national survival now seemed far less pressing than internal ones. The change in policy orientation can easily be traced to the conscription crisis of 1917 and to the emergence of the Progressive movement as a major political force, especially in the prairie west. (In 1919 the Progressives – expressing the grievances of farm and labour groups – won power in Ontario; in 1921 they captured 65 seats in Parliament, outdistancing the Conservatives.) Since the First World War the concept of national unity, implying the need to conciliate regional and ethnic grievances, has occupied a far more prominent place in the consciousness of Canadians than has the goal of national development.

The term *national policy*, however, retained its earlier attraction. Historically minded scholars discovered 'a new national policy' in the federal government's accommodating response to the discontents voiced by the Progressives during the 1920s and later in its endorsement of the principles of the welfare state. Here the salient events are R.B. Bennett's largely abortive 'new deal' of 1934-35 and the Liberals' more enduring project of post–Second World War reconstruction. Equity, not economic nationalism, was the underlying theme of these policy initiatives. 'No people can become a nation,' wrote B.S. Kierstead in 1943, neatly expressing the conflict-avoidance theory of unity, 'if divided in groups conflicting with and exploiting one another in the economic field.'[4] This theory provided an implicit rationale for the new national policy. According to V.C. Fowke, the policy had several elements: the federal government's efforts after 1930 to enlarge its responsibility in the field of social welfare, an agriculture policy concerned less with development than with price supports and crop failure legislation, and a full-employment policy based on Keynesian finance.[5] These initiatives, which formed what we shall call the second national policy, were a response to the instability and inequities inherent in the operation of a market economy, particularly one that was heavily dependent upon the export of staple products.

The constitutional implications of the second national policy, like the first, were strongly centralist at its inception; and the policy remained a centralizing one as long as the fear of post-war depression persisted. For a decade or more after the end of the Second World War federal power continued to grow. The larger and wealthier provinces showed some resistance to the centralizing trend, but only Quebec appeared fundamentally opposed. Its opposition did not count for a great deal, however, perhaps because the federal Liberals (the governing party through most of this period) had a strong electoral base in Quebec and could claim the support of the populace if not the concurrence of the Union nationale government. Moreover, the profoundly conservative character of the Union nationale, and its rural electoral base, gave credence to the argument that Quebec was living in the past. It was easy to suppose that the Quebec government's archaic view of social relations would soon dissolve under the forces of modernization. It was thought that when this happened Quebec, like the other provinces, would recognize the inevitability of responding to national problems on a national scale – that is, under federal leadership.

With the advent of Quebec's Quiet Revolution, ensuing upon the death of Premier Duplessis in 1959, it became clear that this supposition was badly mistaken. A dynamic, reformist government insisted upon augmenting its fiscal resources and upon fully exercising its constitutional powers. Quebec began to demand, from the mid-1960s onward, a series of constitutional changes not only to protect but also to extend its powers as the national government of a distinct Quebec people; the suggestion arose that the whole constitutional structure be recast to accommodate the existence of 'two nations' in Canada.

The demands of the Québécois for equality – for overcoming their minority status within Confederation – were advanced simultaneously on two fronts: in federal-provincial relations, where the object was aggrandizement of provincial power, and in the federal arena itself, where the object was to gain equal influence in all areas of national decision-making both at the political level and within the bureaucracy. In Ottawa the government of Lester Pearson, prime minister from 1963 to 1968, formulated a double response to the emergence of the new mood in Quebec. One element was to implement a policy of official bilingualism; the other was to cede greater powers and responsibilities to Quebec. However, the possibility that the response might extend to offering constitutional recognition of a 'special status' for that province, or might officially endorse the 'two nations' thesis, was closed off when Pierre Elliot Trudeau succeeded Pearson as prime minister in 1968. As early as 1966 the federal government had begun to resist pressures to transfer additional fiscal resources to the provinces, and under Trudeau it steadfastly refused to give Quebec wider constitutional powers than the other provinces possessed. Thus by the late 1960s accommodation of diversity, a policy equated with making concessions to provincial autonomy, no longer appeared to federal decision-makers the panacea for Canada's perennial crisis of national unity. A new affirmation of federal power, particularly in the economic sphere, was to occur.

By the end of the 1960s the era of the second national policy had apparently ended or was at least drawing to a close. With passage of the Medical Care Act (1966) the last major building block of the welfare state was cemented into place. The 1970s were to reveal greater concern with restraining the costs of social programs than with establishing new ones. Promoting full employment and controlling inflation remained major goals; but as governments' inability to meet this dual objective became ever more starkly revealed, emphasis shifted from Keynesian policies to more direct forms of economic intervention aimed at promoting structural changes in the economy.

It had become evident during the years that John Diefenbaker was prime minister (1957-63) that the federal government was beginning to reassume leadership in economic development, as opposed to mere economic management, or stabilization. Not much came of Diefenbaker's 'northern vision,' an electoral slogan that implied an activist role for Ottawa in resource exploitation. However, the Conservatives did begin to show much greater awareness of the regional incidence of federal policies and also became more heavily involved in industrial development through export promotion. After about 1960 the federal government became increasingly inclined to implement policies aimed at expanding specific sectors and to work toward economic transformation of declining regions. Under Pearson and Trudeau – though in fits and starts, beginning with Walter Gordon's ill-fated 1963 budget – the Liberals offered some resistance to American economic penetration. They made an abortive attempt to diversify foreign trade, supported (slightly) by technological development, and implemented a succession of nationalistic policies in the oil and gas sector. Initiatives in these areas formed the kernel of a third national policy.

A THIRD NATIONAL POLICY

D.V. Smiley, in a paper delivered in 1974,[6] already thought it possible 'to delineate broadly an emergent national policy.' The policy, he said, aimed 'for a Canadian economy with a highly developed capacity for indigenous [technological] innovation.' Its 'major and interdependent prescriptions' were, in Smiley's words:

(1) There should be a major cooperative effort involving industry, the universities, and government in applying organized intelligence to industry and thus to enhance the performance and innovative capacity of the national economy.

(2) First priority is to be given to the rationalization of the secondary manufacturing sector to increase the relative importance of this sector in the economy and to make it internationally competitive.

(3) To the extent that the national economy continues to rely on the export of natural resources, these resources should be exported in a state more nearly finished than is now the case.

(4) There should be an ongoing redefinition of certain activities and industries (e.g. aerospace and computers) which are in the forefront of technological advance as key sectors to be reserved for Canadian ownership and control.

(5) Better industrial performance is to be encouraged by the lowering of tariffs through bilateral agreement with the United States or multilaterally.

(6) There should be positive attempts to mobilize Canadian savings for investment in Canada to decrease the existing levels of foreign direct investment.[7]

Smiley noted that this emergent national policy was, like the original one, 'directed toward deliberate action by the federal government to structure the national economy.'[8] We may note that it differed in this respect from the second national policy, which reflected preoccupation with threats to national unity, and the watchword of which was conflict-avoidance. The more highly interventionist role of the federal government, visible in many discrete decisions apparently intended to promote national development, permits one to postulate that a third national policy was beginning to take shape during the 1970s. National development, though it may incidentally involve allaying the discontents of disaffected regions, classes, or ethnic groups, is more emphatically concerned with creating or restructuring an integrated national economy through the agency of a powerful state apparatus. In aiming for this goal the federal government showed itself at times ready and even eager to challenge the power of provincial governments and to provoke considerable interregional conflict.

Development – at least in its economic aspect – was equated with achieving a more 'mature' industrial structure, that is, expanding the production of finished goods, especially high-technology products. It was hoped (and by many still is) that by placing greater reliance on indigenous technology, entrepreneurial talent, and venture capital, the manufacturing sector would be better equipped than in the past both to withstand foreign competition in the domestic market and to expand the export of high-value, highly processed goods. Success in this area would reverse the trend to 'deindustrialization' (as evidenced, at least in the minds of some observers, in the growing trade deficit in manufactures), reduce the extent to which resources are exported in raw or semi-processed form, expand job opportunities in high-wage industries, and lessen the degree of economic vulnerability inherent in heavy reliance upon staples production.

These objectives underlay the prescriptions of the Gray Report (*Foreign Direct Investment in Canada*, 1972), the report of the Senate Special Committee on Science Policy (1972), and various reports of the Science Council of Canada – all cited by Smiley as authoritative statements of the rationale behind the new policy.[9] Such goals are not inherently conflict-generating, but they become so to the extent that the resources sector is made subservient to manufacturing or domestic firms are given advantages over foreign-owned or foreign-controlled ones. And these were, precisely, the hallmarks of the emergent third national policy.

A number of federal policy initiatives during the 1970s greatly reinforced the impression already widespread (especially in the west) that federal economic policy has generally been and is likely to remain at the service of the manufacturing industries located, primarily, in Ontario. (Quebec also has a sizeable manufacturing sector, including some technologically advanced and capital-intensive industries; but many of its older manufacturing industries are in decline.) Several features of federal policy lent credence to charges that it was regionally discriminatory.

1. Whereas mining and the oil and gas industries were targeted for heavy tax increases, notably in the 1974 budget, manufacturing was given advantageous tax treatment and had access to various forms of investment subsidy; the federal

government involved itself directly in encouraging the expansion and development of secondary industry, as well as protecting feeble or declining sectors from the discipline of the market. Necessarily, the costs of such apparent coddling of secondary manufacturing would be borne, through taxes, by other sectors of the economy, especially resource industries. Thus the hinterland regions were seen to underwrite some of the costs of central Canadian industry. Government subsidies awarded in support of manufacturing were of course additional to the indirect, consumer-paid subsidy created by the tariff and by quantitative trade restrictions.

2. The Foreign Investment Review Agency, created in 1974 as a device for selectively approving mergers and takeovers involving foreign-owned firms, was clearly directed to supporting domestic entrepreneurs. Its restrictive impact on foreign investment cost jobs and was evidently directed to strengthening the grip of Canadian capital, mainly based in Toronto, over the economy of the hinterland regions.

3. Since the attempt to strengthen the competitive position of Canadian manufacturing relative to its foreign rivals would require industrial concentration both structurally (e.g. through mergers) and territorially, an implication of federal development strategy would be continued concentration of population in central Canada.

4. Subordination of the resource industries to the needs of the manufacturing sector, and more generally to the interests of central Canada, was clearly visible after 1973 in federal policies relating to the pricing, transportation, and export of oil and gas. Their combined effect was to give Canadian industrial and other consumers secure access to these resources at prices considerably below world levels. The obvious explanation was that more votes were to be garnered from consuming regions than from producing ones. Some Canadian businessmen reportedly feared, in the early 1980s, that other resource industries might be next in line for restrictive policies.

5. In order to implement its preferred development strategy, the federal government sought (in the words of a federal position paper of July 1980) to 'strengthen the Canadian economic union in the constitution.' Realization of this goal would curb the powers of the provinces in economic affairs, reinforcing the dominance of central Canadian business elites over the whole Canadian economy.

Although some suspicions about the motives behind federal policy, and about the intended course of policy in the future, may have been exaggerated, announcement of the National Energy Program (NEP) in November 1980 seemed to confirm them all. Because of the frontal attack it made on provincial powers over resource development, the NEP stands out as the most dramatic event in the recent history of federal economic policy-making.

The NEP both reaffirmed the existing pricing regime (together with its complementary export controls and taxes, and transportation regulation) and imposed a new set of production taxes which were anathema both to the governments of the producing provinces and to the industry. These taxes, in conjunction with price controls, were widely blamed for sharply curtailing exploration and development in the western provinces and for rendering most tertiary (enhanced) recovery schemes on existing reservoirs unprofitable.[10]

When the NEP was announced, it appeared that it had a major undeclared purpose – to use revenues from Alberta production to subsidize exploration and development in the 'Canada Lands' (parts of Canada not within the boundaries of any province), thus effectively shifting the locus of industry activity to remote sites in the Arctic and off the eastern seaboard. Even where operations in the western provinces remained commercially viable, reduced cash flow from current operations would force the industry to raise investment funds on the regular capital markets – not an unacknowledged consequence of, but a declared purpose of the NEP – thus binding the industry to the central Canadian financial community[11] and ensuring its dependence on federal government subsidies (Petroleum Incentive Payments, or PIPs). On top of this, the crown oil company, Petro-Canada, would automatically acquire 25 per cent interest in all Canada Lands discoveries, thus turning all frontier activities into joint ventures with government. This series of measures gave Ottawa extensive control over the whole industry. The measures were designed to ensure that the industry's operations were consistent with 'Canadian' needs – that is, presumably, with the requirements of individual and industrial consumers, the latter being mostly located in southern Ontario and (to some extent) in southern Quebec.

In short, the NEP was, to its opponents, clear confirmation of an already deep-seated suspicion, that the federal government's economic development strategy was one of reindustrialization at the expense (when circumstances required) of the resource industries. It was a central Canadian strategy. The federal government was to be the active ally and partner of manufacturing industry, and federal policies were to confirm and reinforce metropolitan dominance over the hinterland.

PROVINCIAL ALLIANCES

The NEP was sprung upon the industry and the producing provinces in November 1980. The following April eight provinces – all but Ontario and New Brunswick – cemented an alliance to fight the federal government's constitutional amendment package, then blocked in the Commons by dogged opposition from the Conservatives. The two events were not unrelated, for interwoven with the constitutional dispute were economic issues so fundamental that the very idea of Canada – of the existence of a national political community containing within it a number of regional or provincial ones – was called into question. It is no exaggeration to say that the way the provinces lined up on the constitutional question reflected changing perceptions of emerging economic policies and their prospective impact on the regions.

For several years the barometer of changes at the political level had been the relationship between the 'souverainiste' government of Quebec and each of the other provinces. Across Canada the initial reaction to the electoral victory of the Parti québécois in 1976 was one of shock, fear, and anger. Most Canadians had discounted the possibility that Quebecers would vote into office a party committed to secession; and it is said that some premiers were unprepared for the discovery, when they met the new premier, that he and his government were evidently still committed to the electoral program which was then the raison d'être of the party. Be that as it may, René Lévesque's assurances that he would play by the rules of the Confederation game until, by referendum, the population of Quebec released him from the necessity of doing so permitted establishment of quasi-normal relations between Quebec and the other provinces over the five years of the PQ's first mandate. Tension between Quebec and some of the other provinces ran high during the referendum campaign of winter-spring 1980, as several premiers undertook speaking tours in Quebec to urge the voters to reject sovereignty-association. When the other provinces declared that they were not interested in negotiating an economic association with a Quebec that was about to pull out of Confederation, Lévesque and his colleagues accused them of blackmail and insisted that they were bluffing. In the main, however, relations between Quebec and the other provinces were diplomatically correct, if marked by mistrust and ill-concealed antagonism. It is therefore surprising that most provincial government spokesmen reacted to the re-election of the PQ in 1981 with perfect composure. None was hostile; some were openly welcoming. A large part of the explanation for the change in attitude since 1976 was undoubtedly the defeat of the PQ's project for sovereignty-association in the May 1980 referendum and the subsequent promise not to hold another referendum during the party's second mandate, if it were re-elected. It now seemed a lot safer, and more realistic, to treat the PQ as just another provincial government. However, in my opinion, the contrast between 1976 and 1981 indicates more than a vast change of attitude toward the PQ and the threat it posed to Canada's existence. It was symptomatic also of a significant evolution of opinion toward constitutional questions generally.

Among provincial politicians, constitutional issues unrelated to 'the Quebec problem' unquestionably acquired greater immediacy in the late 1970s than was previously the case. Saskatchewan's Premier Ross Thatcher, ousted from office in 1971, used to say that if his province had 100 priorities, constitutional change would be number 101. However, during the 1970s the stakes rose in federal-provincial policy disputes. They quickly spilled over into the constitutional arena. This was most evident in the case of the resource-rich provinces of the west, Saskatchewan among them. But the key case was Alberta.

Following the election of Peter Lougheed as premier in 1971, Alberta adopted an economic development strategy that aimed to promote industrialization based on extraction of hydrocarbon fuels (coal as well as gas and oil).[12] The province sought to use its market power over these scarce resources as an ace card in attracting 'downstream' industries like petrochemicals. Public revenues deriving from resource exploitation were also vital to Alberta's plans for industrialization, since they enable the province to offer manufacturing industry financial inducements to locate there.

The position of Alberta was enormously strengthened in 1973, when the Organization of Petroleum Exporting Countries (OPEC) demonstrated its capacity (which now is known to have been temporary) to manipulate the world price of oil. Not only were Alberta wells almost the sole domestic source of supply when oil suddenly became a scarce commodity on world markets, but the phenomenal increase in provincial revenues (a consequence of rising prices) gave Alberta financial resources far beyond its immediate needs. These factors equipped the province, for the first time, with an effective means of countering the central Canadian strategy of economic development which had been initiated with the first national policy. Provincial ownership of public lands, transferred to the prairie provinces in 1930, was the trump card that Premier Lougheed hoped would enable Alberta – if its hand was played astutely – to challenge the hinterland status hitherto its lot.

The federal government, however, drew upon its own constitutional powers (mainly the power to regulate interprovincial and international trade and commerce) to challenge Alberta's control over resource development and to claim a larger share of the revenues from their exploitation. The National Energy Program was merely the capstone to a series of earlier federal policy offensives on non-renewable resources. The federal initiatives involved, as already noted, control of prices in the domestic market and imposition of export levies; another key measure, introduced in 1974, was refusal to allow corporations to deduct royalty payments to provincial governments from their taxable incomes ('the taxation of royalties,' as opponents of the policy put it). Thus the federal government grabbed more of the resource rents – on mineral ores as well as on oil and gas – for its treasury.

Federal policies relating to natural resource exploitation contributed mightily to the conviction that Ottawa was pursuing an aggressively centralist economic development strategy. They also helped stimulate the formation of a provincialist coalition dedicated to fighting the strategy. For Alberta was not alone in its hostility to federal resources policies. Alberta's position in the Canadian economy, while unique in some respects, typified the situation of several other provinces, indeed, all those provinces that relied heavily – as indeed they still do – on the control of natural resources to stimulate their economic development. Thus, Saskatchewan looked to development of its relatively low-grade reservoirs of oil, its potash (rich enough, it has been estimated, to supply world needs for over a thousand years), and its uranium. British Columbia's economy, as throughout its history, reflected development of its forests, mines, and rivers and the adjacent sea. British Columbia, like Alberta, stood to reap large gains from development of gas resources; its potential here was also threatened by the federal initiatives of 1974 to 1980. Manitoba, though less richly endowed than its neighbours to the west, was also conscious that the key to its future economic development lay in exploitation of natural resources (hydroelectricity and mines). Manitoba's economy could no longer – as in pioneer days – be based on the strategic position of Winnipeg as gateway to the prairie region and commercial centre for marketing of grain. Winnipeg, as the main western node of the Canadian transportation system, had formerly been the prairie outpost of central Canadian industrial and commercial capital; but this role, complementary to its wheat production, could no longer sustain the Manitoba economy.

To the east, Newfoundland was increasingly acquiring many of Alberta's aspirations. These were based partly on the hydrocarbon potential of 'the offshore,' ownership of the resource endowments of which was claimed by both Ottawa and St John's. In addition, however, Newfoundland saw the prospect of wealth, employment, and economic stability deriving from control of the fisheries within the 200-mile economic zone declared by Canada in 1977. As a result of this action it had become possible, for the first time, effectively to prevent overfishing, to rebuild fish stocks, and generally to manage the fishery as a renewable resource. Policy responsibility in this area was being claimed by the federal government, whose constitutional powers in the field were (and are) solidly entrenched – though many of them were being just as determinedly claimed by Newfoundland.

Premier Peckford appeared convinced that with provincial control over licensing of fishermen, Newfoundland could maintain for its own residents priority access to cod stocks over that of neighbouring provinces (mainly Nova Scotia). The province could also, Peckford reasoned, better develop the processing industry – thus providing more employment, and on a more stable basis than hitherto – by insisting that catches be landed in Newfoundland ports. Accordingly, Newfoundland become one of the most outspoken advocates of a transfer of power to the provinces and formed a solid alliance with other provinces, especially Alberta, bent on development of natural resources, both renewable and non-renewable.

Nova Scotia, though at loggerheads with Newfoundland over the fisheries, was also enticed by the prospect of developing oil and gas reserves in the Scotia Banks area. Though it later (1982 and 1986) signed development agreements with Ottawa covering offshore resources (with both parties agreeing to leave the ownership question in abeyance), in the late 1970s and up to the end of 1981, Nova Scotia's position on offshore resources was identical to Newfoundland's.

New Brunswick and Prince Edward Island were in a somewhat ambivalent position, outside the industrial heartland of central Canada but lacking the resource base to provide a powerful engine of economic development. They could not effectively oppose national economic policies rooted in an alliance between the federal government and the most potent segments of Canadian industrial and financial capital. The two provinces reacted to this situation in quite different ways. New Brunswick became the central government's staunchest ally on constitutional and other questions, while Prince Edward Island lined up with the provincialist coalition that began to take shape during the late 1970s.

The provincialist coalition, as I have dubbed it, was dedicated to strengthening provincial constitutional powers against federal encroachment. The coalition was consolidated by the re-election of the federal Liberals in February 1980, replacing the short-lived government of Joe Clark. The coalition consisted of those provinces whose prospects for escaping the economic dominance of Ontario were dependent upon their control of natural resources, renewable and non-renewable. Though Ontario itself was far from deficient in mineral and forest resources, and in hydroelectric power, these were not the most important sectors of its economy. The key to Ontario's prosperity lay in manufacturing (historically oriented toward supplying a protected domestic market) and in Toronto's position as the Canadian metropolis – financial and commercial centre of the country. Toronto had wrested pre-eminence from Montreal during the first half of this century.

The members of the provincialist coalition made common cause in seeking to diminish the importance of Toronto business elites relative to those in other parts of the country. The central Canadian economic development strategy to which the Trudeau government seemed increasingly committed made Ottawa appear the ally and indeed the instrument of industrial Ontario rather than the national government of all Canadians. This viewpoint was the more readily adopted in that it coincided with historically prevalent perceptions of the role of the federal government. The main factor, however, was that Trudeau, when he returned to office after a short hiatus (1979-80), evidently embarked on a program of action to extend federal powers over the economy, especially through vigorous use of the clause on regulation of trade and commerce. His government was also, in the constitutional negotiations of the summer of 1980, overtly committed to strengthening the Canadian economic union by denying certain powers to provincial governments. For example, the proposed Charter of Rights, in a clause that was substantially weakened in the partial accord of November 1981, aimed to prohibit certain forms of provinces' regulation of the labour market within their own respective territories. Other proposed clauses would have guaranteed free interprovincial movement of capital and have eliminated or reduced the capacity of provincial governments to establish non-tariff barriers to trade in goods and services. In these initiatives, federal authorities had the clear support of the Ontario government.

Obviously, the provincialist coalition wanted Quebec in the group. Under the PQ it clearly was. Not only did Premier Lévesque vow to fight the federal constitutional project with every arquebus in his arsenal – this stance one might have expected from the mere fact that the PQ government was committed, whether for cultural or other reasons, to political independence. Equally significant, the PQ government had formulated an economic rationale for independence that emphasized the similarity between Quebec and the traditional hinterland provinces. In fact, the PQ's economic development strategy scarcely differed from those of the other provinces that were trying to disperse industrial development in Canada,[13] escaping the hegemony of Ontario. Although Quebec has a population base and an industrial infrastructure in and around Montreal surpassed only by the Toronto region, and although national policies have generally been thought to advantage the whole industrial corridor between Windsor and Quebec City, many Quebecers (especially in the PQ) began by the 1970s to see their province as part of the hinterland. They complained that the benefits of national policies went mainly to Ontario, while Quebec – like the other provinces on the periphery – had to rely on natural resources as the motor of its development.

In important ways, Quebec's position was thought to be and was analogous to Alberta's. Of course, Quebec has not discovered any petroleum reserves, but the PQ noted with satisfaction that the province's hydroelectricity potential is over 60,000 megawatts[14] (the heat-energy equivalent of about 85 per cent of Alberta's 1981 production of crude oil) -- and that hydro is a non-depleting resource. Quebec therefore set about to force the pace of development in this sector in order to obtain rents from foreign sales, while prices within the province were held down to stimulate industrial investment. Contracts involving sales beyond a certain threshold (five megawatts), it was ruled, would have to be approved by the government in order to ensure that Quebecers obtained maximum benefit in terms of employment and spin-off effects. Exploitation of mineral and forest resources also figured prominently in Quebec's economic development strategy, and here too the province aimed to create, wherever possible, links with manufacturing industry.

Another point of similarity between Quebec and Alberta was that both provinces were (and seem still to be) hinging the modernization of their economies, and their development in every major sector, on an alliance between private capital and the provincial state. Such an alliance is seen as necessary to counterbalance the geographical advantages of southern Ontario and the strength of its economic elite. Policies aiming to do this are frequently expensive, as they involve massive direct or indirect subsidies – hence the importance of maximizing revenues from resource production. But subsidies alone are not enough. Both Quebec and Alberta, and for that matter all provinces seeking to channel and direct their own economic development, require extensive powers over land use and over resource extraction, processing, and sale; they also need limited, but far from negligible, power to influence or control investment and to regulate capital and labour markets.

The position of the Quebec Liberals on these matters had been less clearly provincialist than the PQ's. Any Quebec government, regardless of political hue, is bound to regard the province as 'the primary level of government responsible for the development of their own territories and human resources' (the phrase is taken from the Quebec Liberal party's 1980 Beige Paper of constitutional proposals). However, in 1980-81 the provincial Liberals, under Claude Ryan, were committed to several features of constitutional change that Pierre Trudeau was trying to impose on the provinces. The Beige Paper supported a Charter of Rights that would have limited provincial powers as well as federal ones. It also endorsed entrenchment of constitutional provisions guaranteeing free movement of labour and capital, and it saw the federal government as supplying leadership in devising and implementing a Canadian strategy of economic development. Its view of federal-provincial economic relations was clearly less conflictual than the PQ's – or Alberta's, or Newfoundland's. These provinces may well have thought that Quebec under a Ryan government would be, at best, a shaky member of the provincialist coalition.

Thus, although the PQ was committed to political sovereignty, and in this was opposed by every prominent political leader elsewhere in Canada, there none the less existed a potent rationale for an alliance of convenience between Quebec (as long as it remained under the PQ) and several other provinces. Ontario, which in the late 1960s had been Quebec's best friend among the provinces and an ardent supporter of provincial autonomy (when the most prominent issues were financial, involving extension of the welfare state), had been transformed during the 1970s into Ottawa's most powerful ally, bolstering federal economic power. Against it, toward the end of the decade, formed the provincialist coalition, which included Quebec. This realignment occurred even though Ontario's position had remained consistent over the years. It was still autonomist in matters relating to provision of health, education, and welfare services; and throughout the period since the Second World War it had been a strong supporter of federal power to control economic development. However, the central Canadian economic strategy reaffirmed and extended by Ottawa during the 1970s greatly exacerbated regional conflict; and Ontario's support for this strategy – for example, its insistence on a low price for oil – had become the most visible feature of its relationship to the other provinces and of its policy on intergovernmental relations. As the economic development issue acquired greater salience during the 1970s, the earlier Ontario-Quebec partnership receded into the background.

The provincialist coalition needed to prevent re-emergence of the Ontario-Quebec partnership on a new (or, actually, its historic) economic foundation. Its re-emergence was conceivable under a Ryan government – and this, to my mind, explains the apparent relief of several provincial politicians when the Lévesque government was re-elected in April 1981. By this time, the PQ's teeth seemed to have been drawn by its referendum defeat the previous year. Indeed, during the election campaign the party had pledged itself not to call another referendum on independence during its hoped-for second mandate: thus its constitutional adventurism, if not necessarily a thing of the past, appeared to have been disciplined by the electorate and to be held firmly in check by party strategists. Accordingly, to the members of the provincialist coalition, Quebec under the PQ now must have seemed 'safe' at least temporarily from the PQ's own more impatient 'souverainistes' and from the economic centralism that was a likely consequence of Ryan's classical liberalism.

Quebec's membership in the provincialist coalition was thus confirmed by the re-election of the PQ. Three days later (16 April 1981) Lévesque joined seven other premiers, forming 'the gang of eight,' in drafting a common counter-proposal to the Constitutional Resolution then before Parliament.[15] The federal resolution contained two main elements that the eight premiers regarded as threatening. One was an amending formula permitting the federal government to appeal over the heads of provincial cabinets and legislatures to regional – not provincial – electorates, a feature that might be used to weaken provincial economic powers when a case could be made for national action, say on wage and price controls. The other was a Charter of Rights restricting the powers of provincial legislatures – as also of Parliament – and weakening their capacity to regulate provincial labour markets. (The language provisions of the Charter, though of major importance to Quebec, were not relevant to the other provinces' desire to keep Quebec 'on side' against Ottawa. Other major features of the Resolution – the resources clause introduced on the insistence of the federal NDP, and the equalization clause – were relatively uncontroversial.) In contrast, the eight premiers' 'constitutional accord' made no mention of a Charter of Rights, providing instead for simple patriation and an amending clause that allowed a province to exclude itself from the effect of any amendment derogating from its legislative powers or its proprietary rights (e.g. over natural resources). Under this formula no province had a veto, as any seven provinces comprising half the Canadian population would suffice, but an opting-out province would obtain 'reasonable [financial] compensation' if it provided a service that most provinces had agreed to transfer to federal jurisdiction.

From the spring of 1981 until the night of 5 November, Quebec remained at the forefront of the provincialist coalition. Its eventual exclusion was brought about by two key federal concessions that met the needs of the seven other dissenting provinces, permitting formulation of a deadlock-resolving proposal of which no Quebec delegate was informed until the others were ready to present it. The events producing this outcome were as follows. The court challenge to the original Resolution, launched by the dissenting premiers in December 1980 and supported by the Opposition's delaying tactics in the Commons until Pierre Trudeau promised its referral to the Supreme Court, resulted in a ruling (September 1981) declaring the Resolution legal but also 'unconstitutional in the conventional sense.' The federal government responded by calling a meeting of first ministers for early November, for 'one last try' at reaching agreement. During the course of the four-day meeting, a set of tentative discussions involving federal Minister of Justice Jean Chrétien and several provincial leaders pointed to a possible compromise in which Ottawa would accept the amending formula proposed by the 'gang of eight' in April, except for the financial compensation clause, and the provinces would agree to entrenchment of the Charter with an opting-out provision for some of its key clauses. The double opting-out arrangement removed the threat that a province's powers might in future be clipped, overriding the objections of its government and legislature. Thus fundamental changes in the federal position met the key objectives of all dissenting provinces but Quebec.

With these federal concessions, Quebec became inessential to the provincialist coalition. Its other members, as if relieved at no longer having to rely upon support of a government committed (as they saw it) to secession, cobbled together new proposals calculated to gain also adherence of the federal government and of Ontario and New Brunswick during the night of 5 November. Quebec officials were informed of these events just before proceedings were to start the next day. Thus was the provincialist coalition dissolved, leaving a humiliated René Lévesque to denounce his fellow premiers for their treachery.

A NEW FEDERAL DEVELOPMENT STRATEGY

One of the ironies attending the formation and dissolution of the provincialist coalition is that at the very time the 'gang of eight' was most hotly contesting Trudeau's constitutional initiative, a different economic development strategy was gaining adherents in Ottawa. This strategy did not call for repudiation of any of the features of the emergent national policy as identified by Smiley in 1974; but increased reliance on indigenous technology, entrepreneurship, and capital would have implications for the structure of the economy rather different from those apparently perceived by Smiley or indeed by any other observers prior to the spring of 1981. It became possible to imagine a third national policy that would implement another and in some respects a more traditional economic development strategy.

The new strategy aimed, like the earlier one, to strengthen Canadian manufacturing industry but presumed that the most effective way of doing so was to link manufacturing directly to development of resource industries. The underlying principle was to exploit Canada's comparative advantages. This is consistent with the standard prescription of neoclassical trade theory, which is to encourage development of those industries requiring heavy inputs of the factor of production that is possessed in greatest abundance. In Canada's case the abundant factor is 'land' – the resources of river, ocean, forest, ore-bearing rock, and farmland. Canada, it was argued by the formulators of the new policy, was lucky to have an abundance of natural resources at a time when, world-wide, the advance of technology was reducing employment opportunities in manufacturing; the wise choice for Canada was therefore to make the most of this advantage. By concentrating on further development of the resource sector, Canada would be able also to strengthen its manufacturing industry. Inefficient consumer-oriented industries would have to be converted to service the resource sector (forging 'backward linkages'), and to exploit opportunities for partial processing of resource products (creating new 'forward linkages'). In this way the economy of central Canada, visibly suffering from the declining competitiveness of its manufacturing sector, would be saved by expansion of the peripheral regions – whose markets would, however, continue to lie to a large extent outside the country.

The first sign of this strategy appeared with the publication of the report of the Major Projects Task Force (May 1981). The report, prepared under the direction of Robert Blair, president of Nova Corporation (formerly Alberta Gas Trunk Line), and Shirley Carr, vice-president of the Canadian Labour Congress, was an inventory of 'megaprojects' then on the drawing boards, mostly in the transportation and resource sectors. The significance of the report became evident when the minister of finance published a white paper with the November 1981 budget. The paper, *Economic Development for Canada in the 1980s*, noted that 'the development and exploitation of advanced technology and high productivity goods and services'[16] held growth potential, but it also declared:

The leading opportunity [for economic growth] lies in the development of Canada's rich bounty of natural resources. There is increasing world demand for Canada's major resources – energy, food products such as grain and fish, forest products, and minerals such as coal and potash. The 1980s will see substantial development of energy and energy-based industries such as petrochemicals, and further expansion of agriculture, forest-based industries and mining.

These developments will involve massive investments in productive capability and in the transportation industry's capacity to ship bulk commodities. The recently published report of the Major Projects Task Force, for example, identifies $440 billion of potential projects, predominantly in the energy and resource sectors, which are under consideration for investment between now and the end of the century. At the same time, rapid population growth in the world is placing new demands on the supply of food, and in response to rising world prices further expansion and modernization of the agricultural and food sectors throughout Canada is in prospect.

Linked to this growth dynamic, a second area in which Canada is presented with exceptional economic development opportunities is manufacturing activity, both to supply machinery, equipment, and materials needed for resource development and to extend the further processing of resource products beyond the primary stage. The massive investment in resource development projects will generate many billions of dollars worth of opportunities for supplying these projects or developing new resource-based products, not only in the traditional manufacturing centres but also in the resource-rich regions where industrial diversification is a long-standing objective.[17]

Shortly before this statement was issued, the federal government had negotiated pricing agreements for oil and gas with each of the three westernmost provinces, superseding the price schedules announced in the NEP scarcely one year earlier. The 1981 agreements distinguished between 'old' and 'new' oil. 'New oil' was that obtained from newly discovered reservoirs and also the additional production achievable from tertiary recovery schemes from any field. New oil would be priced at the cost of imports. It appeared at the time that by legislating world prices for new oil, and raising the original NEP schedule of prices for old oil, a major regional grievance against the NEP would be removed. Although higher prices would be somewhat offset by an increased tax and royalty take (undoubtedly a major attraction for the federal and provincial governments alike), firms would have much higher incentives both to discover new oil and to recover more oil from earlier finds. It would make drilling profitable again.

Thus the oil and gas pricing agreement of September 1981 seemingly foreshadowed a switch from the central Canadian, manufacturing-oriented strategy to one based much more on resource development. The new strategy was expounded in the November budget paper. The planned course of action, if successfully pursued, would be a true 'national policy': it would find common ground among the regions, bringing out their latent complementarity. Development of centre and periphery would be mutually reinforcing. Thus I shall call it a *strategy of regional complementarity*.

The attractiveness of a strategy that emphasizes and reinforces the complementarity of Canada's economic regions cannot be gainsaid. There would appear, however, to be a lot of wishful thinking in it too. Within a year of publication of the report of the Major Projects Task Force the idea of megaprojects, centred on energy development, had been dealt a severe blow by the downward trend in world oil prices. Two of the flashiest projects for mining Alberta's oil sands were abandoned shortly afterwards. It remains doubtful whether a strategy based on resource development, but with less emphasis on attention-grabbing megaprojects, could be viable. Even if future world demand and prices, coupled with a far more generous fiscal regime than in the recent past, could justify large-scale investment in resource industries, a strategy of regional complementarity would face two major obstacles.

First, as with any growth strategy based, in the short run, on a prospective investment boom, a key problem could be shortage of capital – not to mention its cost, if (as in the early 1980s) interest rates are high. Recent governments have implicitly recognized the problem. The budget paper foresaw a need for active government participation in mobilizing investment funds. More recently, the federal Conservatives have set about assiduously to court foreign investors in order to increase the inflow of capital from abroad (chiefly, of course, from the United States). However, investment from this source may not be forthcoming in the required amounts, and a future government might, on nationalist grounds, not want greatly to encourage it. If, for whatever reason, capital were less than abundant, one would have to choose between supporting industrial development and supporting resource exploitation. Or rather, the compromises made in seeking to achieve both types of development simultaneously would surely emphasize the extent to which manufacturing and primary production remain competitive rather than complementary.

Second, while the decline of traditional manufacturing industries creates unemployment in some regions, especially southern Quebec, bottlenecks in the supply of labour could occur in certain occupations and in other regions. The budget paper foresaw, incorrectly, a need for considerable westward migration. 'Over half of the investment in major projects in Canada to the end of the century will be in the West. Investments of this magnitude will certainly strain [manpower] capacity. It has been estimated that in the absence of immigration or interregional migration, the West would have a shortage of many thousands of workers by the end of the decade.'[18]

Where would the migrants come from? The Atlantic region was forecast to need all its manpower. It was (and is) anathema to Quebec that its people should leave the province to obtain employment, both because the probability of cultural/linguistic assimilation was high and because the relative political weight of the province in Confederation would decline. Reportedly, federal bureaucrats estimated that Ontario was likely to be the main source of new manpower for the west. However – then or now – it is difficult to see how a federal government with an electoral base in central Canada could pursue an economic development strategy that would entail a significant transfer of jobs and people to the west.

One may reasonably doubt, therefore, the economic and political feasibility of pursuing a development strategy that looks to revitalize central Canadian industry by restructuring it to serve the needs of the resources sector. The historic tension between metropolis and hinterland is unlikely to be so easily resolved. The supposed complementarity of regional interests now seems illusory. Thus any federal government that accepts or claims an active role in the economy (and probably even if it does not) is likely to be confronted with the same problem that faced the Macdonald and Laurier governments as they implemented the first national policy. The problem is to find a formula for pursuing nation-building goals while compensating regional and other interests adversely affected by a central Canadian strategy of economic development.

One choice, as outlined in the 1981 budget paper, is to attempt to combine relaunching of the staples economy with an attempt to strengthen manufacturing. The paper called for restructuring the secondary sector in such a way that, reciprocally, it would support and be supported by the resource industries – while also becoming competitive in high-technology goods (in fields such as nuclear power, aerospace, communications, electronic data processing, and urban transportation equipment). If resource prices head upward again, the 1981 strategy may be revived – in part. In other words, an attempt may be made to move forward simultaneously on all fronts, thus entailing compromise on all objectives and incurring a corresponding degree of political discontent.

THE CONTINENTALIST OPTION

Since 1981 the federal government's enthusiasm for a national policy has waned, and the public mood has turned against interventionism. The signs were evident before Pierre Trudeau's departure from politics but have become more obvious since. Part of the explanation lies in the government's poor record at 'picking winners.' Perhaps a still more potent explanation, though, is that the federal government, having pretty well given up on both the centralist strategy and the strategy of regional complementarity, seems to have run out of ideas. It was apparently incapable of devising a development strategy that gave reasonable promise of working, had the necessary political backing, and could be implemented under the existing or a slightly modified constitution.

The task that was given to the Macdonald Commission in November 1982 was to formulate a strategy meeting the first two of these criteria and to propose any institutional or constitutional changes that might be needed in order to implement it. Opponents of the government saw it variously as a device to relaunch the political career of its chairman (Trudeau was rumoured greatly to prefer Donald S. Macdonald over John Turner as a prospective successor) and as a means of resurrecting the constitutional reform process, which the prime minister had once said would proceed to a 'phase two,' dealing with distribution of powers, after patriation had occurred. Whether either objective was in Trudeau's mind, or both were, I do not purport to know, but the wording of the mandate suggests that it had been formulated on the basis of interventionist presuppositions.

Among the matters the commission was asked to report upon were the very issues that were decisive in evaluating the budget paper of the previous year: 'trends in labour market requirements, ... developments in the supply of raw materials, including energy sources, ... capital requirements, ... trends in productivity, ... industrial adjustment and growth, ... and regional economic development opportunities and constraints in a national economic framework.' The commission was also asked to consider 'the integrity of the Canadian economic union' and to make recommendations on 'the appropriate allocation of fiscal and economic powers, instruments and resources as between the different levels of governments and administrations,' as well as on the structure of national institutions. Perhaps most telling as an indication of the spirit in which the commission's mandate was formulated was the admonition that 'the Government of Canada has the primary responsibility for managing the national economy, for encouraging reasonably balanced economic growth among the various regions of the country and for ensuring that fiscal disparities among provinces are reduced, while at the same time the provincial governments also have important responsibilities in the development and carrying out of economic and social policy.'[19]

Such language strongly suggests that an active role for the federal government was thought to be required to ensure the prosperity of the country as a whole and of its regions and that the provincial governments had to be recruited into supporting that role and, at the same time, prevented from infringing upon the principles of economic union – free interprovincial movement of goods, services, capital, and labour.

The Macdonald report, while confirming the need for drastic change in Canada's economic structure and the orientation of economic and social policies, inverted the suppositions that seem to have informed its mandate. It put forward, not a redesigned national policy for Canada, but the most comprehensive condemnation of the very idea of a national policy ever contained in a Canadian public document. It proposed no strategy or program for economic development except to facilitate adaptation to changing world market conditions, whatever future course they might dictate. In recommending that government 'reassess the relations between state and market, both domestically and internationally,' the Commission urged:

Our long-run concern must be to restore higher rates of growth in both production and employment. To that end, we advocate an increased openness to international competition and, in particular, the conclusion of a free-trade arrangement, encompassing non-tariff barriers (NTBs), with the United States. The explicit premise behind our free-trade proposals is that the Canadian economy must be made more competitive, and that adjustment-retarding policies must be replaced with adjustment-facilitating strategies ... . We must seek an end to those patterns of government involvement in the economy which may generate disincentives, retard flexibility, and work against the desired allocation of resources.'[20]

In short, federal policy should be neutral as between sectors, industries, and firms. 'Free trade is the main instrument in this Commission's approach to industrial policy.' (Internal barriers to trade and to the movement of capital and labour were judged to have slight effect, though the analysis was static rather than dynamic and thus could not address the aspect of the question widely acknowledged to be most important, if most conjectural – see below, pp. 90–1, 203.) Any cushioning of the effects of industrial decline should be targeted, said the commission, at relieving individual hardship, not at supporting or attempting to rationalize the industries in question; government should concentrate on sector-neutral forms of support for economic development such as manpower training and mobility grants; unemployment insurance should be cut back and complemented by adjustment assistance payments which would be conditional upon willingness to upgrade one's skills and/or to move to locations where employment prospects are better.[21]

One wonders whether the commission supposed that a market-enhancing policy, when compared with the interventionism of the preceding years, would soothe interregional conflict and/or the constitutional sensitivities of the provinces. If so, it may be doubted that they were right. To choose a sectorally neutral policy is just as much a political decision as to choose a policy aiming to shape and control economic development, retarding market forces in respect of some industries and forcing the pace elsewhere. Notoriously in the Canadian context, policies impinging differentially upon various industries also impinge differentially upon various regions. Thus it should occasion no surprise that premiers Peterson, Bourassa, and Pawley (respectively of Ontario, Quebec, and Manitoba) have all expressed varying degrees of disquiet about free trade;[22] and no Atlantic premier could conceivably acquiesce in a market-enhancing policy that dealt roughly with the all-too-fragile economic base of the Atlantic region. And as for the constitutional issue: while the attempt to implement a third national policy, particularly under the centralist strategy, struck sparks as federal powers clashed against provincial ones, the market-enhancing policies advocated by the commission are anything but anodyne in their constitutional effects. Indeed, they demand more extensive limitations on provincial powers than anything proposed by the federal government during the negotiations of July to September 1980. Paradoxically, some of the most interventionist provincial governments are also among those most strongly committed to continental free trade. The tension between the two is studiously disregarded. It's a classic eat-and-have situation.

A more thorough analysis of these matters will have to wait; it will be necessary first to step back a few paces and consider some of the characteristics of federalism in Canada and its interrelationship with policy outputs and policy outcomes. (This distinction contrasts *what governments do* with *what results from what they do*.) We shall start with some very general and indeed somewhat abstract reflections on how to assess the policy impact of federalism (chapters 2 and 3) and then examine some features of the Canadian constitution and policy-making process (chapters 4 and 5). This prepares the ground for an inquiry into decentralizing (or is it centralizing?) trends in Canadian federalism and the relation between (de)centralization and interregional conflict (chapters 6 and 7). Finally, the two concluding chapters return to the theme of Canada's national policies, exploring scholarly controversies regarding the effects of the original national policy of Macdonald and Laurier, possible rationales for government interventionism, and (once again, but one hopes with added insight) interrelationships among economic policy, politics, and the constitution.

CONCLUSION

Over the course of little more than a decade there emerged in Canada a vaguely adumbrated and inconsistently applied third national policy, first in a version incorporating a centralist development strategy – though the policy and the strategy behind it were nowhere comprehensively expounded – and then in a version aiming to bring out a new complementarity among Canada's regional economies. The pre-1981 version, which provoked sharp political controversy spilling over into the constitutional realm, was partially superseded when world market trends seemed to make a less conflictual strategy possible. When it became apparent, however, that these conditions were evaporating, which they did almost as soon as they had been recognized, the regional-complementarity version of the third national policy lost its attraction. In its stead a project for achieving closer economic integration with the United States came to dominate the policy agenda.

2

Why the constitution matters,
and to whom

In the campaign leading up to the Quebec referendum of May 1980, federalist forces promised 'renewed federalism' if the electorate rejected sovereignty-association. This promise did much to colour the constitutional debate that followed. On the one hand, it was rightly said that the package put forward by Pierre Trudeau after the failure of the first ministers' conference of September 1980 did almost nothing to meet the grievances of Québécois against the existing federal system. Not one prominent figure in Quebec provincial politics supported either the substance of the Constitutional Resolution as originally presented, or the attempt to force it through the parliaments at Ottawa and Westminster. On the other hand, the resolution was presented outside Quebec as an attempt – all the more galling in view of its seeming futility – to deal a death-blow to 'separatism,' while the urgent task of devising a response to the country's economic woes was shunted to the sidelines. Constitutional adventurism was generally seen as a diversion from the business of running the country or, worse, as an attempt to curb the power of the provinces on the pretext of redeeming a pledge to the Quebec electorate.

Partisan infighting and the shrill cries of political leaders who fear impairment of their powers have undoubtedly narrowed the public's view of the significance of constitutional issues. This may be due in part to the fact that many of those who supported the main features of the 1981 resolution none the less objected to Trudeau's initiative on procedural grounds. Consequently much of the debate was on the extent of provincial consent required, rather than on the merits of the resolution itself. This has helped obscure the reasons why the make-up of a federal constitution matters, and to whom. Why, indeed, does the constitution matter? In my opinion, the answer is to be found by exploring the relation between the institutional framework which imparts some regularity and order to political processes and the substance of the policies that governmental actions and intergovernmental processes generate. This means that the relevant features of the constitution, for our particular problem, are 1) the limitation of governmental power through a charter of freedoms or bill of rights, 2) the structure of representative and decision-making bodies, 3) the federal division of powers, and 4) the constitutional obligation that may be imposed upon each (or either) order of government to obtain advice, co-operation, and consent from the other. If we can identify the potential impact of these features of the constitution on the substance of policy, we shall have taken an essential step toward identifying also its impact upon the interests of various groups. We shall have been able to identify whose interests are at stake, and in what ways, as the structure or operation of political institutions undergoes change, or as proposed amendments to a constitution are carried through or rejected.

Few people have addressed this matter directly, but one can detect quite a range of views implicit in the remarks of politicians and commentators, scholarly and otherwise. I have drawn up a six-point 'impact scale' that ranks opinion according to the magnitude of anticipated policy consequences associated with possible constitutional change. For each point in the scale, we deduce what sort of interests have an apparent stake in constitutional outcomes.

Level 1: At the bottom end of the scale is the opinion that even after root-and-branch constitutional revision, political processes would churn out very much the same policies as before. According to this view, the structural framework in which those processes are acted out is irrelevant to the policy outputs. In other words, the anticipated policy effect of redesigning the Canadian federation, or even of dissolving it, would be negligible. Needless to say, those who believe this to be the case also hold that lesser changes, say in working relations among governments, or in the structure of central institutions, would have still slighter effect.

This view may be widespread. Although one should beware of drawing unwarranted inferences from survey data on a less specific question, it is nonetheless significant that in January 1977 (two months after the election of the secessionist Parti québécois), some 22 per cent of Canadians thought that if Quebec left Confederation, the consequences for the future of the rest of the country would be 'not very serious.'[1] It is likely that many people think that sparring between governments – even when basic constitutional questions are at stake – reflects institutional rivalries and personal ambitions, and nothing else. It is easy, even if logically unwarranted, to extend this supposition and to suggest that the only things motivating constitutional debates are the careers and the self-esteem of those who run the machinery of government – the politicians and bureaucrats.

Level 2: Next on our scale is a position that still regards the policy effect of constitutional change as negligible; it none the less takes account of possible changes in the costs incurred in running the public sector as the constitutional structure is modified.

At the political level, opinion to this effect is implicit in the demand, regularly put forward by several provinces and perhaps even more so by businessmen desiring clarity and simplicity in their dealings with government, for 'disentanglement' of federal and provincial powers. It causes irritation and is wasteful of resources when the federal and the provincial governments are both involved in the same policy area. Federal bureaucrats must spend a lot of time co-ordinating their activities with their provincial counterparts, and vice-versa; inefficient programs are implemented by the provinces because a subsidy is available or because their policy options are restricted by federal initiatives; unwelcomed by-products of one government's activities must be neutralized or undone by the other. For the individual citizen, and for non-governmental organizations, the confusion inherent in overlapping powers and activities is often bothersome and costly.

There is also an academic literature that explores how the costs of governing are affected by governmental structure, especially the allocation of functions between jurisdictions. The most thorough and interesting exposition of this idea is contained in a book by Albert Breton and Anthony Scott, *The Economic Constitution of Federal States* (1978). Although in an earlier article Scott states that 'the permanent assignment of powers and responsibilities to the various levels of governments ... may have a most profound impact on what is actually done,' the larger part of the argument in the book by Breton and Scott suggests that the effect of constitutional change would be negligible except in the sense that it may impose or reduce costs. The incidence of these costs may be difficult to identify. Indeed, the book deals with the distribution of powers within federal (and non-federal) states entirely on the basis of the 'organizational costs' incurred in one or another assignment of functions to various levels of government.[2]

Breton and Scott do not rely on economies-of-scale considerations in the production of public goods. On the contrary, they reject such considerations because they argue that economies of scale can be achieved irrespective of the size of the consuming unit. Thus, to take an example from Scott, a small state can take advantage of economies of scale in providing defence services; to do so it has only to join a military alliance. In consequence, when economies-of-scale considerations apply, Breton and Scott take account of them by positing that organizational costs will be incurred in arranging for joint provision of public goods and services.[3]

Organizational costs are subdivided into four categories: administration, co-ordinating, signalling, and mobility. Administration includes costs involved in setting up the apparatus of government, obtaining information, law enforcement, etc. Co-ordination costs are entailed by the need to reach agreements with other governments, e.g. to provide services jointly, to avoid regulatory confusion, or to negotiate compensation for spill-over effects of public and private activities from one jurisdiction to another. Signalling costs are incurred by citizens in making their preferences known to governments. And mobility costs are incurred by citizens who dislike the bundle of policies implemented within the jurisdiction wherein they live, and who respond by moving elsewhere. The basic proposition expounded by Breton and Scott is that the assignment of functions to various levels of government in a federal state approximates that specific assignment of functions which minimizes aggregate organizational costs: those incurred in administration, co-ordination, signalling, and mobility.

Breton and Scott must logically allow for differences between jurisdictions, either in policy outputs or in the costs of providing public services. Otherwise they could not consider citizens' expenditures on mobility as one type of organizational cost to be set against the other three. Apart from this, however, their argument necessarily rests on the assumption of undifferentiated policy outputs: how many letters to the editor, how many protest marches, etc. – i.e. how much signalling effort – is required before politicians will supply what is wanted? How many hours of meeting time between officials will be necessary to co-ordinate policies of different governments, as if they were made by a central government? How many hours of bureaucratic time are needed under one assignment of functions as compared with another, in order to provide a given level of service? To answer questions such as these, one must discount or ignore changes in policy as one imagines governmental functions shifted around in the let's-pretend context of a simulation exercise. Except in the case of mobility costs, one cannot make sense of the concept of organizational costs other than by presuming a standard set of outputs.

If, then, thinking of the impact of constitutional change in the terms presented to us by Breton and Scott, we consider whose interests are at stake in constitutional change, we have virtually nothing to go on. We are led to consider an undifferentiated public interest summed up in least-cost considerations of running a public sector. The costs of administration and co-ordination will presumably be borne by taxpayers and will therefore correspond to the general incidence of taxation. The costs of signalling and mobility, however, will no doubt be borne disproportionately by minorities that dislike what their governments are doing or find the design of public services inconsistent with their personal preferences – at variance with the values they hold, or inadequate, or too expensive. To our question of what is at stake in constitutional change, the answer must be 'the public interest – with a dollar sign: but nobody's interest in particular.'

Level 3: At one step up on our scale is an opinion that appears to be widely shared and is routinely expressed in the speeches of provincial politicians who favour selective decentralization of legislative powers. They tend to assert or assume that the consequences of decentralization are entirely benign as far as regions other than their own are concerned. They emphasize that decentralization permits differentiation of policy outputs, so that in the aggregate policy is more sensitive to the needs of the various regions and responds better to the values, moods, and preferences of provincial electorates. Mathematics is on the side of the decentralists in this. Scott notes that it can be demonstrated that 'if a nation that is divided among majority and minority parties (or interest groups) is cut up at random into small territorial jurisdictions, the total number of citizens who must suffer as minorities from the policies of majorities will decline; that is, the number of people who are in agreement with government decisions will increase.'[4] A negative way of making the same point, in the Canadian context, is that if central powers were reduced, the federal government would no longer find so many opportunities to impose uniform policies across the country in the mistaken thought that they would solve diverse problems. No longer could Ottawa respond to an Ontario problem with a policy that would aggravate a different problem in New Brunswick, perhaps one that federal bureaucrats hadn't even heard of.

This assessment of the effect of constitutional change is important in the Canadian context (or indeed in the US context, where it forms the rationale for President Reagan's 'new federalism') because it provides the rationale for the view that tensions within a federation can be relieved by transferring more powers to the provinces or states. (For a full discussion of this issue, see chapter 7.) Even the Parti québécois program of sovereignty-association was originally justified on this basis. Quebec's distinctive culture, said the PQ, prompted Québécois to do many things that the rest of Canada preferred not to do; Quebec wished to deal with the standard problems of an industrial society in its own way. PQ spokesmen asserted that while the other provinces did have an interest in maintaining their historic economic ties with Quebec (as did Quebec with the rest of Canada), political independence with economic association presented no threat to the rest of the country. This argument underpinned the assertion that an economic association was in the interest of both parties and that when other premiers insisted that sovereignty-association was a non-starter they did so merely in order to intimidate Quebec's electorate.

The PQ's position on the non-threatening character of its original constitutional option is merely the extreme case of the common view that decentralization is beneficial to all. For a more moderate expression of the same idea, listen to former Premier Lougheed: 'In short, the economic centre of gravity is shifting west. It will continue to do so, but I am aware – as you are – that it neither will nor should shift too far, if we are going to maintain and sustain a strong nation. Frankly though, we can shift quite a way before we reach that point. In my view, without doubt, such a shift is good for Canada. As the regions strengthen, the country strengthens. This is not any exclusive club for Albertans; everybody is welcome, each in his own way and I just urge you, wherever you are, whatever activity, to come aboard.'[5]

To sum up this opinion: the interests at stake in all but the most radical forms of constitutional change are regional in the first instance. But since all regions stand to benefit from decentralization, the national interest too (as an aggregate of regional interests) is served by decentralizing.

Level 4: We now come to the opinion that recognizes regionally differentiated consequences of constitutional change. It is argued that a redistribution of powers, including powers that may be used to swell the public purse (taxing powers, ownership of resources, etc) would shift the costs of providing public services among provinces or among regions. In the case of decentralization, provinces with a narrow revenue base might not only have to raise taxes but might also find it difficult to maintain the same standard of services that the richer provinces provide. Sometimes this is presented as a distinct advantage: provincial governments would cut out wasteful expenditures on vain programs of economic development, when the resources to be developed are elsewhere; lavish social services and income maintenance schemes would no longer hold back emigration from declining regions, etc. Against these arguments, and far more commonly heard, are considerations of equity suggesting that comparable levels of public services ought to be provided in all regions, without undue levels of taxation. In 1982 this principle, committing the federal government to making equalization payments, was enshrined in the constitution.

The issues receiving attention here are the extent of public services available, province by province, and how the costs of providing the services are distributed. It follows that the interests at stake are primarily regional, although there are also suggestions that non-regional interests also may be affected – interests defined by income level, employment status, age, health, and so forth.

Level 5: At the next notch on our scale we find the opinion that a change in constitutional arrangements may raise or lower the level of government services, quite apart from the issue of regional variations in quality, and in cost, of services. It is sometimes argued that federalism makes for 'big government'; not only are many bureaucrats duplicating each others' work (if not actually undoing it), but two orders of government will compete with each other to provide services, with the result that the public sector in a federal state is larger than it would be in the case of a unitary state covering the same territory.

So far as I know, however plausible the argument, there is no empirical support for this view. However, a contrary position has been presented by Harold L. Wilensky in *The Welfare State and Equality.* This book is a contribution to the literature that looks for correlations between certain features of policy (e.g. levels of state expenditure on social welfare) and other variables. The literature finds, in general, that policy outputs correlate reasonably well with social characteristics like per capita income and age of population, and scarcely or not at all with political structures, official or prevalent ideology, or type of economic system. One of the principal conclusions of the literature is that institutions do not seem to matter very much. Wilensky, however, discovered that the one institutional characteristic that seems to affect levels of expenditure on social welfare is the degree of centralization of the regime. He calculated state welfare expenditures as a percentage of gross national product in 22 industrialized countries and discovered: 'Of the top nine welfare-state leaders ... six are clearly among the nine most centralized governments ... [while] of the seven countries ranked lowest in social security [all of them federal] four are among the least centralized'; of the remaining three, one was ambiguous as regards centralization, and two had high levels of military expenditure which presumably restricted their capacity to use state resources for welfare purposes.[6]

Wilensky's evidence about the relation between centralization and social security expenditures can scarcely be taken as conclusive, but the inquiry itself does draw our attention to a different and rather more significant relationship between federalism and public policy than we have considered hitherto. This is the first suggestion that the structure of institutions, as well as the availability of financial resources, may affect what governments do. There is also a difference in terms of the groups affected by constitutional forms. If 'big government' generally favours the less wealthy (because of transfer payments and because of public services disproportionately paid for by the middle- and upper-income groups) then class interests rather than, or as well as, regional ones are probably involved in constitutional questions.

Level 6: Finally, we come to the suggestion that as a result of constitutional change, governments may aim for new or different objectives; they may abandon or trim old ones; and there may be some impact on their policy effectiveness. It is a question not just of levels of public services but of potential changes in the whole range of government activity. For example, the original purpose of creating the Canadian federation was to provide for the physical security of the colonies in British North America, to affirm and achieve distinctive social values ('Toryism,' as Gad Horowitz would have it, symbolized in the affirmation of the British connection; and, in French Canada, Catholicism), and to develop the northern half of the continent as an extension in time and space of 'the commercial empire of the St. Lawrence.'[7] Whether such purposes persist (for example, in the implementation of a third national policy), whether they are replaced or supplemented by others, and who the champions of such purposes are are the matters that most fundamentally underlie constitutional issues in Canada. Insofar as there is a relation between national purposes and institutional structures, those purposes and the capacity of Canadians to realize them through the agency of government are fundamental to the constitutional question, whether this manifests itself in the threat of Quebec's secession, in the demands of the provincialist coalition, in a federal attempt to gain wider powers over the economy, or in entrenchment of a Charter of Rights and Freedoms.

It is evident, though, that in many cases there is no undifferentiated national interest in the pursuit of objectives allegedly held in common. A diverse population affirms diverse purposes. The issues at hand are quintessentially political: some people want to secure objectives that others reject. Various groups of protagonists seek to employ potentially coercive instruments – the taxing and regulatory powers of the state – to accomplish their purposes. Their success in

Policy and the constitution: an impact scale

Presumed impact of constitution on policy outputs	Interests apparently at stake
1 Negligible: constitutional debates in Canada reflect institutional rivalries and nothing else.	The careers of politicians and bureaucrats
2 Negligible, as far as policy outputs themselves are concerned, although the organizational costs of government are affected by factors such as the degree of centralization.	An undifferentiated public interest; alternatively, taxpayers (for administration and co-ordination costs) and consumers of public goods and services (for signalling and mobility costs)
3 Decentralization permits differentiation of policy outputs among regions. Rather than a single central government acting in ignorance of regional needs, regional governments act in accordance with regional preferences; vice versa for centralization.	Regional interests: all regions stand to benefit from decentralization; therefore, in the aggregate, the national interest
4 Cost of providing public services may be raised/lowered in each region individually; possible variations in level or quality of government services by region.	Regional interests: standards of government services may go up/down; interregional shifts in costs of services occur; possible impact on inter-regional migration
5 Raise or lower level of public services, apart from regional variations.	Class, and other groupings defined by a wide variety of characteristics: employment status, age, sex, health, etc
6 Governments may aim for new or different objectives, may abandon old objectives, may become more/less effective in achieving specific purposes.	Regional (in the sense of incompatibility of regional objectives) and non-regional (i.e. interests within each region, or within some regions)

doing so will depend on the extent and effectiveness of state power, on the allocation of powers and financial resources to the federal and the provincial governments respectively, and on the ability of various interests (regional and otherwise) to influence or control the various governments in the exercise of their powers.

We have so far been concerned to identify various opinions on the relation between constitutional forms, the substance of public policy, and the interests apparently at stake in constitutional change. I have provided an exposition of these opinions on the basis of a rank ordering that sees an increasingly close relation between structural factors and policy outputs and that correspondingly perceives increasingly large stakes in constitutional questions. A summary of the scale in tabular form may be useful (see the accompanying table).

It may be objected, as one looks over the table, that it does not actually provide a rank-ordering of opinions; it merely identifies several different ways in which a constitution may affect policy and hence the interests of various groups of people. Indeed it does. However, category 2 absorbs category 1, category 3 absorbs categories 2 and 1, and so forth. For example, a person who is concerned about constitutional questions because he thinks constitutional change might lead to variations in the quality of public services in the various regions would have no difficulty in acknowledging that amendments to the constitution might well also affect the careers of politicians and bureaucrats, might raise or lower the costs of government in the aggregate, and might affect the sensitivity of government to the needs of the various regions.

What is important is not the logical compatibility or incompatibility of the categories, but the fact that the more one focuses on the lower end of the scale, the easier it is to lose sight of the upper end and thus to fail to perceive what is ultimately or potentially at stake in constitutional questions. In particular, the more we argue about issues like the costs of running the apparatus of government, important though this issue is, the more likely it is that other issues, perhaps of even more far-reaching significance, will be neglected.

This chapter has put the question of how federalism – or more generally, the structure of a constitution – may affect policy and thus touch the interests of various segments of a population. The discussion has dwelt upon the categories in which we might expect an answer to be formulated, rather than exploring specific effects of a specific constitution or possible changes in it. In this sense it is but a prelude to empirical inquiry.

3

Explaining public policy:
the relevance of federalism

In this chapter we ask: Among various factors influencing policy formation in a federation, what is the relevance of the federal structure itself? Such a question ought to be an abomination to any tidy-minded social scientist. I did not realize this at first. Then, as I wrote and as the unwisdom of proceeding according to game-plan became uncomfortably clear, it seemed that the simplest way to expound the ideas that were developing in my mind would be to recruit the reader as an accomplice in my intellectual misdemeanours, inviting him to join me in breaking the rules of social-scientific inquiry.

A question that is badly formulated may still be worth asking. In this case there was a political motive. My aim was to appreciate why the constitutional status quo in Canada was supported by certain segments of the Canadian political community and to understand some of the constitutional grievances of other groups. The reasoning here was that if people like a given set of decisions, they will like the decision-making rules, and if they are dissatisfied with the main thrust of public policy, they will be sympathetic to changing the institutions and processes through which policy is made.

Before proceeding we should note that this project may seem dubious for the most fundamental of all reasons: irrelevance. Perhaps if our concern is ultimately with political loyalties and emotional ties to a national community, it would be better to deal frankly with matters of the heart. Why impute to ordinary folk the fine calculations of political arithmetic? The answer is that if there are those who live at the level of the passions, there are others who look to their own advantage; and the two are perhaps not entirely unrelated. Indeed, the latter has a reputation for being the more enduring. As Proust said of Swann, regarding his infatuation with Odette:

Probably if anyone had said to him, at the beginning, 'It's your position that attracts her,' or

... 'It's your money that she's really in love with,' he would not have believed the suggestion ... But even if he had accepted the possibility, it might not have caused him any suffering to discover that Odette's love for him was based on a foundation more lasting than mere affection, or any attractive qualities which she might have found in him; on a sound, commercial interest; an interest which would postpone for ever the fatal day on which she might be tempted to bring their relations to an end.[1]

With such thoughts, I set out to explore the relation between federalism and the main features of public policy.

There remain, however, methodological problems – in fact two of them. One is that what we wish to explain (the explicandum: 'policy outputs') lacks precision; the other is that the form of the question gives priority, for no apparent scientific reason, to a single independent variable (federalism).

On the first point, that the explicandum lacks precise definition, we should note that in scholarly inquiry the success of one's investigations depends heavily upon having the wits or insight to put one's questions in a useful way, that is, to select the right dependent variable. This in itself may be a difficult task – at least in the social sciences – since we must do so within categories that permit us to compare or survey a number of similar events.[2] The singular event becomes amenable to explanation only to the extent that it is seen as similar to, or as sharing characteristics with, a larger set. We cannot hope to explain 'policy outputs' as such, or any single policy decision, except within categories that draw attention to the ways in which certain decisions compare with others, for example, that they favour a particular group or class, that they entail heavy public expenditure, or that they betray a government's inability to do unpopular but seemingly necessary things. When we ask about the relation between federalism and public policy, no useful answers will be forthcoming at least until some relevant features of policy are selected for explanation.

Our second problem concerns the form of the question. It does not ask, 'What explains "x"?' but rather, 'What does "y" explain?' Though the reference to policy outputs does give a useful clue to the meaning of the question, the project design is still unpromising. When one's scientific work begins with an independent variable and takes the form of looking for consequences, one's judgment becomes unreliable. A surprising range of facts can be 'explained' by a single independent variable, though in most cases the cogency of the explanation would soon vanish if the researcher undertook to survey all plausible explanations of a given phenomenon and then queried which one of them (or which combination) seemed most powerful, within the most economical argument. It is almost as futile to ask what impact federalism has upon policy as to ask what consequences flow from the Second World War. One hardly knows where to begin.

Neither of these criticisms, however, weakens our reasons for wanting to trace the effect of federalism on policy. There are many questions which, though posed in a naïve way, remain interesting; and the effect of constitutional arrangements on policy is one of them. When a question is put 'the wrong way,' we may have to scale down our expectations about the quality of the obtainable answers, but that is not always sufficient ground for abandoning the question itself.

Perhaps the best way of proceeding is to heed the rule that advises one to look for explanations rather than consequences, but to forget at least temporarily that 'policy outputs' is a fuzzy and hence probably unrewarding definition of the explicandum. We shall touch upon a number of different sorts of explanation of policy, as found in the scholarly and popular literature.[3] None of them has to do with federalism. But perhaps we can, none the less, see how 'federalism' relates to some of the more conventional explanatory categories.

ALTERNATIVE EXPLANATIONS OF POLICY OUTPUTS

The most obvious way of explaining public policy is to deal with discrete decisions and the people who make them: their personalities, their life-histories, formative events in their previous experience, and whom they associate with – not to mention accidents of the moment such as a cocktail party chat, a memo leaked, a late airplane, an act of spite to settle an old score. It is the attractiveness of this form of explanation that leads historians to take up biography. Outside the academic world, it is the style of explanation preferred by politicians and other participants in the processes of decision-making or close observers of affairs: journalists, civil servants, and chambermaids in the White House.

Such a manner of explanation is seldom very satisfying to political scientists, for whom accident is an embarrassment. All inquiry pretending to 'scientific' status demands regularity and (ideally) predictability. Accordingly, political scientists try to look beyond what is momentary and adventitious, to see if they can find correlations of apparent significance, suggesting law-like explanation. This predilection leads them to extend the search for explanatory factors into more and more unchangeable features of a political situation: from weather to climate, as it were. Their answer to the question 'What explains policy?' leads them through several stages of abstraction.

A first step in this direction is to look not at individuals but at whole groups of participants in decision-making processes. The archetype of this form of study (though scarcely part of the 'policy analysis' literature) is probably C. Wright Mills' *The Power Elite*.[4] It is clear that for Mills the behaviour of the power elite is determined by the socialization patterns of its members. Presumably, too, the character of the key decisions taken by government and other agencies of public significance in the United States – mainly the large corporations – can be traced to the characteristics of the decision-makers, who are said to form a cohesive and homogeneous group of think-alikes.

In Canada, the broadening of the range of policy outputs at the provincial level since 1960 has occasionally been attributed to the recruitment of a first-class provincial public service, first in Saskatchewan, then in Quebec, and subsequently in provinces like Ontario and Alberta. We are also familiar with interpretations of cabinet government according to which real power is alleged to lie with the civil service. It is almost a corollary of such opinion that the explanation of policy is to be found in the character of the bureaucracy: whom it recruits, how it inducts neophytes into its habits and mysteries, and how it expels the non-conformist.

A third type of explanation of policy outputs focuses on the changing configuration of the political and economic situation. It tends to view decision-makers as victims of circumstance. They are often portrayed, and may retrospectively portray themselves, as being at the mercy of events, driven by occurrences beyond their control, responding pragmatically to the crises and moods of the day – a collapse in the world price of oil, an outbreak of labour unrest, a sudden rise in public concern about pollution, a drop in the birth rate and its eventual consequences on the age-distribution of the population and thus on demands for public services such as education and health care. Policy-making consists, in this context, of problem-solving; and the character of political outputs is determined by the problems that arise and the order in which they appear.

Another form of explanation pays particular attention to longer-term factors such as the composition of political forces that impinge upon governmental authorities. This approach is especially well suited to a pluralist perspective on political life, which emphasizes the multiplicity of political cleavages and views political decision-making as a resultant of interplay between the elite leaders of the interested groups. Of course, one of the features of pluralism is that its adherents assert that no group is dominant across all areas of policy formation. Consequently, pluralists view political action as involving the constant recombination of temporary coalitions. They deny the existence of a single political elite and affirm the existence of multiple, overlapping elites, mainly outside government. Elite actors make their influence felt upon office-holders, who (in the extreme case) may merely record the result of intergroup bargaining. To the extent that this style of explaining policy outputs manages to escape the ephemeral and the accidental, it does so by searching for demographic, economic, and cultural trends that explain shifts in the 'winning coalition' that backs up successive governments.

The search for factors having a longer-term impact upon the character of public policy may lead away from the interplay of groups and encourage us instead to focus on the structure of the institutions that make such a pluralist bargaining process possible – or render it irrelevant to the key decisions. If we do this, we look to the framework, not to the myriad of events that unroll within it, for an explanation of policy. Rather than engaging in case studies of key or typical decisions, we may think it most telling to examine the characteristics of the decision-making process itself.

This approach is attractive for two reasons. One is that access to positions of political authority, and the behaviour of role-occupants, are indeed likely to be affected (though not always in precise or demonstrable ways) by the structure of the institutions and the conventions that are built up around them. The other reason for examining the structure of the regime – a reason of especial importance for our argument – is that political forces are necessarily channelled through a system of representation that has the dual function of making for the effective expression of some group interests and diverting or even suppressing other interests. In other words, there is no representation without distortion: what decision-makers respond to (or are constrained by) is not a perfect scanning of public opinion but a set of political forces as shaped by and channelled through interest organizations and a wide range of partisan, legislative, and bureaucratic institutions. The make-up of those institutions accordingly may be presumed to have some effect on the character of the outputs from the governmental process.

One may choose, again, to look beyond the particular institutions to the political culture of a society, on the supposition that the political culture influences all behaviour within the institutional framework. Almost everyone now recognizes that institutions cannot simply be transported from one social setting to another with the expectation that they will work the same way in both. Social structure, religious traditions, and political culture – cognition of political objects and attitudes toward certain types of behaviour – are responsible for such differences. It is scarcely surprising, then, that those who study politics comparatively, particularly if they study non-industrialized countries, tend to be more impressed by patterns of political culture than by the formal structure of governmental institutions.

One factor rarely taken into account in explaining policy outputs is the composition of the political community. It is commonly ignored for the simple reason that political boundaries are normally taken as given; but in some circumstances definition of the political community may become a matter of controversy. In Canada the controversies of the late 1970s over the possible secession of Quebec, or even some of the western provinces, arose partly because of emotional factors, but partly too because people assumed that different policies would be implemented by governments if the province or provinces concerned achieved political independence. Such an event, it was acknowledged, would trigger other changes in the composition of the Canadian political community or a general redrawing of political boundaries. Consequently, a different set of political communities would become relevant to decision-making. One might anticipate corresponding changes in the relevant political culture, and certainly in the composition of the political forces impinging upon the actions of decision-makers.

For some analysts, even the drawing of national boundaries may be regarded as a factor that is overshadowed by other considerations. In Canada this is especially true of the contemporary followers of Harold Innis, some of whom affect to

Marxism. Political economists of this persuasion tend to see Canada's place in the world economy as a factor underpinning all those other factors to which allusion has already been made. From the geo-economic situation of the country is said to derive the structure of classes, the drawing of political boundaries (i.e. the very idea of a Confederation), prevalent cultural patterns, and the political power of the coalitions upon which governments rest. It is an implication of this position that a redrawing of boundaries, or any lesser form of institutional change, would be powerless fundamentally to affect the functions performed by the state in furthering the interests of the economically dominant class or class fractions.

To summarize the presentation so far, here is the list of factors we have surveyed, each of which plausibly impinges upon policy: 1) the personalities of key decision-makers; 2) the characteristics of groups of decision-makers, for example as determined by socialization patterns (applies especially to bureaucracies, public and private); 3) the changing configuration of political and economic situations, which cast up an ever-changing lot of problems with which decision-makers must grapple; 4) the composition of political forces; changing coalitions of interest groups (pluralist perspective); 5) the structure of institutions of representation, and the character of decision-making processes; 6) political culture, and generally the prevalent values and preferences within the political community; 7) the definition of the political community, or the drawing of political boundaries; and 8) the geopolitical position of the country, its place in the world economy, and related factors of class structure and politico-economic domination.

This typology of explanations goes from the particular and adventitious to the general and secular. The factors that appear toward the bottom of the list are correspondingly better suited to inclusion in more highly theoretical work. However, these factors can explain only the most general features of policy, which may be observable only from a substantial distance. The very act of taking one's distance in this way, however, makes the detail difficult to see. Explanation must focus increasingly on the general features of policy and not on its particularities.

In conclusion of this part of our essay, we may observe that one probably has to choose between a fine focus on the details of policy, where explanation tends to draw upon the items near the top of our list, and a more distant perspective which more easily takes account of the factors near the bottom. The former tends to be only superficially theoretical and often fails to observe the more general features of the policy landscape, while the latter offers a greater chance of obtaining theoretical insight, but at the cost of ignoring what seems most significant to participants in the policy process.

To put the matter succinctly: we embarked on a search for explanations of policy outputs; we drew up a long and diverse list, but we discovered that the list was long mainly because we had implicitly shifted our definition of what was to be explained.

EXPLAINING POLICY: WHERE FEDERALISM FITS IN

Another way of stating our discovery is to say that different types of explanation of policy tend to focus on different characteristics of policy outputs. Some explanations draw attention to the minutiae, others only to the broadest features. If we try to fit 'federalism' into our list of explanatory factors, we find that it is encompassed by, or else has some bearing upon, items 4–7, and perhaps 8 (more on this, below). This would suggest that if federalism has any detectable impact on policy, the prospects for generalizing about it would be relatively good, in the sense that its effect might be expected to extend to the main outlines of policy and not be limited merely to the details. In fact, we do find in the Canadian literature a number of attempts at making such generalizations, such as: that federalism imparts a conservative bias to policy; that it augments the political power and influence of regional elites and regional majorities, thereby impeding government action pursuant to the goals of national majorities; and that it promotes continentalism.

Conservative bias: Much of the writing on federalism during the 1930s decried federalism as an outmoded form of government which prevented Canada from dealing effectively with the problems posed by the world economic crisis. It was this feeling – expressed, for example, in the writings of Frank Scott – that led most Canadian socialists to support the extension of federal power. The centralism of the Co-operative Commonwealth Federation (CCF), however, was criticized by Pierre Elliott Trudeau,[5] who noted that federalism encouraged experimentation in policy and permitted innovation in the exercise of governmental powers in one province while national majorities (or, he might have added, vested interests wielding power at the federal level) prohibited federal initiatives in the provision of services. Trudeau argued that the success of policies introduced in one part of the country might well lead to their emulation elsewhere: thus federalism could equally be seen as a progressive form of government.

More recently, Donald Smiley[6] has argued that federalism, at least in its Canadian form, has encouraged expansion of government activity, as the two major orders of government compete with each other for the support of the electorate; such competition results in higher taxes and higher levels of spending than would be likely in a unitary state. The argument is plausible, especially in the context of a discussion of the federal spending power: a federal government may initiate programs (such as medicare) in the knowledge that it will not have to bear the full cost that the program entails or will eventually prove to entail. As I noted in chapter 2, however, such data as are available on this subject would seem to be inconsistent with Smiley's hypothesis.

In the presence of conflicting arguments and data, it is difficult to know what to make of the allegation that federalism imparts a conservative bias to policy. The question is interesting, but in posing it we accomplish no more than to point to the desirability of finding a way of researching it.

Regional versus national majorities: Almost by definition federalism augments the political power and influence of regional elites and regional majorities, diminishing the sway of national elites and national majorities. In any case, this statement dwells on the structure of power, not on its policy consequences. These may be several. One consequence, which is a truism, is that when some policy responsibilities are confided in regional governments, regional differentiation in policy may result; thus, within a federation it is almost certainly possible to accommodate a wider range of policy preferences than in a unitary state. A more interesting set of consequences, however, may also arise in relation to matters within the purview of the central government. Depending on the structure of central institutions and the character of decision-making processes within the federation, regional elites and regional majorities may have a larger say in common policies (those applicable to the whole country without regional differentiation) than they would under a unitary form of government. There are three separate reasons for thinking so: regional voices get amplified by provincial politicians, who are professional spokesmen for regional interests and also have ready access to the media; power structures are modified by intergovernmental bargaining; and the existence of regional governments actually creates vested regional interests, often in the form of organizations that cluster around and support governmental institutions at the regional (provincial/state) level.[7]

All three arguments lead us to suppose that even those policy decisions taken at the centre will be influenced or constrained by regional elites and regional majorities that are able, through federalism, to exercise a degree of power that would be denied them within a unitary state. However, the effect the regions have on central policies is much greater in some federations than in others. Are these differences among federations explained by differences in the structure of institutions, or must we conclude that federal institutions produce such an effect in some circumstances but not in others, that is, that federalism has policy effects that are contingent upon non-institutional factors? Obviously, there are some thorny problems to sort out here. And, to formulate a question that so far has been left obscure: how can one sort out institutional interests – those of provincial or state governments – from the policy preferences of regional majorities?

Federalism and continentalism: Garth Stevenson has made the intriguing if somewhat Sybilline remark that in Canada the constitutional powers of the provinces (especially their ownership and control over natural resources) have acquired such importance that the federal government has become incapable of performing the functions of a national government and that economic elites therefore turn to Washington instead.[8] Whatever this may mean, Stevenson subscribes to the view that federalism weakens the central government, that the provinces have an interest in promoting continentalism or, at a minimum, are incapable of resisting it, and that accordingly federalism is a major factor contributing to Canada's economic and political dependence upon the United States.

It is obviously not a generalization applicable to federalism as such, that it emasculates the central power to the point that it cannot perform the functions of a national government. For example, no one has claimed this of the United States. Our problem, then, is to know – if we accept the view that public policy in Canada has promoted continentalism or has been ineffective in resisting it – what weight to assign to federalism as an explanatory variable and what weight to 'non-federal' factors.

What conclusion may we draw about the effect of federalism on policy? Our earlier attempt to identify the factors impinging on public policy led us to identify eight categories of variable, ranging from the personalities of key decision-makers through to the geopolitical situation of Canada and its role in the world economy. It is my contention that federalism is not an explanatory variable opposed to the others already mentioned. Rather, whatever effect it has, it has through them or in conjunction with them. One ought to see 'federalism' as an aspect of, or as something affecting, several items on a standard list of variables applicable to federal and non-federal countries alike. Looking at the subject this way, one obtains a relatively comprehensive view of the various ways that federalism may affect policy, and thus one equips oneself with a checklist of things to think about or to look for in the conduct of empirical research.

It is, ultimately, the knowledge obtained through case studies that will enable one to make an informed judgment about the impact of federalism on policy – its alleged conservatism, the extent to which it augments the political power and influence of regional elites and regional majorities, the encouragement it offers (in the Canadian case) to continentalism, and so forth. If, on the basis of several case studies, one attempts to formulate generalizations about the effect of federalism on public policy, it is unlikely that those generalizations will apply to any but a single country. The theoretical achievements of even an extended inquiry into federalism and public policy are likely to be slight or non-existent. This is a corollary of our earlier point, that one should attempt to assess the impact of federalism through, or in combination with, other factors that point to the uniqueness of each federal country and to the particular historical context in which it is being examined. Thus we conclude, first, that one can assess the impact of federalism only by making an implicit comparison with a posited alternative – a unitary state, a confederal regime, or independence for at least some of the component states or provinces. Obviously it makes a great deal of difference which of these alternatives is implied in the federal–non-federal comparison.

Second, the structure of the federation – its distribution of powers and the make-up of governmental institutions – is likely to be as important as federalism itself. Indeed, if one is concerned with the probable impact of constitutional change on policy, it would be of limited use to formulate the alternatives as crudely as 'federalism,' 'a unitary state,' or 'dissolution of the federation.'

Third, contingent factors, such as the place of a given federation in the world economy, or the distribution of population and natural resources within it, cannot be ignored. On the contrary, as was earlier stressed, federalism should not be contrasted with such explanatory variables, but should be examined in context with them, its effects thus being tied in with, and inseparable from, factors unique to a given case.

We come back, then, to the list of variables that have been invoked from time to time to explain public policy. Not all of them seem to have much to do with federalism; but the following do seem relevant: the structure of representative and decision-making institutions (number 5 on the list); the drawing, or significance, of political boundaries (7); politically relevant attitudes, values, preferences, and loyalties (6); and foreign economic relations in relation to domestic class structure – that is, in a general way, the composition of political forces (8, 4).

Institutions: The division of powers may create areas of 'policy vacuum' where neither order of government can deal effectively with certain problems or act efficaciously to achieve certain policy aims. Conversely, it may create areas of overlap in which both orders of government may become active. In either case there may be governmental interaction in policy formation, such that policy is really a joint product of the activities of both orders of government. Many observers and indeed many governmental actors have complained about the duplication, confusion, and delays endemic to policy-making in such circumstances. Frequently governments work at cross-purposes, with one order of government sometimes neutralizing the actions of the other; then unfortunate citizens may be caught in the cross-fire.

Even in the absence of such effects, when policy-making in a given field is shared between orders of government, relations of mutual influence arise. These complicate and alter the system of representation. They do so partly because federalism is integral to the design of the institutional circuitry – packed with transformers, semi-conductors, resistors, and condensers – which filters and amplifies the signals through which citizens' needs and desires are communicated to decision-makers. Even more important in this context is the fact that federalism restructures power within the system, multiplying the centres of decision-making and setting up a process of intergovernmental bargaining in which the participants 'represent,' in effect, different interests.

Political boundaries: The classical conception of federalism, while it ignores governmental interaction in policy formation (and therefore cannot consider its policy consequences), is very much attuned to the significance of the distribution of legislative powers. However, its perspective being legalistic, it is more concerned with questions of legislative competence than with policy responsiveness – or lack of it – in relation to the needs and desires of various groups.

The subject of political boundaries may be brought into focus by posing the question, in relation to any given area of government activity: What is the relevant political community? We may presume that in any liberal-democratic state policy-making responds to, or is at least ultimately constrained by, the interests most obviously implicated. Policy decisions are, at least in some degree, affected by the composition of the political community. If its boundaries are redrawn, the constellation of political forces relevant to policy formation changes, and policy choices previously unthought-of, undesired, or politically 'dangerous' may be selected and implemented. The same is true when territorial boundaries remain fixed but functional boundaries, that is, the policy areas assigned by the constitution to specified orders of government, are moved. Any constitutional allocation or re-allocation of legislative powers specifies the political community/communities (federal or provincial) relevant to policy-making in each field. This effect is most simply conceptualized within a classical form of federalism, where it is posited that each of the orders of government acts independently in its own sphere; but it also applies equally to federalism as we know it in Canada, where policy-making frequently involves extensive governmental interaction. In the latter case, both the attractiveness of given policy options, and the political resources of the various governments, may be significantly altered by any changes in the division of powers.

Attitudes, perceptions, values, loyalties: It has been pointed out, notably by J.A. Corry,[9] that political support is frequently as important as the possession of constitutional powers in determining the de facto distribution of policy responsibilities in a federal system. Governments may possess powers, such as the disallowance power in Canada, that have fallen into disuse; their exercise would be unexpected and would be widely regarded as illegitimate. Conversely, governments may exercise the 'prime initiative' in policy formation in areas where they lack constitutional powers, as the central government in Canada has done in several aspects of social policy, through exercise of its spending power. The practical realities of policy-making give great weight to political support, or the lack of it, although necessarily what is done must not contravene the constitution. The significance of the legal aspect of the constitution may, however, be limited by the difficulty of bringing certain policy matters before the courts and by the courts' reticence in pronouncing on matters they deem 'political,' or more appropriate to a legislature.

All this points to the importance of attitudes, preferences, and loyalties, in determining the character of the working constitution of a federal country. Perhaps this is now a commonplace observation, but it is well to be explicit in recognizing that purely subjective factors may underpin the processes of governmental interaction in policy formation and the locus of policy responsibilities ('functional boundaries'). In other words, what we have said so far about the policy relevance of federalism must take account of the subjective element. Further, and this is perhaps the key point, federalism may itself have a powerful effect on attitudes, perceptions, values,and loyalties.

The question of loyalty, or the focus of political loyalties, is crucial in determining whether a given policy dispute is seen as regional in character – that is, as implicating regional interests or regional communities – or is a 'national' issue in the sense that the interests at stake are seen in non-territorial terms (as is the case, for example, with the issue of equality between the sexes). Federalism provides a dual focus of political loyalty and may perpetuate or even create a dual sense of community ('national' and regional). Indeed there may be, as in Quebec, a widespread tendency to view the provincial political community as comprising the nation which, together with one or more other nations, have formed a federal union. This implies, for many Québécois, a sense of distinctiveness built upon a value system that differs from that prevalent in other provinces; for them, federalism is an institutional device that was explicitly designed to protect and perpetuate Quebec's cultural distinctiveness. Doubts about its effectiveness in this regard contributed significantly to *indépendantisme* – a desire to escape the constraints imposed on the Quebec polity by its participation in a federal union. Other provinces too have inherited or acquired a sense of political community that may conflict with or challenge a Canadian sense of political community. To the extent that this occurs, the policy consequences are likely to be pervasive.

However, the tendency toward what one writer has called 'the maturation of the regions'[10] should not be viewed as inexorable: it apparently has not occurred in other successful federations, or not to the same degree as in Canada. This fact simply underscores the importance of viewing federalism in context with other factors relevant to policy formation and seeing its policy effects in conjunction with them.

Composition of political forces: The wisdom of assessing the policy effect of federalism not in isolation from but in conjunction with other factors is most clearly illustrated with reference to Canada's evolving political and economic ties with other countries, particularly the United States. Associated with such ties are changes in the political forces bearing upon Canadian governments both federal and provincial. Allusion has already been made to the work of Harold Innis and his successors on this subject. The key question for us here, however, is whether a relation of reciprocal causation has been set up, in which economic factors (and the domestic class structure associated with them) largely determine the design of political institutions – including the federal aspect – which then acquire an independent causative effect on policy by strengthening certain interests and enfeebling others. This appears to be the position taken by Alan Cairns,[11] though he neglected to stress the complementarity of institutional and non-institutional factors in shaping the evolution of the power structure, and of policy, within federal regimes. Thus he attributed to federalism, apart from the historical and geographical context of particular federations, an effect or a degree of importance which it manifestly has not had in all of them.

The preceding remarks have adumbrated a series of problems which the remainder of this book will explore. Institutions and processes are discussed in chapters 4 and 5. Chapter 4 deals with the categories through which jurisdiction is conferred under the Canadian constitution and with the difficulties attending any attempt to return to a more 'classical' form of federalism. Chapter 5 examines different forms of governmental interaction in policy formation.

The question of 'functional boundaries' and their policy consequences invites a general discussion of centralization and decentralization: what these concepts mean, how (de)centralization may be measured, and some of the possible effects of (de)centralization. These topics are the subject matter of chapter 6.

Regionalism, a subjective phenomenon, denotes a sense of community encompassing territorial subdivisions of a country; it implies that the region is a focal point for political loyalties and that people tend to think that policy disputes implicate regions more than they do strata, such as occupation or class. Chapter 7 reflects upon regionalism and interregional conflict in Canada and upon the relation between (de)centralization and interregional conflict.

Chapters 8 and 9 discuss the capacity of governments in Canada, given the structure of the federal system and constraining external factors, to implement national policies for economic development; and they attempt to identify, given Canada's position as a trading nation, what rationale there may be for having a federal system with extensive central powers over the economy. They ask, in effect, whether the objective of maximizing aggregate welfare requires a relatively centralized form of federalism, or whether this objective is more effectively promoted through a looser political structure in which government in general (whether federal or provincial) has only limited powers to channel and reshape market forces.

Since the subject of the present chapter extends to the remainder of the book, the reader will scarcely expect conclusions at this stage. Nonetheless, one observation is in order. We defined our task as being to trace the effect of federalism on policy. This explanatory variable has now been embedded within others, to which it bears a reciprocal and evolving relation. Policy, too, has its own impact on the changing structure of the federal system and on the other factors in conjunction with which federalism has its putative policy effects. What we have to seek to understand is the dynamics of a complex, changing relation, not the cause-and-effect simplicity of a static world whose structure can be grasped in terms of dependent and independent variables.

4

Entanglement: why the constitutional thicket can't be pruned

Federalism has often been equated with the division of powers. Today, however, there is no federal state in which policy responsibilities are allocated in even moderately watertight compartments to the two (or more) orders of government. Both the division and the sharing of powers have become essential aspects of contemporary federalism. While the distinctiveness of each federal regime is due in no small measure to the two aspects being combined in various ways (with the one or the other predominating), neither may be neglected if we wish to explore the effect of a federal system on policy.

The advantages (and equally, some of the deficiencies) of federalism are usually seen as flowing from the division of powers. Is federalism a 'good' form of government? If the implicit comparison is with independent statehood for the component parts, then federalism is a device for achieving an otherwise unattainable degree of uniformity in policy, whether for politico-cultural, security, or economic goals; but critics may see it as an undesired form of constraint on the autonomy of the units or as a device whereby a national majority dominates and exploits a regional minority. If, by contrast, the implicit comparison is with a unitary state, then federalism is a device for permitting regional diversity in policy, generally to accommodate distinctive regional preferences. However, critics of federalism may decry the incapacity of government, due to the inadequacy of central power, to achieve policy objectives that the constituent parts are presumed to hold in common.

These issues will receive our attention in chapters 6–9. It is necessary first to focus attention on the sharing of policy responsibilities between orders of government, which we do in this chapter and the next. In these chapters we look at areas of jurisdictional vacuum into which both orders of government move but that neither is empowered to fill, at the interlocking of exclusive powers within a single policy field (demanding co-ordination among governments to accomplish policy goals), and at the overlapping of constitutional powers.

The pejorative term for these phenomena is entanglement. It gives rise to considerable irritation and some serious criticism. There are several reasons for complaint. First, when no single order of government has adequate and exclusive powers to form policy in a given field – the typical situation in Canada – it complicates life for the citizen and for interest organizations. It is unclear where responsibility lies, with the result that people do not know who to deal with (i.e. citizens incur inflated 'signalling costs,' to use the term suggested by Breton and Scott).[1] Governments, too, waste time trying, with only partial success, to co-ordinate their activities. Things may get done, but with unnecessary muddle and at avoidable expense.

Second, not only does entanglement (say the critics) increase the cost of government: often things don't get done at all, or they get done too slowly, because politicians won't co-operate with each other. The complaint is that politicians spend their time bickering, trying to protect and extend their jurisdictions, when they should be concentrating on rendering service to the public. The negative consequences of this situation are particularly severe when both orders of government claim authority, engaging in jurisdictional battles in which private individuals and corporations get caught in the cross-fire.

Third, policy objectives may not be met, because neither order of government has the necessary powers, and even concerted action may not work. Historically, this has been a problem in Canada regarding controlled marketing of natural products, although (as I shall argue in the next chapter) interdelegation seems to have resolved the difficulties experienced in the 1930s.

Fourth and finally, when governments do co-ordinate their activities and implement policy jointly, through a process that has been labelled 'executive federalism,'[2] their behaviour is sometimes criticized for being undemocratic, exacerbating the problems of legislative control and responsibility to the electorate.

This indictment of the sharing of policy responsibilities in a federation requires us to ask, and to try to answer, two questions. First, is there any way of avoiding or significantly reducing entanglement, short of abolishing the federal system itself? This question breaks down into several others, which are addressed in this chapter. Second, what political expedients have been devised to cope with a constitutional division of powers that leaves jurisdictional gaps, divides policy fields in an impractical and apparently illogical manner, and creates areas of overlap where both orders of government can become involved? This question leads us to examine modes of government interaction in policy formation, which we do in chapter 5.

HOW ENTANGLEMENT OCCURS

It is now part of the conventional wisdom that the day of 'classical federalism' is over. This concept posited the existence of co-ordinate governments that acted, within their own spheres, independently of the other governments in the federation.[3] This was probably an idealized picture of how federalism worked, even in newly established federations, but it formerly bore at least some semblance to reality. As J.A. Corry has pointed out, the demise of classical federalism in Canada, as elsewhere, may be attributed to integration of the national market, greater mobility of persons, and expansion of the range of services demanded by the citizenry.[4] In short, according to Corry's thesis (which I think is widely accepted), factors external to the decision-making process have impinged upon it and have resulted in changes in the working constitution.

This I take for granted. The question remains, however, whether Canada has moved further from the classical model of federalism than required by the above-mentioned factors – none of which has to do with the structure of political institutions or with the actions of politicians or bureaucrats. In other words, in Canada policy responsibilities are now shared between orders of government to a degree which, judging by public criticism of federal and provincial politicians' inability to co-operate with each other, many people consider to be not only undesirable but also unnecessary. It is this point that I wish to discuss.

It is commonly said that the Constitution Act is outmoded, since the categories of 1867 (still largely intact) are no longer suitable. After all, the argument goes, the Fathers of Confederation could not have foreseen the development of technologies such as telecommunications or undersea mining, they thought of labour relations in terms of master and servant rather than of collective bargaining, and they lived in a world of private charity rather than of public welfare rights. Since 1867 both technological change and the restructuring of social relations have invoked forms of state regulation and types of public services undreamed of by the Fathers. As Paul Weiler has said, expressing his thesis in general terms but illustrating it with Canadian examples:

Social change eventually renders most of the original federal bargain outmoded ... The original law-making functions which were explicitly allocated by the constitution substantially alter their character in ways which are significant to their proper distribution (e.g. the emergence of the rehabilitative ideal in the criminal law). New social problems arise and demand legislative responses which were not foreseen by the draftsman, and thus must be dealt with in terms of the residuary clauses in the constitution (e.g. orderly farm marketing). The governmental units themselves change their character and capacities for legislative action (e.g. Canada's international status). New fundamental values evolve within the nation, and so alter the principles which shaped the original federal bargain (e.g. the claim to equalization of basic social security protections in different regions).[5]

Weiler was not here concerned with the question of entanglement, but every one of the policy problems he cites points to the breakdown of classical federalism. By court decision or by simple political initiative, the policy fields referred to by

Weiler have been divided into a federal and a provincial aspect or have become the subject of joint intervention, co-ordinated or not. Thus, to some extent the prevalence of entanglement in Canada is arguably due to the obsolescence of the written constitution. If we find the constitution doesn't suit our needs, we have the option of not applying it (as is Weiler's preference, discussed below) or of modernizing it to reduce the squeaking and lurching, like retrofitting a Red River cart with shock absorbers.

A competing explanation of jurisdictional gaps and overlaps and of tortured distinctions among exclusive constitutional powers – all of which contribute to entanglement – is the tendentious claim that the Constitution Act has been badly interpreted. The extreme statement of the case is that of the O'Connor Report, 1939. O'Connor, who was counsel to the Senate, echoed many of the complaints voiced by constitutional lawyers and others during the 1930s, to the effect that the Judicial Committee of the Imperial Privy Council had emasculated the central government's capacity to enact laws for the peace, order, and good government of Canada and had inflated the significance of several provincial powers, notably the 'property and civil rights' clause. He complained that the Judicial Committee had ignored the fact that 'all Dominion legislative powers, according to the text, are exclusive' and consequently had found provincial aspects in many subjects properly under federal control: 'I cannot follow Lord Watson's references to "matters" as if there could be dual legislation in relation to some "matter" or that rightful exercise of jurisdiction under section 91 can result in "trenching" on section 92. To my mind a matter is within section 91 or 92, or out of it.'[6]

A counter-proposition of greater subtlety was put forward some fifteen years later by W.R. Lederman, who wrote:

The categories of laws enumerated in sections 91 and 92 are not in the logical sense mutually exclusive; they overlap and encroach upon one another in many more respects than is usually realized. To put it another way, many rules of law have one feature that renders them relevant to a provincial class of laws and another feature which renders them equally relevant logically to a federal class of laws ... For a simple illustration, take the well-known rule that a will made by an unmarried person becomes void if and when he marries. Is this a rule of 'marriage' [federal] ... or of 'property and civil rights' [provincial]? ... The decision as to which classification is to be used for a given purpose has to be made on non-logical grounds of policy and justice.[7]

This is, in my view, a much more easily defensible position than O'Connor's. It suggests that the joint occupancy of policy fields in Canada reflects the very terms of the Constitution Act and is due neither to its obsolesence nor to faulty construction of its terms.

Fine. But does this mean that the British North America Act was sloppy patchwork from the beginning, or does it mean that even the cleverest draughtsman cannot eliminate the logical ambiguities that Lederman discerns? Lederman's view, which I agree with, is that no matter how one defines the categories, mutual exclusion – in the logical sense – cannot be attained. Thus, even disregarding the political difficulties involved in the amending process, there is only very limited scope for making revisions to the division of powers such that the overlapping of governmental powers and activities will be reduced.

We shall come back to this subject, but first it is necessary to ask whether the existing distribution of powers, which is a complex one anyway, is further and unnecessarily complicated because our politicians have disregarded the spirit if not the letter of the constitution. Is it not true that each order of government has extended its policy tentacles into every discoverable crevice in the other's jurisdiction?

Perhaps so, but this is not necessarily reprehensible; and I do not think that we ought, except perhaps in some particular instances, to condemn politicians for failing to respect the constitution. If one thinks they do, that is because the Canadian constitution is often thought to say more than it really does. For the general public, political debate is the readiest source of information on constitutional questions, and political debate – here as in other matters – oversimplifies the issues. It would be well to reflect that politicians are unreliable mentors in constitutional law, even when they themselves have some schooling in it, because electoral motivations and administrative convenience cause them to stretch and shrink the clauses of the Constitution Act. Sometimes the constitution is a convenient shield, held up by politicians to protect themselves against charges of inaction or ineffectiveness. More commonly it is invoked in an attempt to clear the field of other governments, the recitation of constitutional powers being like the trill of a songbird laying claim to desirable territory. Here, for example, is Ontario songbird John Robarts at the 1969 constitutional conference of first ministers, with Newfoundland's Premier Smallwood amplifying false notes:

Honourable J.P. Robarts: ... surely our problem is the stress we feel about the unlimited spending power of the Federal Government when it is used to move into a field that the Federal Government cannot get into under any other constitutional heading.

Right Honourable P.E. Trudeau: This is what I cannot see. Are there some fields where we cannot give money to individuals? We are not talking of shared-cost programmes. We are not talking of joint grants. We are not talking of highways. We are talking of giving money to a Canadian citizen because he is either young or very old or blind or something like that.

Honourable J.P. Robarts: My problem would be this: education is a provincial constitutional jurisdiction. Are you then free to make grants to students in the elementary school system of the Province of Ontario? ... You cannot get into the field of education so you use another door to achieve the same thing and thus thwart the provisions of the British North America Act ...

Honourable J.R. Smallwood: Premier, let me ask you this: now, at this moment, under the

B.N.A. Act, as it is now and has been right along, could the Government of Canada offer money to every student in Canada that it wishes to?
Honourable J.P. Robarts: Well, I believe that this is the proposition we put.
Honourable J.R. Smallwood: Can it now, at this time? Is it constitutionally able to do so?
Honourable J.P. Robarts: Well, I am not a good enough constitutional lawyer to answer that question, but I would say that the unrestricted use of the spending power has been used to circumnavigate or get around certain areas of provincial jurisdiction, which is I suppose
...
Honourable J.R. Smallwood: If you can now make a [family allowance] cheque every month to help clothe and house and feed the children in the family; if the Government of Canada can do that now, could they not do it to help educate these same children?
Honourable J.P. Robarts: They can.
Honourable J.R. Smallwood: But does it do it constitutionally and properly?
Honourable J.P. Robarts: If you read the British North America Act, it simply says education is the responsibility of the province. Now, I am quite certain the Federal Government can do this if it chooses. All I am saying to you is that you are going to change your Constitution without rewriting one word of it if you allow that sort of thing to go on.[8]

Robarts' case was not constitutional in the juridical sense, but political. The Constitution Act allocates certain powers to the provincial legislatures and other powers to the federal parliament; some powers it allocates concurrently to both. It does not, however, impose a *responsibility* to use those powers in a particular way or to use them at all: it merely defines the *jurisdiction* of each order of government.

A government's sense of responsibility to use its powers for certain ends derives from electoral impulsion or perhaps from the consciences as well as from the ambitions of government leaders. Upon the politicians lies a responsibility to use the powers of the state, sometimes vigorously, sometimes with restraint, and sometimes not at all. Implicitly, what Robarts was saying in the passage quoted was that his government had responsibilities in the field of education and the federal government had a responsibility to avoid interfering. His was an argument that should not concern a court of law.

The distinction between jurisdiction and responsibility alerts us to an important question. Acknowledgment of a responsibility, whether political or moral, implies recognition of an obligation to act consistently with the achievement of certain purposes. Ought we to expect jurisdiction – the definition of legislative powers and hence also of administrative authority – to be couched in the same terms as those we use to express the responsibilities of government? If so, our constitution does not measure up: under the Constitution Act governmental powers are not congruent with current conceptions of where governmental responsibilities do lie or should lie.

Should there not, then, be a reallocation of powers in terms more consistent with current conceptions of the policy responsibilities of governments? Would not such changes in the constitution reduce the entanglement of governmental powers and activities? I think the answer is that it might do so, slightly, by eliminating some cases of divided jurisdiction. However, new concurrent fields would almost certainly open up, producing a different sort of sharing of policy responsibilities and virtually eliminating judicial enforcement of the division of powers.

In cases of divided jurisdiction a given policy field is split into two mutually exclusive parts, one federal and the other provincial. For instance, in the marketing of farm products, the provinces may regulate intraprovincial sales and the federal government may regulate interprovincial and international sales, and neither may encroach upon the other's jurisdiction; thus any effective policy must be implemented by co-ordinated action and through recourse to expedients such as the delegation of federal powers to provincial marketing boards or vice versa. By contrast, concurrency denotes a situation where essentially the same law may be passed by either order of government, with either the federal or the provincial law being paramount, i.e. overriding any conflicting provisions in legislation enacted at the other level.

In policy fields where, by judicial decision, jurisdiction has been divided, the courts are periodically called upon to refine or extend their rulings delineating the scope of federal and provincial powers. One option they have is to relax judicial constraints on the exercise of governmental powers, thus effectively expanding constitutional concurrency. Indeed, this is precisely what Paul Weiler would like to see the courts do, because he thinks the courts are unsuited to making the essentially political judgments involved in most cases that turn on questions of ultra vires. Consider the following passages from, respectively, Lederman and Weiler. Lederman:

Canadian judges do not have to consider the substantive merit of a challenged law in this sense [i.e. in the sense that a freedom guaranteed in the constitution may conflict with some vital public interest – the statement antedates the Canadian Charter of Rights and Freedoms]; indeed they are accustomed to labour the point that they are not concerned with whether such a law is good or bad, necessary or unnecessary. They say in effect that the malady and its proper cure are not their concern, rather that they have to ask only, Who is to be the physician? [However, a challenged law may have] features of meaning relevant to both federal and provincial classes of laws. Then our judges cannot be content simply to ask, who is to be the physician? They must rather ask, who is the better physician to prescribe in this way for this malady?[9]

And Weiler:

It is impossible to separate the meaning of a legal proposition from the context of the procedure by which it was originally enacted, the demands of the situation within which it was created and the purposes or intentions of those who drafted it ... Gradually the significance of the original [federal] scheme recedes as the gap widens between the frozen constitutional language and the rapidly changing society. As this happens, the courts inevitably begin to elaborate a new federal scheme in the course of adjudicating many novel and unforeseen problems. As we look back, we can see that this is the objective effect of the work of the courts even though judges may have disguised their personal responsibility for the results – from themselves as well as from others – by adoption of a very formal style of legal reasoning. The major thrust of constitutional literature in Canada in the last thirty years or so has been built on this insight into judicial responsibility for constitutional innovation. Writers have not only described the nature and extent of judicial alterations to our federal structure but have also tried to articulate the factors which ought to influence the courts in their allocation of legislative power to one jurisdiction or another. This whole effort is directed at one basic constitutional question: 'which is the better physician for a social malady, the dominion or provincial government?'[10]

Weiler's conclusion is sweeping: 'Federalism questions are not amenable to stable legal principles.' He urges that the Supreme Court should simply stop declaring statutes and regulations ultra vires. The result would be joint occupancy (in the legal sense) of many policy fields and political negotiation to determine the respective scope of federal and provincial activities. Cases of conflict between federal and provincial laws would be dealt with by a standard rule of federal paramountcy, such that federal laws would override provincial laws in any and all cases of conflict. Though this would give 'the national government the legal power to erode the federal system through a gradual process of self-aggrandizement, … we can and must rely on the political constraints of the federal system to ensure that this does not happen.'[11]

And there, neatly expressed, we have the dilemma. If the courts recognize (implicitly, one presumes) that the constitution necessarily ages over time and that to 'enforce' it really means to substitute for the original federal bargain a new federal scheme of the judiciary's making, and if consequently they relax all jurisdictional rules and avoid declaring legislation ultra vires, the provinces inevitably lose all protection against self-aggrandizement by the federal government. The regions lose whatever protection federalism offers them against domination by national majorities. This is an ineluctable consequence of universal concurrency together with a standard rule of federal paramountcy. If, however, the courts accept responsibility for umpiring the federal system, they find themselves obliged to apply frozen constitutional language to a continuously evolving situation, with results that may be castigated (as they are by Weiler) as arbitrary and frequently indefensible, even in logic.

The courts' dilemma is a grave one. The policy responsibilities of government change over time, and it is necessary to adapt our institutions (including the division-of-powers aspect of the federal system) to changing needs. However, the regions – or groups that form a majority in one or more provinces, but occupy a minority position in the country as a whole – demand protection against unanticipated or unwanted changes in the rules of the political game. To some extent this dilemma has been resolved, though obviously not to everybody's satisfaction, through changes in working relationships among governments. As will be more fully argued below, however, not only do political events and processes transform the working constitution: the written constitution underpins a set of political processes (interaction among governments) through which much of Canadian policy is made. Unless, through reform of political institutions at the centre, regional majorities find an alternative means of protecting and pursuing their interests, they will have to continue to rely upon the provincial governments and – as guarantors of provincial powers – the courts, to prevent their being overwhelmed by national majorities. However convenient it might be for the justices of the Supreme Court to follow Weiler's advice and retire from the business of declaring statutes ultra vires, they would have to realize that to do so would be as political an act as (in Weiler's acid phrase) 'making up the rules as they go along.'

There is also another problem arising from judicial interpretation of powers, a problem which, though of lesser political importance, is more germane to the matter of entanglement. If the courts generally opt for the rule of mutual exclusivity of legislative powers rather than for the rule of legislative concurrency (as Lederman tells us they prefer to do),[12] jurisdiction may be divided between the two senior orders of government. There then occurs a particular form of entanglement: co-ordination of federal and provincial policy initiatives may be required if shared policy goals are to be achieved; alternatively, when policy disputes arise between orders of government, a more destructive form of entanglement may occur, as governments attempt to neutralize or counteract the policy initiatives of the other and to assert their own supremacy in the field.

However, entanglement – in the sense of governments working at cross-purposes – cannot necessarily be avoided when the sharing of policy responsibilities occurs through concurrency rather than through the division of legislative powers. Ideally, under concurrency, governments will reach a tacit or negotiated agreement on the sharing of policy responsibilities in the field. In the absence of such agreement both may legislate, and both legislations will be valid except in cases of pure duplication (which presumably doesn't matter much) or in cases of actual conflict in the rigorous sense that obeying one law involves breaking the other.[13] But the legislations may, without conflicting in this way, still express incompatible policy goals, as when federal and provincial tax regimes aim to influence investment in different ways. In all such cases, too, the clean separation of federal and provincial policy responsibilities becomes impossible. The policy landscape cannot acquire the appearance of formal gardens, with neat edges and trimmed shrubs; it is an overgrown field, invaded by a rampant constitutional thicket that resists pruning by court and legislature alike.

It is true, as Weiler argues, that the framers of the BNA Act drafted a list of governmental powers whose meaning derived from the conditions of the day and that they could not have foreseen the wide range of activities that the state, a hundred years later, would be required to assume. Conceivably, as O'Connor and many others have argued, the courts have been too ingenious in finding constitutional justification for the exercise of provincial powers and too restrictive in the interpretation of federal ones. And it is certain that politicians at both levels have exploited opportunities offered them by the act to extend the range of their activities in directions and to an extent that a simple reading of the act would not appear to justify. All these factors may help to explain the blurring of jurisdictional boundaries; but the basic reason for the overlapping of federal and provincial activities – for entanglement – is that contemporary conceptions of the policy responsibilities of government do not match the categories in which jurisdiction was conferred under the act.

ALLOCATING JURISDICTION: THE CATEGORIES EMPLOYED

Might not the division of powers be reformulated in such a way as to achieve a clear and simple allocation of responsibility for the various policy fields, some being federal and others being provincial? Perhaps so. But then, I shall argue, virtually all judicial control over the extent of federal and provincial powers would disappear, and the 'balance' of the federal system would be determined entirely politically. (Weiler would approve.) Even if this did not result in unrestrained aggrandizement of central power and emasculation of the provinces, it would certainly extend the sharing of policy responsibilities between the two senior orders of government. We would have to learn to swallow our misgivings about entanglement and to embrace it, hoping for intergovernmental co-operation.

Governmental responsibilities for specific policy fields could be clearly and simply set out in the constitution in a way that might assist the public – say, newspaper editorial writers – in judging the legitimacy of a policy initiative. One presumes that few specific objectives would be given special constitutional status (thus the 'equalization' clause in the Constitution Act of 1982 would probably be atypical); but certainly a constitution could assign, say, 'health care' to one order of government or the other without specifying the standards to be achieved or the means for doing so. If one went down the list of governmental activities in the late twentieth century, assigning each to a federal, a provincial, or a concurrent list, and if one inscribed the lists in a revised constitution, such a document would contain a much clearer delineation of policy responsibilities than does (or ever did) the BNA Act of 1867.

A government that declared that it was doing a particular thing to fulfil a policy responsibility assigned to it might be judged by public opinion to be acting wisely and in a way that respected the revised and constitutionally enshrined federal bargain, or to be overstepping the bounds of its moral authority. Possibly, even, a constitutional court might be created to make such judgments, which it would do on the explicit grounds that an impugned law or regulation was justified (or not) given its stated purposes; but the function would not be judicial in any traditional sense, and it is hard to imagine what sort of institution other than an elected legislature could legitimately make such pronouncements. Certainly our own Supreme Court, if one may make inferences from pre-Charter jurisprudence, would shy away from the task. (Post-Charter jurisprudence may suggest a different conclusion, but it is too early to tell.)

The general point is that if we expect judicial enforcement of the division of powers, we are unlikely to get it (nor do I think we would want it) if jurisdiction is defined in terms of policy responsibilities, that is in terms of the purposes or objectives of government action. If powers were defined in terms of the goals to be realized or aimed for, the courts would be called upon to assess the efficacy of specific measures in relation to their stated purposes. With such an obviously political task, judges would undoubtedly disqualify themselves, and would say (but in nice legal language), 'Anything goes.'

The point may be illustrated by referring to the judgment of Mr Justice Beetz in the Anti-Inflation Act reference case (1976). Lawyers for the federal goverment and for the province of Ontario had argued that the subject of the act was containment and reduction of inflation. This subject is not one reserved to the provinces and is therefore (it was claimed) within federal competence under the residuary power. If the Supreme Court had been willing to accept this argument, the control of wages, prices, and profit margins would have been permanently brought within federal jurisdiction as a matter relating to the peace, order, and good government of Canada. Mr Justice Beetz (supported in this part of his judgment by a majority of the court) wrote:

I have no reason to doubt that the Anti-Inflation Act is part of a more general program aimed at inflation and which may include fiscal and monetary measures and government expenditure policies. I am prepared to accept that inflation was the occasion or the reason for its enactment. But I do not agree that inflation is the subject matter of the Act ...

The 'containment and reduction of inflation' does not pass muster as a new subject matter. It is an aggregate of several subjects some of which form a substantial part of provincial jurisdiction. It is totally lacking in specificity. It is so pervasive that it knows no bounds. Its recognition as a federal head of power would render most provincial powers nugatory.[14]

Mr Justice Beetz was not denying that the federal government had responsibility to do what it could to combat inflation; he merely said that in doing so it must find instruments within its jurisdiction. Were jurisdiction defined (in this case, by judicial decision) in terms as broad as 'the containment and reduction of inflation,' no subsequent court could impose any serious limitation of federal economic powers if Parliament were to assert, or appeared to have presumed, that its actions were aimed at curtailing inflationary pressures.

Examination of the Constitution Act reveals that the categories used to define jurisdiction fall into groups, each group reflecting a different criterion for assigning powers. The more specific the criteria, the readier the courts have been to validate legislation arguably based upon them. Here, then, are four criteria ranked in order of increasing vagueness and decreasing willingness of the courts to give them much significance in their interpretation of the Act:

Clientele: The sole example, so far as I know, is 'Indians' in the clause 'Indians and Lands reserved for the Indians' (section 91:24). That the Constitution Act enumerates an item of federal jurisdiction in this way has enabled the Parliament of Canada to define 'Indian' as it wishes – for example, to include children of Indian men who marry non-Indians but not those of Indian women who marry non-Indians – and to legislate comprehensively on matters affecting them. Under this clause the federal government does many things in relation to Indians that are otherwise handled by the provinces (e.g. in education).

Instruments of policy: The pre-eminent examples of instrumental powers are the two clauses on taxation (sections 91:3 and 92:2). Other clauses also appear to have an instrumental character or are so used. For example, the federal power over criminal law has been used as an instrument of competition policy, and the provincial licensing power (section 92:9), although its use is expressly limited to the purpose of 'the raising of a Revenue for Provincial, Local, or Municipal Purposes,' has none the less been employed with regulatory effect (for example, to prohibit certain kinds of entertainment in taverns). And the very sweeping provincial jurisdiction over 'Property and Civil Rights in the Province' (section 92:13) is often used instrumentally, thus employing the powers conferred by this section for purposes by no means apparent in the phrase itself. A major example is regulation of the larger part of industrial relations. Indeed, there are many other matters that also could be interpreted as falling within the category of rights arising out of contracts – in the case of industrial relations, contracts between employer and employee. In this matter, and many others, the instrumental power of 'Property and Civil Rights' has proved more powerful than the subject of 'The Regulation of Trade and Commerce' (section 91:2).

Subject, or the substance of policy: Examples are education, agriculture, naturalization of aliens, and navigation and shipping. Admittedly, it is hazardous to try to classify the various clauses of the act according to their instrumental or their substantive character. Many (perhaps most) clauses appear substantive but are capable of being used instrumentally. That is, they may have a bearing on a number of substantive policy areas whether enumerated in the act or not. The reason for making a distinction between instrument and subject, even though it is difficult to apply, is to emphasize the disjunction between what a law is 'about' (in a policy, but not necessarily in a constitutional sense) – the control of inflation is an example – and the capacity of a legislature to draw on its powers in order to fulfil its responsibilities as it sees them.

When achievement of substantive purposes calls for use of instruments vested in another legislature, the courts have been readier to look at the instruments than at the substance. For example, the federal agriculture power (held concurrently with the provinces, but with provision for federal paramountcy) was restricted by the courts to matters affecting production, while intraprovincial commerce in agricultural produce, however important to the well-being of farmers, was declared to lie outside federal competence. Thus, as already noted, the marketing of farm products became one of the classic areas of divided jurisdiction. Admittedly, there have been cases in which instruments have transparently been employed in such a way as to encroach on an object of policy outside the legislature's jurisdiction, and legislative power has been held ultra vires because the use of the legislative power was regarded as 'colourable.' On the whole, however, instruments seem to outweigh subjects in judicial interpretation.

Purpose or objectives: The only example I know of where jurisdiction is couched in terms of purpose is the famous 'Peace, Order and Good Government' clause (the opening paragraph of section 91). As is well known, the practical import of this clause is slight except in emergency condi tions, when it becomes (in Donald Smiley's apt phrase) 'Canada's other constitution.'[15]

In sum: the terms in which jurisdiction is conferred in the Constitution Act do not correspond to the responsibilities of government or to the purposes of government action. It is, however, responsibilities and purposes that usually concern us in studies of federalism and public policy. One must not make sweeping statements about 'responsibilities' as if they were, or could wisely be, conferred upon political authorities by a constitution.

These observations carry, in my opinion, a significant lesson for anyone who would like to redefine governmental powers under the Canadian constitution to achieve some measure of disentanglement. The thought that disentanglement is not only desirable but ought to be a guiding principle of constitutional reform (if ever amendment of the division of powers is reinscribed on the political agenda) presupposes a neater correspondence between governmental responsibilities and the categories in which jurisdiction may usefully be conferred. 'Disentanglement' may be an appropriate objective for politicians, but I do not see it as a practical objective for any redefinition of constitutional categories.

One reason for not attempting to rewrite our constitutional categories in terms of policy responsibilities – quite apart from the obvious objection, that it would become much more quickly outdated than our own constitution has done – is that judicial enforcement of the division of powers would become well-nigh impossible. Whatever the shortcomings of the Supreme Court as an 'umpire of the federal system,' it is probably no exaggeration to say that to retire it from its role as umpire would be the end of federalism in Canada. If this seems extreme to some readers, I would remind them that in those federations in which there is no effective judicial restraint on the exercise of central powers, the make-up of political institutions at the centre compensates for this. For example, in the United States and in West Germany, central institutions provide far more effective regional representation than seems to be achieved through parliamentary institutions on the Westminster model.

There is also a second reason for not making policy responsibilities into constitutional categories. This reason is a corollary of the first. If jurisdiction were defined in terms of policy responsibilities, overlapping of federal and provincial activities would be hugely extended, not reduced. The probable effect would be to turn the provinces into administrative agencies of the central government. To the extent that they retained any real policy-making role, in practice their powers would be concurrent rather than exclusive. The intent might be to reduce entanglement, but the means employed would accomplish exactly the opposite.

INTERPLAY OF LAW AND POLITICS

As we have seen, a variety of instruments may be used to implement policy or to fulfil policy responsibilities assumed by politicians either on their own initiative or in response to citizens' demands. Some instruments are under federal control while others are under the control of the provinces. Still others, like the direct taxing power, may be wielded by both orders of government. It seems that the wider the choice of instruments for the implementation of policy, the less restrictive the constitution in the relevant policy areas.

Accordingly, the constitution appears no longer to be as potent as it formerly was in prescribing the scope of (respectively) federal and provincial action. There are several reasons for thinking so:

The increasing importance of the service activities of government: When the BNA Act was written, the role of government was perceived in basically negative terms: it could regulate or proscribe certain activities but – even though in the Canadian case the federal government was expected to play an entrepreneurial role in opening up a country from sea to sea – service functions were much less prominent than they are today. This is true especially of people-oriented services like education, health care, and social welfare, but it applies also to assistance to industry and active participation of government in the economy. On the whole, a constitution is better adapted to prescribing what a government may or may not regulate, or the instruments it may or may not use in regulation, than it is in defining the scope of service activities. Complications arise, however, when a service is introduced which has a regulatory effect. An example is the subsidies offered by the Canadian Dairy Commission (a service activity), which are allocated in such a way as to control production (a regulatory activity).

The huge resources now available to governments: In part the resources in question are financial, as governments can now extract a hitherto unheard-of proportion of national income and use it for public purposes. In part governmental resources are of a technical nature and reflect its capacity to acquire and process information, to draw on skills of the rarest character (to estimate reserves of hydrocarbon fuels, for example), and to control vast administrative structures. When such resources – both financial and technical – are available, the range of instruments that may be acquired and manipulated by policy-makers is broad and diverse. In consequence, a government's possibility of finding some instrument within its jurisdiction to do what it wishes is materially enhanced. Diversity of instruments means fewer restrictions imposed by the constitution.

The opening up, by judicial interpretation, of new areas of concurrent jurisdiction: Only two subjects are expressly concurrent according to the original terms of the BNA Act: agriculture and immigration. In both cases there is provision for federal paramountcy, i.e. in the case of conflict, federal law prevails. Since 1867, many other areas of concurrency have been opened up by judicial interpretation, again with federal paramountcy; and by constitutional amendment the contributory pensions field is now also concurrent, though in this case paramountcy lies with the provinces. While one should not neglect the importance of knowing where paramountcy lies, the opening of concurrent fields does diminish the importance of the constitution in determining which level of government takes the lead in, or exclusively controls, policy formation in any given areas.

The use of the federal spending power: In the case of service activities, particularly if they are expensive, conditional federal payments to provincial governments may influence policy formation. This has been of great importance in the fields of social security and health care. Not only has there been some effect on provincial spending priorities, since for specified programs the provinces can obtain a subsidy from the federal government, but the scope and character of the programs have been influenced by federal policies. For example, in the Medical Care Act of 1966, the federal government demanded that the provincial plan meet four criteria in order to be eligible for the federal subsidy: '(1) comprehensive coverage of physicians' services, both general practitioners' and specialists', (2) universal coverage on uniform terms and conditions, (3) administration on a non-profit basis by the province or a provincial agency, and (4) portability of benefits between provinces ...' Since 1977 (with the introduction of Established Programs Financing), federal payments to the provinces no longer depend on program costs in medicare, hospital insurance, and post-secondary education. Nonetheless, in the two health-related programs, Ottawa insists on provincial compliance with federal policy and has reformulated and tightened the criteria which, if infringed, will entail financial sanctions, as under the Canada Health Act, 1984.[16]

The above factors – increasing scope of service activities, augmented governmental access to financial and technical resources, extension of concurrency, and use of the spending power – may have contributed to the impression, apparently held by some observers, that the constitution has virtually no effect on what Canadian governments (federal and provincial) actually do. These people think that the constitution, as a legal document, has already been replaced by political processes as governments, flouting the spirit if not the terms of the Constitution Act, muscle in on each others' territory.

In my opinion this view misrepresents the interplay between political and legal elements in Canada's working constitution. The constitution does not effectively separate the policy areas in which federal and provincial governments, respectively, are active, but it does impose limits on the range of powers – often defined in instrumental rather than substantive terms – that each may legally exercise. An analogy might be that the constitution supplies each order of government with certain tools, which in some cases are adapted only to quite specific uses and in other cases are quite versatile; but it does not prescribe the extent to which the tools are to be used, or even for what purpose. When both senior orders of government consider that they have policy responsibilities in a given field, the powers they have at their disposal may be used in ways that supplement, reinforce, or counteract the effect of those powers that are exercised by the other order of government. Thus the law of the Canadian constitution is best understood as underpinning a set of political processes or a set of interactions between federal and provincial authorities.[17] Policy, in many fields, is then a joint product, the result of a rather messy decision-making process in which more than a single order of government is involved. Call it entanglement or shared responsibility, as you will.

5

Government interaction
in policy formation:
power relations in the federal system

A leitmotif of the literature on the processes of government interaction in policy formation[1] is that good machinery promotes intergovernmental co-operation, which most writers regard as beneficial to the public. A complementary theme is that observance of behavioural norms building up mutual trust is often just as important as devising suitable institutional mechanisms or maintaining regular patterns of communication. Some attention is also paid to factors such as location and timing of meetings, which may affect the social chemistry of interaction among participants at intergovernmental conferences. In short, the main thrust of the literature is that the 'right' machinery, supported by a variety of conditions conducive to intergovernmental agreement, may help to resolve difficulties arising out of divided jurisdiction and concurrency, or the sharing of policy responsibilities between orders of government.

A shortcoming of writing in this genre is that it seldom considers how government interaction in policy formation expresses and may affect the structure of power within the federal system. The analysis tends to be strangely non-political. Or let us say that it frequently neglects to take adequate account of factors militating against resolution of policy differences among governments. If 'politics' is an activity wherein some segment of a larger group attempts to impose a policy upon the whole or upon some other segment, while others prefer a different policy or no policy,[2] an adequate analysis of a political situation must take pains to identify the opposing interests, the seriousness of the conflict between them, and the capacity of one interest to predominate over another.

An overview of the institutions and processes of government interaction in policy formation, if it is to take proper account of the political – as opposed to the administrative – aspect of the subject, should distinguish three rather different situations.

First, governments may share the same goals, in which case the problem is to devise machinery and to regularize practices that will circumvent any obstacles to co-operation among them. This problem occupied the attention of several Canadian writers during the 1930s, who saw federalism – particularly when judges attempted to contain the powers of each order of government within the 'watertight compartments' supposedly constructed in 1867 – as an inconvenient and possibly outmoded form of government.

Second, governments may have policy differences but share some underlying objectives, such that mutual concessions will produce a mutual benefit. Most of the recent literature on intergovernmental relations evokes this class of cases. It details the processes of negotiation through which a common policy denominator is sought and through which compromises to translate it into action are devised.

Third, governments may be antagonists, either because their interests as institutions are incompatible or because they give expression to interests external to themselves, one of which seeks to prevail over the others. One result may be continuing, unresolved conflict; another may be a modus vivendi on some range of issues, essentially because one government recognizes the other's superior political and/or constitutional position and seeks to minimize costs flowing from its own weakness. These categories of cases receive insufficient attention in the literature.

Where governments seek mutually incompatible goals, it is futile to propose more co-operation or to design machinery capable of achieving fuller intergovernmental co-ordination or more regular liaison. Under these conditions it makes sense to pay close attention to the components and sources of governmental power, defined as the capacity to realize one's will against resistance.

In this chapter I follow that injunction: we will examine how power relations in the Canadian federal state, as expressed in a variety of modes of governmental interaction in policy formation, relate to the constitutional structure. In keeping with this objective, the first section identifies and distinguishes seven modes of interaction. A second section discusses how various institutional or constitutional factors give rise to one or other of these modes; here it will be important to bear in mind that substantive policy questions, as well as the machinery devised to handle them, determine the character of interaction processes. The chapter concludes with a comment on power relations within the federal system. It is acknowledged that these relations impinge upon institutions and processes that are the primary focus of the literature on intergovernmental relations. It is also argued, however, that any attempt to redesign institutions and processes of intergovernmental relations, with a view to achieving greater harmony and better co-operation, would probably alter the power relations in ways that are arguably undesirable.

MODES OF INTERACTION

The modes of government interaction we shall examine are those involving policy formation by: a process of thrust and riposte; one government's voluntary vacancy of a field; exchange of information, followed by independent action; joint funding of programs; delegation or interdelegation of powers; legislative and/or administrative supplementation; and the federalization of political institutions at the centre. Broadly speaking, the modes of interaction involving unilateralism (such that policy is formed through a sequence of unilateral actions, accompanied or not by 'federal-provincial diplomacy') are listed at the top of this typology, and those modes involving collaborative action are found toward the bottom.

Policy-Making by Thrust and Riposte

If in some instances government interaction in policy formation seems to take on the characteristics of treaty-making among allied nations, in other instances it may be more akin to a form of signal-sending between rival powers, in which words are either absent or are routinely taken as bluff or propaganda. Such interaction is what war games are made of, the stock-in-trade of the Strangelove scholars who simulate international crises. The domestic brinkmanship of federal and provincial governments is pallid by comparison; but it exists none the less, and in Canada some policies are formed by engaging in it. It is one style of government behaviour leading to formation of policy by a sequence of unilateral actions.

A case in point is taxation of firms engaged in the exploitation of non-renewable resources − with all the implications that taxation of the resources industries carries for the pace of resource development, processing of raw materials within the province of production, and distribution of the wealth derived from the sale of energy and mineral ores. In 1971 the central government announced plans to reduce its taxes on mining profits, 'accompanied [as R.D. Brown notes] by a denial of any deduction for provincial mining taxes.' This combination of policies would 'leave tax elbow room to the provinces to develop their own tax policies for the industry.' Brown comments:

These federal proposals represented in part an abdication of federal influence over the mining industry in favour of the provinces. The reduction in the level of federal taxes on the mining industry, coupled with the establishment of a federal system of taxation which is completely independent of, and does not allow any specific deduction or relief for, provincial mining and income taxation, was obviously designed both to satisfy the demand of the provincial governments for greater influence in mining taxation, and to allow for the development of independent federal and provincial tax systems.[3]

Some provincial governments (notably British Columbia's) moved quickly to take advantage of this federal initiative and started to take their share of economic rents through revised royalty schedules rather than through mining taxes. The former were deductible; the latter would no longer be so after 1976.

This was also the period of the first rapid escalation in world oil prices, and Alberta introduced new royalties on 'old oil' to skim off about two-thirds of the increase in corporate profits resulting from the actions of OPEC. Only the remaining third could be tapped by Ottawa – and then only partially – through the corporation income tax. The federal response, presented in the May 1974 budget, was to declare that henceforth royalty payments to provincial governments would no longer be deductible in calculating taxable incomes. The new provision applied equally to mining firms and to oil and gas producers. Again, Brown's comment is apposite:

The dramatic increase in provincial resource revenues following the recent provincial tax and royalty increases would naturally tend to result in a decline in the proportion of the total tax and royalty burden on the industries going to the federal government. Without further federal initiatives, this decline would probably continue in the years ahead, consequent on the scheduled reduction in the effective federal tax rate on mining profits after 1976 and probable future provincial increases in mining taxes and oil royalties. The result was that the federal government would receive a sharply lower proportion of what was turning out to be an extremely lucrative tax field, as well as having a declining influence generally on the industries.

This position, on reflection, obviously did not seem attractive to Finance Minister Turner, and he moved to redress the balance by increasing his government's share of resource income.[4]

In this federal-provincial dispute, resource firms were caught in the cross-fire. The situation resulting from the May 1974 budget was clearly untenable, since in some cases an increase in the price of the commodities would result in a combined marginal royalty-plus-tax burden of more than 100 per cent. This uncomfortable situation was prolonged by the defeat of the federal government and its budget in the House and an ensuing election. By the time the budget was reintroduced in the fall, Alberta had agreed to reduce its royalty schedules, and in the budget the federal rates of tax were moderated somewhat.

This was a form of policy-making by thrust and riposte. Neither order of government could oust the other from the field, and each was conscious that its actions would affect decisions taken by the other. Policy (looking at it from the perspective of the companies or from that of the energy-consuming and tax-paying public) was the sum of federal and provincial actions. The situation was by no means comfortable for the firms caught in the cross-fire, but perhaps no other mode of policy formation was possible unless one order of government simply vacated the field. The incompatibility of objectives – both orders of government aimed to tap a larger share of the economic rents – made a less conflictual form of interaction difficult and may have made it impossible.

The energy policy disputes of 1980-81 took very much the same form as the

1974 controversy, though in the more recent case the range of issues was broader. Prior to announcement of the National Energy Program (NEP) in November 1980, the federal government found itself in the awkward position of trying to hold back on price increases demanded by producing provinces, urged upon it by most professional economists, and increasingly supported by central Canadian business interests which saw higher prices as necessary to achieve long-term security of supply. All these pressures were reinforced by the increasing drain on the federal treasury resulting from the policy of subsidizing imports which were growing steadily in relation to exports. Critics, citing all these facts, decried the low-price policy as short-sighted and irrational. However – and this is the key point – in the eyes of the Liberal government it was, for both political and economic reasons, absolutely impossible significantly to increase prices without first, or simultaneously, solving the problem of revenue-sharing between the industry and the public sector and between orders of government.

In the absence of a new federal policy initiative, the only weapon that Ottawa could use to bring about a new sharing arrangement was to sit tight on prices, and this was becoming increasingly difficult. As long as the two issues were treated separately, as they had been by the Clark government, Ottawa had to ask Alberta to do it a big favour in the matter of revenue-sharing, but Alberta was not about to give away its birthright. To establish a bargaining position, Ottawa brought in the NEP, an aggressive policy thrust which, predictably, engendered a vigorous Alberta riposte: restrictions on rates of production. Production cuts hurt the industry as well as the federal government, so what the province could do along these lines was limited; its restrictions would have to be for the short term only. The stand-off created by the NEP and the Alberta response to it set the scene for several months' negotiations of which the upshot was the pricing agreements of 1981 (see chapter 1).

Voluntary Vacancy

One should not suppose that if policy is formed through a sequence of unilateral decisions the results will necessarily be bad; nor will relations between governments necessarily be hostile. The cases we have just looked at are ones where the interests of the governments were diametrically opposed; but where their objectives are coincident or (with some mutual concessions) at least compatible, a less conflictual form of unilateralism may obtain. Policy-making by thrust and riposte is not the only sort of sequence of unilateral decisions that one might imagine to exist, or indeed that one observes.

In some functional areas, one order of government may actually withdraw in order to leave the other with a free hand in policy formation. Perhaps this can only weakly be termed a form of policy-making by governmental interaction, but a tacit or explicit agreement to leave a field to another order of government is something that we ought not to let pass unobserved. It will be recalled that the chain of events that led to the 1974 fight over resource profits was initiated by a 1971 federal budget decision to assume a lower profile in taxation and control of mining operations; it was only when the incompatibility of objectives was revealed by subsequent events that the brouhaha occurred.

In other situations what I should like to call a 'passive partner' arrangement has persisted for a considerable length of time without apparent disagreement or animosity. The institutional rivalries and tendencies toward bureaucratic aggrandizement, as noted separately by Cairns and by Simeon,[5] have not (for example) destabilized a long-standing de facto sharing of policy responsibilities in relation to agriculture. In this concurrent field, the two orders of government have fairly satisfactorily dovetailed their activities. One instance of this occurs in the dairy industry, where Parliament has authorized the Canadian Dairy Commission to control the supply and marketing of industrial milk (for processing into powder or cheese, as well as for making products such as glue), while the provinces market fresh milk. The division of responsibility presumably has occurred because liquid milk, being perishable, is necessarily restricted to a local market, with the consequence that the provinces can effectively regulate prices and production; the federal government has accepted responsibility for milk products that can more readily be shipped and stored.

We might note, parenthetically, that if a province vacates a field, it does not always do so voluntarily. Provincial legislation is still, under the Constitution Act, subject to reservation by the lieutenant-governor pending instructions from the governor-general in council (i.e. the federal cabinet) or to retroactive disallowance by the same body. Although these powers have now fallen into disuse, they once gave the federal government a means of preventing the provinces from undertaking initiatives at variance with federal policy; and as long as they remain in the written constitution, it remains conceivable – though unlikely – that they could be invoked again. An effect similar to dissallowance can also be secured in certain strictly delimited areas when Parliament legislates in a concurrent field, suspending any conflicting or duplicative provincial legislation then in force. Moreover, in an emergency situation, the 'Peace, Order and Good Government' clause can temporarily give Parliament virtually unlimited power to legislate in fields normally within exclusive provincial jurisdiction, nullifying any conflicting provincial legislation.

Exchange of Information, Followed by Independent Action

Fiscal policy is an important area in which all governments share partially compatible goals but where differences between them arise because of the multi-faceted aspect of the field and because opinions on how to realize the goals may diverge. Also, regional variations in the degree of stimulus or restraint may be desired. As a result, attempts at co-ordination are frequently half-hearted, and interaction appears weak; policy is the result of a series of unilateral decisions. Ottawa's desire, during the early post–Second World War period, to assume overall responsibility for economic management has been thwarted by the growth of the provinces. Provincial governments and provincial crown corporations are now the large-scale investors in public works. Their investment policies (and particularly their practice of borrowing on foreign money markets) necessarily greatly affect the relative magnitudes of public spending and public revenue collection, whether through taxes or borrowing. As a result, fiscal policy in Canada emerges from a largely unco-ordinated series of decisions taken in Ottawa and in the provincial capitals, mostly without consideration of their impact on economic stabilization or the exchange value of the dollar. At other times the provinces may deliberately counteract federal policy. An example is described in the following comment by H. Ian Macdonald, formerly chief economist for Ontario:

Canada is not a unitary state ... We are a federal state and a highly decentralized one, with immense economic and fiscal powers in the hands of the provinces. Today, the provinces and their municipalities account for what is approaching two-thirds of public expenditure in Canada and about eighty per cent of that highly significant sector – public capital investment. As a result, a determined provincial administration, in conjunction with its municipalities, can exert a significant counter-influence on fiscal policy to that of the federal government and, in conjunction with large agencies such as a hydro-electric power corporation, can have a major impact on domestic capital markets and, through foreign borrowings, on capital flows and exchange rates.

The countervailing influence of provincial fiscal policy is exactly what happened in 1970 and 1971 in Ontario and I have been surprised that it did not attract more attention. At that time, the federal government was seeking to offset inflation and was practising a policy of fiscal restraint, with particular discretionary attention directed at the urban areas of Ontario. However, in the view of the Ontario Government, unemployment was the more serious threat at the time and a deliberate effort was made, through the 1970 and 1971 budgets, to stimulate the economy, particularly in the basic investment sector.[6]

So far we have considered various forms of policy formation through sequences of unilateral decisions. The 'thrust and riposte' process involves deliberate and antagonistic unilateralism; antagonism is probably impossible to avoid when policy objectives are incompatible. In less conflictual situations, governments may divide up a concurrent field, resulting in a 'voluntary vacancy' or 'passive partner' situation. When voluntary vacancy occurs, policy-making can be mostly unilateral for the simple reason that there has been agreement about the division of the policy field into areas of federal and provincial responsibility. Again, governments may exchange information, after which each proceeds to do what it thinks best. In such cases there may be some scope for the exercise of mutual influence (otherwise there would be no point in exchanging information), so we are beginning to move away from unilateralism. Nonetheless, the feature common to each of the policy processes considered so far is that in all of them co-ordinate governments act independently of each other. They do not act 'each in its own sphere,' since in the areas we are looking at the constitution does not make a clear distinction between what is federal and what is provincial; but decisions are unilateral in the sense that, in each instance, a single government makes them. In all cases, there is a policy. Something gets done, agreement or no agreement. This is not true of the remaining modes of interaction, discussed below.

Joint Funding

Co-ordination between governments is not always unconstrained. It may be elicited by one government's exercising its fiscal muscle. In doing so it brings to bear upon other governments a whole set of political and financial inducements to action. This is almost necessarily the case when a program is launched through a cost-sharing arrangement.

Unilateral decisions, then, may also be involved in modes of government interaction other than the ones discussed above; but there is an essential difference. Where joint funding is constitutionally or politically necessary nothing gets done unless the inducements work and a program is, with good will or bad, launched by mutual agreement resulting in reciprocal action.

One of the standard forms of joint funding is the shared-cost program. The literature on this subject is extensive, and there is no need to add to it here. However, the variety of joint-funding arrangements and the sheer pervasiveness of this technique for mounting programs within the Canadian federal state may not be widely appreciated. A 1985 inventory of federal-provincial programs and activities[7] runs to over 300 pages and lists, in addition to major fiscal transfers under the Fiscal Arrangements Act and those relating to Established Programs Financing: 99 cost-sharing agreements involving federal payments to provinces and municipalities, plus 12 development agreements with provinces or territories; 5 cost-sharing agreements involving provincial or municipal payments to the federal government; 50 agreements involving intergovernmental transfers for the purchase of goods or services, 35 of these providing for payments from the federal government to provinces or municipalities; 11 agreements under which the federal government makes payments to provinces or municipalities for transfer of title to land or for improvements to physical assets; 15 agreements for loans to provinces or municipalities; 93 agreements on joint activities where each order of government independently finances a share of the costs; 16 agreements regarding intergovernmental liaison and joint administrative bodies; and 34 other agreements.

The diversity of joint funding arrangements within each of the above categories is too great for me to convey much about their character just by the odd illustration. Even so, the tally reported above does give some impression of the variety of forms that joint funding may take. As already noted, collaborative action may be achieved only in the sense that, while the federal government ultimately sets the terms of the agreement, no program gets started in a given province unless and until the province accepts what eventually comes down to a take-it-or-leave-it proposition.

However, the history of shared-cost programs does reveal that federal policy in these areas has been considerably influenced by provincial demands. There is enough common ground in the areas covered by joint funding arrangements to produce extensive bargaining, even though the central government maintains the whip hand because it is the one handing out a subsidy. As the 1983-84 medicare dispute (over 'extra-billing' and 'user fees') shows, it is even possible for Ottawa to tighten its criteria for allocating funds under a program which is not, in the traditional sense, a shared-cost one.

Delegation or Interdelegation

Legislatures in Canada cannot delegate powers to each other, but they can delegate regulatory authority to boards or commissions set up by another government. This is the basis of Canadian policy on the marketing of farm products.

The common form of delegation is from Parliament to provincial marketing boards, as occurs under the Agricultural Products Marketing Act of 1949. This act enables provincial boards to exercise the same powers outside the province as provincial legislation authorizes them to exercise within it. Thus if a provincial marketing scheme is established for a particular product, a producer cannot avoid the compulsory feature of the plan by selling outside the province. On the basis of this delegation of powers, and of appropriate legislation by the provinces, provincial marketing boards are sole agents for the sale of various regulated products not only within the province but also in interprovincial and export trade. Delegation occurs because the two orders of government share the same goal: they co-operate to avoid one of the historical difficulties of divided jurisdiction.

One thing that cannot be accomplished effectively under delegation from Parliament to provincial boards is 'supply management,' a euphemism for what non-agribusiness folk call production control. Production controls applied to, say, New Brunswick potato producers cannot but work to their disadvantage as long as producers of other provinces can sell whatever quantities they like in New Brunswick and elsewhere. Effective supply management requires national marketing schemes. The machinery for doing this was established by the Farm Products Marketing Agencies Act of 1972.[8] Under the terms of the act, national marketing agencies may be established by cabinet order and may exercise powers delegated to it by provincial governments as well as by the terms of the federal order-in-council. The powers may include those necessary to impose production controls and may place an agency in a position to determine which provincial producers will supply any given provincial market. A province could, as a result, find that 20 or 85 per cent of its market for (say) pork bellies had been divided up among the other provinces according to some ratio set by the relevant agency.

In cases pertaining to the Farm Products Marketing Agencies Act, interdelegation is not necessarily a sign of complete congruence between federal and provincial objectives. Although, during protracted debate on the bill, the minister of agriculture insisted that no province would be under compulsion to delegate any powers to any agency, and might at any time withdraw any powers it had delegated in the past, critics were not convinced that the legal right to do so would have much practical significance. Their argument made a lot of sense. A surplus province (producing in excess of its own needs) could be excluded from other provincial markets if an agency were set up for the product concerned; its right to remain aloof was therefore absolute but also rather empty. A deficit province – one producing less than its own needs in a given product – might have greater latitude; but it would not be in a position to control imports into the province, and it might be levered into joining a scheme in order to obtain an extraprovincial market for another regulated product.

The foregoing account of one of the features of the Farm Products Marketing Agencies Act emphasizes the interdependencies to which the delegation or interdelegation of powers may give rise. In the area of agricultural marketing, interdelegation has been the only way to work within the Canadian constitution to achieve a specific policy objective. Where delegation occurs, the revocability of delegated powers gives the delegator a fulcrum on which to rest the lever of its political resources and thus to influence the way delegated powers are exercised. But the extent of this influence necessarily depends upon the credibility of a threatened withdrawal from the scheme.

Supplementation: Legislative Concurrency and Administrative Devolution

It will be easier to identify this form of government interaction in policy formation in Canada if we look first at a foreign example, that of West Germany. Its 1949 constitution contains a short list of exclusive federal powers and a longer list of concurrent powers with federal paramountcy; subjects not appearing on either list are within the purview of the states or Länder. Concurrency enables the federal parliament to enact general laws and thereby to achieve, in the words of Gunter Kisker, an 'indispensable minimum of uniformity.' These laws may be supplemented by the Länder. Kisker notes that in practice there has been a wholesale transfer of legislative activity toward the centre, so much so that 'as far as legislation is concerned there is not much left of Länder autonomy; in this realm the Federal Republic of Germany is today pretty close to a unitary structure.' He continues:

On the other hand, other elements of the traditional structure are still very much alive ... Matters of administration are Länder matters. As under the constitution of 1871 even federal statutes in principle are executed by the Länder. The execution of federal statutes by the Bund [the federal government] is provided for in exceptional cases only. This means that the federal government still depends on the administrative machine of the Länder. It exercises supervision to ensure that the Länder execute the federal law correctly. But the Bund has still got no disciplinary power to control the Länder bureaucracy. So as in the nineteenth century the system cannot work but on a cooperative basis: the federal legislator therefore will consider carefully the proposals and objections of the Länder bureaucracies. In return the Länder bureaucracies will loyally execute the federal statutes.[9]

Of course the chief institutional means for involving the Länder in policy-making at the centre is through the Bundesrat or upper house, the members of which are appointed by and act under instructions of the Land governments. The Bundesrat must consent to every statute that contains rules for its execution by the state administrations (i.e. it must approve the large majority of federal statutes).

The administration of federal laws by state bureaucracies is not unknown in federations based on the sharp delimitation of legislative powers (broadly speaking, those of British emanation, involving two parallel governmental systems); it is for example a notable feature of Indian federalism. In Canada such supplementation, whether by legislative or administrative action, has generally been avoided. Nonetheless, there are exceptions.

One of the most interesting exceptions has recently been the subject of constitutional litigation. Under the Constitution Act, the criminal law power, including procedure in criminal matters, is exclusively federal (section 91:27), whereas one of the exclusive provincial powers is 'The Administration of Justice in the Province' (section 92:14). In view of the division of powers that a juxtaposition of these two sections would seemingly suggest, it has been fairly widely presumed that the federal Parliament has no option but to rely upon the provincial attorneys general for criminal investigations and prosecutions, as historically has been the case. As Campbell Sharman has shown, this has resulted in some surprising interprovincial variations in Canadian criminal law as actually enforced.[10] Indeed, Sharman's point has been underlined by a decade-long history of prosecutions for abortion offences, a history that shows how provincial governments may in practice determine the character of parts of Canadian criminal law.

Dr Henry Morgentaler established an abortion clinic in Quebec in 1968 and from 1973 to 1976 was repeatedly charged with contravention of the abortion provisions of the Criminal Code, notwithstanding repeated jury acquittals. The federal minister of justice, under fire for hounding a man whom juries would not convict, took refuge in alleged constitutional incapacity to do anything about it. He emphasized that the power of decision in matters of prosecution lay with Quebec's minister of justice, not with federal authorities. Eventually, with the election (1976) of the Parti québécois, Morgentaler obtained surcease, for the PQ dropped the charges against him, effectively neutralizing – for Quebec – the relevant clauses of the Criminal Code. However, Morgentaler subsequently opened clinics in Manitoba and Ontario and is being prosecuted in those two provinces under a law that is not being applied, or not being applied in the same way, in another part of the country.

The irony is that it now appears, as a result of a ruling by the Supreme Court in October 1983, that provincial enforcement of the Criminal Code derives not from the Constitution Act but from the Code itself.[11] The federal government had for years investigated and prosecuted, on its own, certain classes of offence (narcotics, espionage) under special statutes, not under the Criminal Code. Some provinces became edgy about extension of federal law enforcement into non-traditional areas and sought through litigation to affirm provincial exclusivity in administration of justice. They were concerned that criminal-type laws could be enacted outside the code, giving rise to a dual system in which federal offences would increasingly be enforced federally and provincial offences enforced provincially. A federal government dissatisfied with provincial law enforcement in some area could simply transfer the relevant offences to federally administered acts. However, when the provinces pressed the issue, the Supreme Court decided that federal law enforcement powers, in relation to acts of the Parliament of Canada including the Criminal Code, are not constitutionally limited and that such provincial authority as exists is conferred merely by federal legislation. Conceivably, this could result in the federal government's exercising supervision and control over the provinces' administration of justice for all federally created offences.

Although in relation to the field of criminal justice we may be moving away from provincial action to modify, extend, or apply federal policy, in a number of other areas this mode of interaction may be on the increase. In certain cases federal programs have been designed specifically with provincial supplementation in mind, and in other cases a similar situation arises because of the opening up of areas of concurrency by judicial interpretation. I shall give two examples of each.

The family allowances program was modified in 1974 to permit provincial governments to vary payments in such a way as to co-ordinate the program with other provincial social security measures or to fit in better with the provinces' conceptions of what makes good policy. The federal policy called for a standard dollar average of payments ($20 per child, increased annually by indexing for inflation) but allowed the provinces to pay less in respect of some children (depending on their age and on the number of children in the family) and more for others. Quebec, Alberta, and Prince Edward Island have taken advantage of the opportunity to do so. In addition, provinces may supplement federal payments with their own.

The student loans program is administered by the provinces on a basis that integrates federal loans with provincial grants to post-secondary students. The mix of loans and grants varies by province, and some provinces require students to take out a loan – the magnitude depending on the province – before the student becomes eligible for a provincial grant, which is non-repayable.

In the field of highway safety an area of concurrency has been established by the courts. The most serious driving offences come within the Criminal Code, and other offences are defined by provincial legislatures. The two legislations together make up a sort of highway code that varies a little among provinces. In general, as W.R. Lederman has explained, provincial legislation that is purely supplementary to federal statute law is valid. The provinces have been enacting supplementary legislation in concurrent fields with increasing frequency.[12]

In the area of consumer protection, both federal and provincial governments have enacted legislation to prohibit certain trade practices (e.g. misleading advertising). Parliament has done so on the basis of its criminal law power, while the provinces have been active in the field through their control of contract law (property and civil rights). On this basis the provinces may create offences, breach of which results in the imposition of a penalty – and is therefore akin to the criminal law – but it may also provide civil remedies, i.e. restitution to the aggrieved party. For this reason the provinces have generally preferred to act under their own legislation and have done little to prosecute offences under the Criminal Code. At one point, the federal government appeared to be worried about this and was considering transferring its trade practices legislation to the Competition Act, in order to place enforcement powers directly in federal hands. Had it proceeded with this legislation, or should it do so in the future, its intrusion into a traditionally provincial area would cause a loud ruckus.[13]

These examples show that supplementation of federal policy by provincial governments, through some combination of legislative and administrative measures, is not entirely foreign to Canada. Where it occurs, however, it does so by way of exception to the normal practices of that form of federalism that emphasizes parallel structures and independent action by each government within the federation. Policy supplementation seldom occurs outside of fields where federal and provincial policy objectives are congruent, or nearly so.

Federalization of Political Institutions at the Centre

Virtually no steps have been taken in Canada to 'federalize' political institutions at the centre so that provincial governments involve themselves in a formal way with decisions taken for the country as a whole. Comparatively speaking, the most obvious contrasting case is that of West Germany. Not only is the Bundesrat made up of delegates of the Land governments, but formal special-purpose intergovernmental bodies exist to co-ordinate activities of the Länder in a way that also involves the federal government. The latter has been described in a most interesting way by Gerhard Lembruch:

The far-reaching constitutional amendments adopted in 1967-1969 are characterized by what might be described as 'cooperative centralization'. That is, the function of coordinating the economic and financial policies of the federation and of the *Länder* was not entrusted to the federal authorities as classical conceptions of federalism might have suggested. Instead, different consultative bodies and 'planning commissions' composed of representatives of the Federal and *Länder* Governments were established: 1. The *Finanzplanungsrat*, the function of which is the coordination of budgetary (five-year) planning. 2. The *Konjunkturrat* coordinating anticyclical policies of the Federation, the *Länder* and local authorities by preparing, e.g., decisions regulating the borrowing by territorial authorities or obliging the Federation and the *Länder* to keep interest-free reserves on a Federal Bank account. 3. The planning commissions for the *Gemeinschaftsaufgaben* ('joint tasks') which have largely replaced the former grants-in-aid and are jointly financed by the Federation and the *Länder*. There are three commissions, for regional economic development, for agricultural development and for the construction or enlargement of universities. 4. The *Bund-LanderKommission fur Bildungsplanung* (Joint Commission for Educational Planning), established in 1970 by an agreement of the Federal and Land governments as a planning body for the long-term development of the educational system.

In comparing these bodies to the institutions of traditional 'horizontal' co-operation [i.e., among Länder] there appear some significant patterns. As they belong to the domain of 'vertical' coordination the federal government is now an important partner. (The most important exception is the KMK [*Kultusministerkonferenz*] which continues to coordinate much of the educational policies of the *Länder*, in spite of the existence of the Joint Commission mentioned above.)[14]

In Canada, by contrast, interprovincial conferences at the ministerial level generally exclude observers from the federal government and have far less capacity to influence or control provincial governments.

From the mid-1970s until the early 1980s constitutional debate in Canada reflected considerable interest in some features of West German federalism, particularly in the Bundesrat as a model for a second chamber to replace the Senate. Gordon Robertson, former secretary to the cabinet for federal-provincial Relations, notes: 'Each of the central institutions of our federation is to some degree flawed as a forum for the fullest expression and reconciliation of regional interests ... If the central institutions, where much of the responsibility for this advocacy and brokerage function lies, could be overhauled to be more effective in this sense, there would be less need for federal-provincial conferences.'[15]

Presumably ideas such as these were behind the federal Bill c-60 proposal of June 1978, to create a non-elected House of the Federation with some members appointed by the central government and others by provincial governments, in both cases on a basis of proportional representation (i.e. reflecting the popular vote in respective elections). This restructured second chamber may have been intended to give central institutions greater legitimacy as agencies for expression of regional interests and thereby to enable them effectively to challenge claims of provincial governments to be the sole authentic articulators of such interests. By contrast, a recommendation of the Task Force on Canadian Unity was more directly modelled on the Bundesrat; the Task Force proposed a Council of the Federation composed of provincial delegates. Similar proposals were put forward by the governments of British Columbia and Ontario, by the Quebec provincial Liberal party, and by a committee of the Canadian Bar Association.[16]

Another suggestion that has cropped up from time to time, but has received far less public attention, is the idea of making central regulatory agencies into joint federal-provincial bodies. It has been suggested that, at the minimum, the federal government should consult with provincial governments before appointing members of commissions such as the Canadian Radio-Television and Telecommunications Commission (CRTC) and the National Energy Board (NEB); a more far-reaching proposal is that the provinces be accorded formal power to appoint some members of regulatory commissions. If this were done with the intent of preventing commissions from being used as instruments of central power, it would be logical also to eliminate the power of the federal cabinet to issue instructions to them.

An obvious reason for wanting to federalize political institutions at the centre is to curb federal unilateralism. An advantage might be reduction of overt federal-provincial conflict. One may wonder, however, to what extent this result might be achieved through genuine harmonization of federal and provincial policy objectives and to what extent merely by neutralizing some existing instruments of federal power. It would be naïve and I think perverse to ignore the fact that federalizing central institutions would have major implications for the exercise of power within the Canadian federal system. We shall return to this subject after discussing, in a more general way, the impact of the constitution on modes of government interaction in policy formation.

THE CONSTITUTION: A DETERMINANT OF INTERACTION PROCESSES

Formation of policy through a process of thrust and riposte may be unique to Canada and is almost certainly more common here than in any other federation. Aggressive unilateralism also marks some of the other modes of governmental interaction in Canada, to a greater extent than in other federations. Why so? No doubt it is due in part to the highly regionalized make-up of the country (cultural pluralism and divergence of economic interest among provinces). Perhaps Canadians have more to fight about among themselves than, say, Americans. But this is not very convincing. Linguistic dualism aside, it is doubtful that Canada is more regionally diverse than the United States. Some of the bitterest intergovernmental disputes of the past decade have arisen over economic issues and have not involved Quebec in a primary way. Since it is implausible that Canadians are by nature more self-assertive than their neighbours to the south, one concludes, through a process of elimination, that the design of political institutions is a relevant factor. Three features of the constitution come to mind.

One such feature is the scheme for allocating legislative powers, with most activities of government being covered expressly or implicitly in two largely exclusive lists. As a result, both orders of government are endowed with powers that may be exercised without fear of override by the other and in a competitive way. It would be otherwise if there were wide areas of concurrency together with (as one would expect) constitutional allocation of paramountcy in respect of each concurrent power. In these circumstances the provinces would exercise their constitutional powers in the knowledge that in some areas their legislation would prevail notwithstanding anything on the federal statute books, while in other areas their legislation would be subject to suspension or effective repeal by the federal government. Similarly, the federal government would know when its legislation would prevail and when it would not. This situation would give maximum encouragement to each order of government to exercise its powers co-operatively with the other, in those areas where they would be subject to override.

A generous interpretation of the federal peace, order, and good government clause could easily have produced this result. A wide array of exclusive provincial powers would have become subject to suspension through the rule of federal paramountcy if the Judicial Committee of the Privy Council had not, in a series of decisions shortly after the First World War, turned the clause into a reserve of emergency power to deal with extraordinary situations. For example, wage and price controls and the whole field of industrial relations might easily have become concurrent, with federal paramountcy. Although a general extension of federal power on a concurrent basis would not have eliminated federal unilateralism – and might easily have produced more of it – the constitutional basis for continuing conflict, with a thrust-and-riposte style of policy formation, would have been eliminated. Similarly, with wider concurrency there would not be the same reason to establish shared-cost programs in areas of provincial jurisdiction or to seek delegation or interdelegation of legislative and administrative powers. These too, are firmly rooted in a constitutional scheme that relies mainly on the principle of exclusivity in the division of powers.

This observation is important because it draws our attention to a perhaps unsuspected point: unilateralism and the frequently acrimonious processes of intergovernmental negotiation (of which unilateralism is an underlying condition) may be a necessary price to pay if we are to avoid the general primacy of one order of government over the other. If governments are able to throw legislative thunderbolts at each other, it is a sure sign that neither level has become subservient to the other, or quite eclipsed by it.

Widespread concurrency would probably result in extension of federal power. Although concurrency has been expanded by judicial interpretation in recent years and would be further expanded in a major way if attempts were made to update the constitution by defining powers in terms of current policy responsibilities, the Supreme Court's preference for exclusivity of powers (where practical) has left it playing an active role as judicial umpire. In the absence of political mechanisms to give the provinces a large role in decision-making at the centre – a matter discussed below – the court's preference for exclusivity stands as a continuing protection against emasculation of provincial power.

A second feature of the Canadian constitution that has been widely commented upon over the years, as militating against conciliation of regional and other conflicts in the federal (i.e. central) political arena – thus throwing them into the intergovernmental one – is the parliamentary form of government. The cabinet's insistence upon treating all major policy questions as matters of confidence conduces to the concentration of power in the executive and, since the advent of television, in the hands of the prime minister. A corollary is the existence of disciplined parties, centrally controlled, which are more likely to break up than to tolerate widely divergent opinion on major policy issues. The party system and Parliament thus find it difficult to accommodate and resolve conflict. The classic statement of this thesis was made in 1954 by S.M. Lipset:

Contemporary Canadian politics should be seen as the product of the failure of British parliamentary institutions to work in a complex North American federal union. The British system with parliamentary government and the single-member constituency elected by a plurality of the voters can only operate in a homogeneous country in which there is one basic source of political difference. In Britain, it is clearly the class difference. Differences based on regions, religious or ethnic allegiances, urban-rural conflicts, or past historical feuds are largely non-existent, or affect groups which are too small to organize on their own behalf.

Actually, the underlying structural cleavages in Canadian society are more comparable to those existing in the US or in France [where cleavages are multiple and cross-cutting] than they are to those of Great Britain ... Canada's political party problem is a result of the fact that its social structure and bases for political division are essentially comparable to the American and French pattern, but it retains a form of government which requires disciplined parliamentary parties, and which does not permit cross-party alignments in the House of Commons, sharp divergences among the federal programs of the parties from province to province, or democratic methods of solving internal party cleavages.[17]

Lipset was here concerned not with federal-provincial relations but with the structure of the party system. However, the relation between the two was commented upon, in the American context, by M.J.C. Vile in 1961:

The federal structure of the United States ... exhibits a type of flexibility not so apparent in more centralized political systems ... The importance of the body of constitutional law and legal institutions cannot be denied, nor can the significance of the party system and the plethora of interest groups. A party system on the American model may not be a necessity in a federal system, but it certainly helps. The decentralization of political power so that no semi-permanent majority can be formed which will seek to control both Federal and State government machines and bring into existence a rival monolithic opposition to compete with it, ensures that the machinery of the Federal Government never comes into the possession of a group dedicated to the destruction of the power of the States. No group is strong enough to attempt this and it will always be faced by a stronger combination devoted to the defence of the States as a means of defending their own interests from domination by any single group. In Australia the unity of the parties in the Federal legislature is frequently rudely shattered when it comes to fundamental problems of social and economic innovation, so that the federal system continues by the destruction of party unity, whereas in the United States such unity is not even sought.[18]

The implications of these facts for intergovernmental relations in Canada were drawn out by Richard Simeon in 1972:

In Canada and Australia parliamentary government with strict party discipline, together with centralization within both levels of government, appears to have been a sufficient condition to inhibit the effectiveness of national legislative bodies as arenas for adjustment and so to facilitate the development of a new set of institutional arrangements, the federal-provincial conferences. This contrasts with the United States, where lack of party discipline and decentralization within governments has meant that the Congress has served as an important arena for adjustment. Moreover, the larger number of units and the fact that senior executives cannot easily authoritatively commit each other in the United States would make federal-state conferences on the Canadian model difficult if not impossible.[19]

Thus, according to Simeon, 'federal-provincial diplomacy' has become an important feature of policy-making in Canada. The quasi-diplomatic activity depicted by Simeon is, however, but one aspect of several of the modes of governmental interaction identified in this chapter. It is one feature of a relationship characterized also by unilateral policy initiatives and often by faits accomplis. Ensuing or accompanying negotiations may lead to agreement and collaboration or to breakdown and impasse – or, if its powers are adequate, to Ottawa's implementation of the policy in defiance of some or all of the provinces.

A third feature of the Canadian constitution conducing to unilateralism is that the design of central institutions leaves provincial governments without a direct voice in national policy-making. If the previous point (developed by Lipset, Vile, and Simeon) contrasts the Canadian constitutional structure with the American, this point contrasts it with the West German federation.

Allusion has already been made to proposals for federalizing Canadian political institutions at the centre or (as some writers would have it) for importing and adapting a system of 'intrastate federalism.'[20] In view of the diversity of such proposals, generalizations on the subject are hazardous, but it seems safe to say that those versions proposing a Bundesrat type of institution, in which delegates of the provincial governments would participate in the policy process in Ottawa on a regular and direct basis, aim at limiting exercise of federal unilateral powers. These include the emergency power, the spending power, and the declaratory power. Some proposals have also suggested a more general suspensive veto on legislation, or a broad advisory role for the new institution, as well as requiring its assent for certain appointments such as those to the Supreme Court. The precise composition and powers of the proposed body are, however, less relevant to our present argument than the intent of the proposers, which implies a particular diagnosis of the causes of intergovernmental conflict.

The institutional innovations that have been suggested all rest on the assumption that the degree of conflict engendered by governmental interaction in policy formation ('aggressive unilateralism' as I put it earlier) could be reduced if the provinces had more say in central decision-making. Essentially, what is aimed for is institutionalizing and regularizing interaction among governments in policy formation. The implicit contention is that irregular, ad hoc interaction concerning exercise of mutually exclusive powers generates more conflict than sharing of power within institutions designed to that end.

POWER RELATIONS

The key point about some of the proposals of the late 1970s or early 1980s for instititional innovation, creating some form of intrastate federalism in Canada, is that the only powers it was suggested be shared were federal ones. Designs for federalizing central political institutions were inspired by a wish to inject the provincial governments into central decision-making processes while leaving the division of powers largely intact, or extending provincial powers.[21] In this they contrasted with a basic feature of intrastate federalism – at least if we take the West German system as a model – since the latter system places comparatively little emphasis on division of powers and rather more on joint exercise of policy responsibilities in concurrent fields. Protection of regional interests is sought through political processes and political representation at the centre rather than through allocation of exclusive powers to regional units.

By contrast, the intent of Canadian proposals to transform the Senate into an intergovernmental body (or to create a new institution as a sort of 'third house') was apparently to import half the intrastate model into Canada, combining exclusive provincial powers with a provincial presence in central institutions. The effect would have been unambiguously decentralizing – though how greatly so would have depended on the extent of the powers assigned to the new institution.

There are three possible reactions – or three I can think of – to this observation, besides simple refusal to contemplate any form of change in federal institutions and policy processes. One is to opt for changes in central political institutions that would make them more sensitive to regional needs and demands but without involving provincial governments; a second is to deny that the effect of partial intrastate federalism in Canada would be as one-sided as I have described it; and a third is to affirm that to rein in central unilateral, or overriding, powers is long overdue and would be more consistent with federal principles than is the design of our present system. Let us look at each of these views in turn.

1. Two types of intrastate federalism have been distinguished by Alan Cairns, who notes that 'two distinct options' for recasting Canadian federalism along intrastate lines have been put forward: '[one] giving power and influence at the centre to provincial governments, [and a second] making the central government more responsive to territorial diversities in ways which bypass provincial governments ... [These] may be labelled respectively provincial intrastate federalism, and centralist intrastate federalism. The centralist intrastate version is clearly designed "to obstruct the growing power of the provinces." '[22]

To describe the latter arrangement as a form of intrastate federalism strikes me as inappropriate, but that merely expresses my preference for affixing the label only to a fairly specific constitutional arrangement on the West German model. What is important is the underlying idea. Briefly, an attempt may be made to restructure power at the centre, giving added prominence and perhaps a form of veto power to certain regional interests without confiding a representative and controlling role to the provincial governments. One device for reaching this objective, contained in Pierre Trudeau's Bill c-60 proposal (1979), was briefly described earlier in the chapter. Another suggestion has more recently been put forward by Gordon Robertson, for an elected Senate with a mixture of permanent-veto and suspensive-veto powers.[23] One aim of such proposals may be, precisely, to undermine the provinces' claim to be the sole authentic articulators of regional interests; but a further consequence, more germane to the subject-matter of this chapter, might be that a more regionally sensitive central government would behave less aggressively toward provincial governments. Or, alternatively, provincial governments might feel less well equipped to engage in battle with the central government. Either way there might be a greater proclivity to settle federal-provincial policy disputes without engaging in thrust and riposte or other modes of interaction marked by competitiveness and unilateralism. And in both cases the effect would be to augment federal power at the expense of the provinces.

2. The question arises whether creation of institutions involving the provinces in federal policy-making actually would (as some have supposed) incapacitate the central government in the performance of its policy responsibilities and/or sap its legitimacy. The latter effect is of particular concern to Alan Cairns, who warns that constitutions not only reflect existing power relations but may prefigure the future

direction of political loyalties and perceptions of community. In the Canadian context it may be dangerous, says Cairns, further to institutionalize regional forces, even in ways that do not expand the role of the provinces as articulators of regional interests: 'Intrastate versions of an appropriate constitutional future tend, to the extent of their permeation of central government institutions, to inhibit national perspectives, country-wide definitions of issues, egalitarianism, and the sense that Canada is more than the sum of its parts. We give an extra nudge, and institutional support, to tendencies that are already strong.'[24]

However, as Cairns also recognizes, this is not the only possible result of federalizing political institutions at the centre. In West Germany the effect of intrastate federalism would appear to have been centralizing, although the intent of the framers of the 1949 constitution was to keep a tight rein on the power of the Bonn government and to reduce its potential for unilateral action at the expense of the Länder. Arguably, centralization has occurred only because of the wide range of concurrent powers under the 1949 constitution, which permitted gradual extension of Bonn's decision-making power as long as spokesmen of the Länder governments had a say in those decisions.

It is also possible, however, to claim that intrastate federalism typically has a unifying effect. The reasoning is that when regional governments have a share of responsibility for national decisions, their leaders might come to acquire a national perspective. There is a difference between being a critic of decisions made by another government, in which case only the negative fallout of its actions receives attention, and being forced to consider all the policy alternatives and to choose the one with the largest net benefits or, on balance, the fewest disadvantages. It is possible to suppose that if delegates of the provincial governments shared responsibility for difficult decisions, they would come to behave like national rather than regional figures.

However, to suppose this result is to be resolutely optimistic; and one must acknowledge that, in itself, sharing of policy responsibilities carries no guarantee of harmony. Provincial governments would remain responsible to provincial electorates – and this fact would stand in the way both of intergovernmental harmony and of any transformation of provincial politicians into public figures espousing a national over a provincial view. Though their behaviour might change marginally, the effect of giving them a veto over national decisions would necessarily hamper the exercise of central power.

3. To bring provincial governments into decision-making processes at the centre, while retaining or expanding the existing list of exclusive provincial powers, thus does appear one-sided. Acknowledging this, one response is to say that it is a necessary corrective to what is now a one-sided, unbalanced form of federalism. This, indeed, is the explicit justification for devices to establish some provincial control over exercise of the federal spending power, the emergency power, the powers of reservation and disallowance, and the declaratory power. All

have the effect of suspending provincial powers, transferring them to the central government, or involving the central government in their exercise. It is argued that this transgresses federal principles[25] – or perhaps, more exactly, the principles of interstate federalism. In lieu of abolishing such 'unilateral powers' altogether, it may seem preferable to give the provinces a say in exercising them.

This issue is perhaps argued less usefully on the basis of federal principles (for the species within this genus are many) than on the basis of perceptions regarding the present-day functioning of the Canadian federal state. What one must decide, and can only be decided by forming an opinion on the policy responsibilities of government in an industrial or post-industrial society, is whether the central government is equipped with the powers and resources it requires and whether the provinces have sufficient autonomy to respond adequately to the needs expressed by provincial electorates. Views on this question obviously differ. The remaining chapters will identify reasons why they do so and will discuss the merits of various opinions on the matters.

So saying, I am not necessarily reintroducing the thorny issue of formal constitutional change. One of the lessons to be learned from a study of government interaction in policy formation is that through governmental interaction, processes of centralization/decentralization, and accompanying restructuring of power relations, are going on all the time. They are continuous processes, unlike the intermittent spates of concern, at least outside Quebec, with revising the written constitution. Shifts in working relations among governments, and consequently in the power that each order of government can effectively exercise, occur as part of everyday politics, not ostensibly concerned with constitutional questions. New policy responsibilities arise; old ones shift. It behooves us to ask whether such shifts as have occurred in Canada have been centralizing or decentralizing in their effects and whether – or from whose perspective – the direction of change has been consistent with the public interest.

6

(De)centralization:
meaning, measures, significance

Over more than a century we have seen a deep-rooted process that tends increasingly to centralization of the true levers of political power.

Claude Morin (1973)[1]

Over the last two decades, contrary to the myth of ever increasing centralization, we have seen a weakening of the fiscal and economic muscle of the federal government and a corresponding increase in the fiscal and economic muscle of the provinces or at least of the richer provinces. Inevitably there has been a corresponding shift in political power. I do not say that this phenomenon has been unhealthy but the risks are great when it goes too far.

Jean Chrétien (1981)[2]

Much of the recent history of Canadian federalism has been marked by intense intergovernmental rivalry. Each of the two senior orders of government has claimed that the other has sought to expand its powers, overstepping the role assigned to it in the constitution. These allegations have been ammunition in a propaganda war; each order of government, by portraying its rival as a usurper, has sought to bolster the legitimacy of its own cause.

Though they have served an ulterior purpose, such complaints and allegations are not mere cant. The politicians who have made them appear to have been genuinely frustrated by their incapacity to implement policies that they considered necessary and sometimes urgent. Provincial leaders have complained about centralization because they were incapable of meeting provincial needs as they perceived them. Federal leaders have complained about decentralization because they could not adequately perform what they regarded as the duties of a national government. In both cases the politicians were also worried about loss of political support. Is it not possible, they have said, to restore the balance of federal and provincial power?

This proposal seems unexceptionable, though it is not completely clear which direction to move in, let alone how to accomplish what is desired. For one thing, the very meaning of centralization (and its obverse, decentralization) is unclear. This is a conceptual problem; and it is compounded by a research problem – for even if we agree on a definition of 'centralization,' it is hard to identify indicators capable of establishing that a trend exists, whether in one direction or the other. (Alternatively, if we compare two federations how do we know which is the more centralized?) Unfortunately neither the conceptual problem, nor that of devising reliable indicators, has a satisfactory solution.

When we examine how students of federalism have handled this research problem, it becomes evident that international comparisons among federal systems, or comparisons over time for a given federation, are implicitly made on the basis of two quite distinct methods and criteria for establishing the degree of centralization. One method is to examine the extent of central and regional powers and/or the scope of governmental activity at the central and the regional levels respectively. This method implicitly assumes that the two orders of government operate more or less independently of each other, as in K.C. Wheare's classical federalism. This is an ideal type distilled from what Wheare thought to be the essence of those federal regimes established in former British dependencies (the United States and the present Commonwealth).[3] It is commonly acknowledged, however, that even in these countries the classical model no longer applies and that there is now – as illustrated in the previous chapter – extensive governmental interaction in policy formation. This being the case, an alternative method for judging the degree of centralization must be employed: to search for evidence regarding the extent of central government influence on decision-making at the regional level and also for signs of the regional governments' influence on central decisions.

The view that the Canadian federation is highly decentralized is based on the first criterion, which largely disregards the interdependence of governments. This interpretation is supported by various indicators of government activity, notably public finance data, and by observations on the extent of provincial involvement in the development of their economies, entailing actions that impede the free flow of goods, services, and capital within Canada. In these areas there has been a marked trend toward extension of provincial activity since the Second World War.

An opposing interpretation, that Canada is highly centralized and becoming more so, is based on the second criterion, the one that directs our attention to the extent of influence or control each order of government exerts upon the other. The indicators here are less obvious than in the other case. Still, many provincial politicians and civil servants claim that their policy decisions are circumscribed by federal action and that the primacy of the central government has been growing steadily over the past fifty years or more. This view is apparently widespread in Quebec, even outside governmental circles, and may increasingly be shared elsewhere in Canada. In its extreme formulation, it asserts that the provinces are being reduced to administrative agents of the centre.[4] A more widely held view suggests that the range of federal policy aims, most of which are pursued independently of the provinces, is expanding. Not only is Ottawa allegedly insensitive to regional needs, but it is said to intrude upon traditional areas of provincial jurisdiction, constraining and counterbalancing the policy choices of the provincial governments.

THE RISE OF THE PROVINCES?

In English Canada, at least outside provincial government circles, the conventional wisdom is that Canada has experienced pendulum-like swings in the relative strength of federal and provincial governments, with the provinces enjoying a phase of ascendancy between the late 1950s and the late 1970s. The American political scientist William Riker asserted in 1975 that 'among the ... federations of the modern world, most writers would agree that Canada is about as decentralized as one can get,' and in 1978 a committee of the Canadian Bar Association, sympathetically noting demands for decentralization, none the less cautioned: 'There is a clear limit to decentralization. The central government must be strong enough to manage the national economy, to provide for defence and generally to function at home and abroad as the government of all Canadians. Already Canada is one of the most decentralized federations.[5]

The evidence on the centralization/decentralization question that is easiest to collect – and most easily misused – is supplied by budgetary data: revenues collected, intergovernmental transfers, and levels of spending. Richard Bird points out that even if one restricts oneself to public finance data, 'there are many possible measures of centralization, not all of which necessarily move in the same direction at the same time, and all of which are potentially revelant for one purpose or another.'[6] A major difficulty in interpreting the data arises from intergovernmental transfers, which result in discrepancies between the provinces' 'own-source' revenue share and their share of public-sector expenditure. The large size of federal transfers to the provinces – since 1970 they have made up 19 to 23 per cent of total federal spending – is used by some observers as an index of decentralization (because it limits discretionary federal spending while contributing to an expansion of provincial programs) and by others as an index of centralization (because it increases the dependence of at least some provinces on the federal government). In addition, there are serious definitional problems relating even to apparently simple categories like 'taxes,' 'revenues,' and 'expenditures.' For example, how should one classify the revenues and expenditures of public corporations, which in some cases operate virtually as government departments and in other instances are commercial or industrial enterprises?

Puzzles such as these reduce the usefulness of the data, but the data are

Government revenue and expenditure: the federal share (all figures are in percentages)

	I 'Own-source' revenues*	2 Current expenditures, excluding transfers to other governments	3 Transfer payments to persons†	4 Current expenditure on goods and gross capital formation
1950	65.2	51.9		
1955	67.1	58.1		
1960	60.8	50.5		
1965	54.3	43.0		
1970	48.6	38.1	58.9	27.4
1975	49.4	40.8	64.9	25.0
1976	48.0	39.3	62.5	25.3
1977	44.8	39.2	62.7	25.8
1978	42.8	39.5	62.8	25.2
1979	42.8	38.8	60.0	24.5
1980	43.5	38.7	58.2	23.3
1981	46.0	39.7	58.5	23.8
1982	44.1	41.3	61.7	24.4
1983	43.3	41.2	62.5	23.3
1984			61.6	24.0

SOURCES

Columns 1 and 2: Canadian Tax Foundation: *The National Finances 1984–5*, Tables 3.6 and 3.10
Columns 3 and 4: Statistics Canada: *National Income and Expenditure Accounts* (Catalogue 13-201), 1970–1984 (table 43)
*Includes capital consumption allowances
†Excludes Canada and Quebec Pension Plans and service charges on the public debt

frequently cited all the same. Bird, who warns that 'playing with such numbers is not a very useful way to approach Canada's current political problems,' none the less remarks that 'it seems fairly safe to say that most measures suggest that Canada's public finances have indeed become more decentralized in recent years.'[7] One could scarcely conclude otherwise, given the data (for a sampling, see the accompanying table). However, the phase of marked fiscal decentralization on the expenditure side seems to have occurred during the latter 1950s and the 1960s; expenditure shares have been fairly stable since 1970. Whereas the federal government predominates in transfer payments to persons (e.g. family allowances, old age security, and unemployment insurance), provincial and local governments predominate in the purchase of current goods and services, subsidies, and capital assistance (see columns 3 and 4; items excluded from these columns are interest charges on the public debt and transfer payments to other orders of government). On the revenue side, the federal share dipped noticeably in 1977 and 1978, with the transfer of tax points to the provinces under the Established Programs Financing arrangement.

The data do not, however, really tell us all that much about the degree of centralization in the system. It remains an open question to what extent either order of government is truly able to determine its own expenditure priorities except by dipping more heavily into the taxpayer's pocket – that is, through an expansion of the public sector relative to the private one. The limitation is particularly evident in the case of the provinces, some of which obtain more than half their revenues from the federal treasury and all of which are subject to the vagaries of federal decision-making through the device of tied funds and the five-year revision of the whole system of fiscal transfers, including equalization. Finally, and I think most tellingly, the public accounts give no information at all about the field of government regulation, where important changes in policy can be implemented with only slight fiscal consequences. Attempts to remedy the shortcomings of fiscal indicators by devising other types of measures such as numbers of employees supply only the faintest glimmer of additional insight into the centralization question.

The deficiencies of the fiscal data approach force us to fall back on ordinal ('more-less') measures of the extent of government activity in particular policy areas. Here we ask what policies are being pursued and by which order of government. But there are problems with this manner of proceeding. One difficulty is that judgments are necessarily subjective, which conduces to disagreement. Another is that one cannot easily aggregate one's findings if there appears to be centralization in one field and decentralization in another. It is impossible to surmount these problems completely. However, it is not too difficult to understand the force that ordinal measures probably have for all participants and observers, affecting even what one sees in fiscal and other data. Thus it is scarcely surprising that among federal politicians and bureaucrats, as also among some businessmen, Canadian nationalists, and economists, voices are raised in alarm over growing provincial government involvement in economic development, which is sometimes held to challenge the integrity of the Canadian common market and to weaken the federal government's capacity for economic management.

There is now a fairly large literature on interprovincial barriers to economic exchange in Canada. While recent estimates of the quantitative impact of such barriers indicate that their overall economic cost may be slight, the results of such studies are not necessarily conclusive and in any case may not have a great deal of bearing on their political importance. In 1980 the federal government published an 'illustrative survey' of internal barriers in one of its position papers on the constitution (*Securing the Canadian Economic Union in the Constitution*). Some of these barriers, it should be noted, result from federal and not from provincial action; but most are provincial. Among those imposed by the provinces, the survey makes reference to procurement policies, imposition of differing product standards and technical specifications, restrictions on extra-provincial sale of unprocessed natural resources, trucking regulations, and hiring restrictions in various industries. The survey also notes differences among provinces in licensing of professionals and certification of skilled tradesmen, restrictions on extra-provincial takeover bids, requirements that insurance firms invest a certain percentage of their assets within the province, fiscal incentives for local investment or expansion, and provincial tax credits for investment in provincially domiciled corporations. It might, in addition, have noted restrictions on labour mobility implicit in Quebec's language legislation and the mobility-reducing effects of the widely discretionary powers exercised by provincial agencies that subsidize industrial investment. For example, a subsidy may be made conditional on the firm's obtaining engineering services within the province or upon the employment of provincial residents.[8]

A major purpose of Confederation was to create an integrated economy on the northern half of the continent. Many Canadians continue to regard this as one of the principal justifications of Canada's existence as a nation. For those sympathetic to the continuation of the historic 'national policies' or to their redesign and vigorous implementation, adoption of provincial development strategies and the consequent growth of interprovincial barriers to mobility of goods and factors of production are sure signs of the aggressive and illegitimate extension of provincial power.

This situation is not without its ironies. A Canadian policy for economic development, even if it calls for economic integration on a continental or world scale, must be predicated upon integration of the domestic economy. Provincial policies restricting the outflow of capital or of unprocessed resources, impeding the inflow of labour, controlling the external takeover of local firms, subsidizing manufacturing, and/or aiming for greater provincial self-sufficiency in agricultural products are the antithesis of national economic integration and development strategies based upon it. So, however, are centrally directed policies of regional development other than those aimed at speeding up the process of economic adjustment – that is, adapting industrial structure quickly to the dictates of the market and shifts in regional patterns of comparative advantage. On the whole, regional development policies retard adjustment to changing technologies and market conditions rather than promote it. But this fact is less readily noted by Canadian nationalists than is 'provincial protectionism' or 'economic provincialism.' Thus, policies that are similar in intent and character may be viewed by Canadian nationalists as reinforcing Canadian unity if centrally directed and as challenging Canada's national existence – the ultimate expression of decentralization – if designed and implemented by the provinces.

A CENTRALIZING TREND?

The provinces, Ontario excepted, do not seem gravely worried about each others' engaging in 'economic provincialism.' There are flashes of complaint against other provinces' policies (particularly where restrictions on the free movement of labour are concerned), but generally speaking the provinces seem more concerned about the regional incidence of federal policies than about each others' infringement of common market principles. And certainly, they are worried about a declining capacity to exercise their own powers as they see fit.

There appear to be three main reasons why the provinces are edgy about losing control of policy instruments that they have wielded in the past: joint programs tend to be negotiated with the provinces individually, especially in regional development; federal regulatory powers are often exercised in ways regarded by several provinces as insensitive to regional needs or prejudicial to regional interests; and provincial aspirations in the field of economic development have broadened, incurring judicial invalidation of some provincial initiatives and the frustration of others when federal policies (in traditionally federal fields, such as the control of interest rates) interfere.

The Spending Power: Bilateral Negotiation of Joint Programs

A traditional justification for federalism, as will be discussed in the next chapter, is that it centralizes authority in areas demanding a common policy (from defence to standardization of weights and measures) while permitting accommodation of regional differences in values, preferences, and needs. It is difficult, however, for provincial governments to fix priorities and design programs suited to regional or local conditions if they are fiscally dependent upon the central government.

E.R. Black, recognizing this, has devised a 'policy limitation index,' which attempts to gauge the extent of constraint on provincial independence in policy-making[9] by relating the magnitude of conditional grants to a province's 'net general revenue.' However, as Black would be the first to acknowledge, such measures must be treated with extreme caution. Not only is it necessary to recognize the inevitable arbitrariness of any formula that might be devised, but one must avoid inferring that any 'policy limitation index' could be a general measure applying equally to all policy areas. It cannot do so, as some policies may be implemented without much cost – at least to government – with the result that financial considerations have scarcely any weight in the decision-making process. For example, public expenditure is presumably a negligible factor in deciding upon most aspects of the law of industrial relations in the private sector; the design of public education curricula (though not, evidently, in the level or quality of schooling offered); the drawing of municipal boundaries, the design of municipal institutions, and the assignment of powers and responsibilities to them; the marketing (compulsorily or otherwise) of farm products through provincial boards; censorship ('community standards'); environmental protection laws and their enforcement; and the management of forest resources, and generally the licensing of firms for the exploitation of both renewable and non-renewable natural resources. This list is haphazard but may give some impression of the wide range of policy areas under at least partial provincial jurisdiction that frequently engage wide public controversy but make only slight demands upon the public treasury. In these areas a 'policy limitation index' scarcely applies.

Of course in many policy areas cost is an important if not the prime consideration in decision-making, and there the presence or absence of fiscal inducements, to which the exercise of the federal spending power is the key, may well be the decisive factor in provincial policy formation. The best-known case is that of medicare. Although originally most provinces opposed the introduction of public medical insurance (medicare) on a shared-cost basis, once the federal act was in place (1966) no province was able for more than five years to withstand the fiscal inducements and electoral pressures to enter the scheme. Inevitably, the financial burden thus assumed by the provinces, or imposed upon them, has reduced the funds available for spending in other areas.

One way in which the medicare case is instructive is that it stands out as a model of one type of shared-cost program, highlighting the differences exhibited by some others. In medicare fixed criteria were set, determining when a province was eligible for the subsidy. Although some of the criteria, such as the clause requiring universal coverage, are not easy to apply, none the less the same conditions are imposed on all 'agreeing provinces.' For example, it is a matter of judgment whether or not 'extra billing' infringes the principle, but once a decision on such a matter is made, it may be uniformly applied. A contrasting situation arises with some other programs   regional development grants being the textbook case – where bilateral negotiations establish the list of projects and activities to be jointly funded. Agreements made with one province cannot be extended to others; only a general rule of fairness, implying that if two provinces were in the same situation similar agreements would be offered to both, can apply.

In the period 1973-81, program and project decisions relating to regional development were made within a framework set out by a series of General Development Agreements (GDAs) separately negotiated with each province. (The sole exception was Prince Edward Island, where another agreement applied.) As Donald J. Savoie noted in 1981:

GDA-sponsored initiatives can be developed in a variety of policy fields. In fact, GDAs are essentially loosely defined legal frameworks and in themselves do not provide for specific action. Project and cost-sharing arrangements are, instead, presented in subsidiary agreements [with the federal share running to 90 in Newfoundland, 80 in Nova Scotia and New Brunswick, 60 in Quebec, Manitoba, and Saskatchewan, and 50 in Ontario, Alberta, and British Columbia] ...

Over the past several years, and in particular since the introduction of the GDA, [the Department of Regional Economic Expansion's] financial resources have come to play a significant role in the priority determining process of the "have-not" provinces. In the case of New Brunswick, for example, the great majority of new projects in the general economic development spending category are cost-shared under the GDA approach. One provincial Treasury Board official commented that GDA-sponsored projects account for "over" 70 percent of discretionary spending in New Brunswick ...

The Government of New Brunswick has now reached the point where every one of its departments – other than those strictly concerned with providing internal administrative support services – has entered into some kind of cost-sharing arrangements with the federal government ... The Government of New Brunswick can no longer point to a single policy area for which it is unambiguously and solely responsible. Admittedly, the province could turn down federal cost-sharing schemes but this ... is both politically and economically impractical, since non-participation means forgoing federal funds.[10]

The import of these comments is somewhat limited, because there is no readily accessible evidence to show how far they were valid for other provinces, and even more so because the situation has evolved considerably since Savoie wrote. Abandonment of the GDA approach was announced in January 1982; in their stead the federal government has negotiated with each province an Economic and Regional Development Agreement, or ERDA, in which emphasis is on parallel rather than joint delivery of programs. The difference is that some projects are now identifiably federal and others identifiably provincial, instead of all projects being supported through a cost-sharing agreement and administered by the province. However, the two orders of government do not quite act independently of each other; negotiation of the ERDAS and related or subsidiary agreements enables Ottawa to influence provincial decision-making for economic development. In effect, the federal government offers to undertake certain projects provided the province agrees to go ahead with complementary or similar ones. Thus there remain financial inducements that may insinuate a federal presence into the decision-making process in every province, to the extent that budgetary pressures constrain policy choices.[11]

A collaborative style of decision-making, though undoubtedly preferable to an adversarial one, may none the less stifle provincial autonomy. Savoie maintains that in the GDA period Ottawa so fully decentralized operations of the (now defunct) Department of Regional Economic Expansion, and so extended its working relations with provincial bureaucracies, that one could scarcely say whether a particular project was the brainchild of provincial or of federal officials. To provincial politicians this simply underscored the fact that there was scarcely a policy area where they were free of the federal embrace; in New Brunswick it even happened that some provincial officials were partially paid out of federal funds.[12]

Briefly, a collaborative style blurs the line between the federal and the provincial administration. The more that intergovernmental relations are characterized by collaboration, the more apposite the following comment by Anthony Careless, made in the context of a study of intergovernmental relations and regional economic development in the pre-GDA period:

Commentators on Canadian federalism have failed to read both sides of the greater federal flexibility in dealing with provinces. While, indeed, bilateralism may indicate greater concessions won by individual provinces, it may also serve as an entry for 'divide and conquer' techniques in intergovernmental relations. Rarely have provinces been aware of each other's special relationships with Ottawa in shared-cost programs ... The often different nature of relations between Ottawa and each province and the reluctance of each to reveal its own particular arrangements have created a situation whereby the provincial regimes cannot comment upon national development patterns apart from what Ottawa – i.e., the federal government – wishes to say they are. Thus the apparent victory of provincialism may actually have fragmented collective action and left only Ottawa in a position to establish broad national objectives.[13]

There is evidently plenty of scope for divergent assessments of working relations between federal and provincial governments and hence of the centralizing or decentralizing impact of federal regional development policy. Flexibility, or the tailoring of federal programs to the specific needs of each province, is one side of a coin whose obverse is the steady shrinkage of independent provincial decision-making power. The virtue of sensitivity is also the vice of centralization. Or so at least it is with joint programs, bilaterally negotiated. It may be a different story with the exercise of regulatory powers.

Federal Regulatory Activities

In 1976 the premiers of the four western provinces issued a conference communiqué in which they 'expressed their concern over the increasing tendency of the government of Canada to legislate in areas which historically and constitutionally had been considered to be within the provincial sphere.'[14] The follow-up to this statement was the creation of a Western Premiers' Task Force on Constitutional Trends, which published three reports (1977, 1978, 1979) sometimes known as 'Intrusions Papers.' The term speaks for itself, but a little misleadingly. Although the reports do detail some instances of doubtful constitutional morality (if we may borrow a term from J.A. Corry), the vast majority of cases they cite merely illustrate the virtual impossibility of neatly separating the policy responsibilities of the two senior orders of government. Others cases, such as negotiation of international trade agreements, were explicitly acknowledged not to be intrusions but were none the less included in order to claim the right to participate in federal decisions. The striking thing about the task force reports, upon close reading, is that they are really a catalogue of complaints about federal insensitivity to provincial needs. In some cases they also allege federal discrimination against western interests. The character of the documents is clear from the fact that almost every item in the inventory of 'apparent intrusions'[15] (there are 57 of them in the 1979 report) is followed not simply by a demand to cease and desist but by a request for consultation and co-operation to achieve objectives that are, the reports imply, the legitimate concern of both orders of government.

Quebec, of course, has frequently taken a much stronger position than this, insisting upon federal withdrawal from disputed policy fields. However, in most of the cases listed in the 'Intrusions Papers' – and I suspect in almost any regulatory area where federal actions have been the subject of provincial complaints – withdrawal could not be equated with pulling back to an earlier demarcation line between federal and provincial spheres, re-establishing a status quo ante. In most cases the pre-existing situation no longer has meaning or has become irrelevant: either the range of matters within the public domain has expanded or the circumstances that made the earlier demarcation line workable have so changed that traditional policy objectives can no longer be realized without undertaking new programs or selecting new instruments. Conditions change, rendering the old partition of responsibilities outmoded. When, responding to a change in circumstances, the initiative is taken by one order of government, the other may resent it as an intrusion into its own area of jurisdiction.

This perspective on the subject of federal 'apparent intrusions' is not to be taken as a claim that provincial complaints (whether from Quebec, the west, or any other region) are without foundation. I do wish to suggest, however, that they are founded less upon an attempted federal takeover of traditional provincial powers and responsibilities than upon grievances arising from the manner in which federal powers, especially those pertaining to regulation, have been exercised.

Since this interpretation of the facts will probably be contested by some readers, an explanation is in order. The 1979 'Intrusions Paper' contains an inventory of 57 grievances, which for our purposes may be divided into five categories.

1. Nineteen items are not relevant to the present discussion, as they do not have to do with the exercise of regulatory powers,[16] with which this part of the argument is concerned.

2. Seven items allege inadequacy or misdirection of federal policies in fields that the report acknowledges to be within federal jurisdiction, either in exclusivity or concurrently. Examples are deficiencies in transportation ('The Task Force did not question the federal government's jurisdiction in the interprovincial transportation field, but rather the manner in which the authority was exercised'; agricultural stabilization and farm credit; international trade; and industrial development ('care should be taken to ensure that the policies developed are complementary to the aspirations of the provinces.')[17]

3. Six items concern partition of the rapidly expanding field of communications: electronic payments systems, pay television, cable, video games, etc. These are subjects of dispute opened up by technological advances which, in the eyes of the provinces, are not within the ambit of federal jurisdiction over broadcasting, established by the 'Radio case' in 1932. The conflicts that arise in these areas are

less germane to the centralization issue that to the problem of reaching an intergovernmental modus vivendi in a new and complex field.

4. Twenty-two items are disputes arising out of policy innovation in fields where jurisdiction is divided, generally as a result of partial applicability of several heads of power in the Constitution Act. Twelve impinge upon control or taxation of natural resources (mostly non-renewable); others concern market regulation (trade practices, competition policy, consumer credit, trust companies and credit unions), television advertising, educational communications, family law, and investigation of transportation accidents.

5. Three items pertain to land use, a traditional provincial regulatory field. Of these, one concerns zoning around airports, another relocation of rail lines and urban planning studies, and one establishment of national guidelines for land use policy, effective only if adopted by the provinces individually.

Of these five categories the most important in my opinion is the fourth, which pertains to policy disputes arising within fields where jurisdiction is divided between orders of government, each having exclusive powers over part of the field. It is in such fields, it will be recalled from the argument in the previous chapter, that governmental interaction is most likely to be marked by unilateralism and persisting acrimony. Thus it is, with this 22-item list culled from the 1979 'Intrusions Paper.' Some or all of the grievances about exercise of federal powers may be justified; I do not wish to address this issue. But it is clear – and this is what is germane to the present argument – that the grievances are about the substance of federal policy objectives rather than about federal involvement per se. The point may be illustrated by referring once more to the resources issue, which (as already noted) accounts for more than half of the 22 items on the list.

Notwithstanding the provinces' wide regulatory power over the production and management of natural resources, deriving from their jurisdiction over property and civil rights, Parliament has always had the power to regulate interprovincial and international sales of resources (as of other products), controlling prices and prohibiting or limiting exports. This power is not impaired by provincial ownership where it obtains; it is as extensive in those cases where the resource is owned by the province as in cases where freehold rights have been transferred to private interests. Nor, probably, will it prove to be seriously limited by the resources clause enacted in 1982. The federal government also has a significant measure of control over development and production of natural resources through its power of corporate taxation. However, its power to tax provincially owned resources is more limited.

The federal government's power in relation to pricing, export, and taxation of natural resources was more actively exercised during the years 1973-84 than at any previous time in Canada's history. Nonetheless Ottawa's involvement in these areas was not a new phenomenon, as federal controls over export of electricity – provoking bitter controversy with Ontario during the late 1930s and with British

Columbia in 1961-63 over the sale of Columbia River power – dramatically showed.[18] In both cases an aspect of the dispute was that the central government refused to allow the long-term sale of hydroelectric power to the United States, on the grounds that an established pattern of exports could not be cut back in the future without causing an international crisis, and Canada would be prudent to reserve its energy resources to fuel future Canadian industrial growth. This policy also underlay the original version of the Columbia River Treaty, signed by John Diefenbaker in 1961. However, with the defeat of federal intentions through a series of brilliant manoeuvres by BC premier W.A.C. Bennett, the federal government was forced to abandon its long-standing policy. In any case the rationale for the policy had been weakened by Ottawa's insistent efforts to expand US markets for surplus Alberta petroleum; with such a policy, the refusal to license the export of electricity appeared to discriminate against one form of energy production relative to another. Perhaps more seriously, it discriminated against several large provinces – British Columbia, Ontario, and Quebec.

Dissimilar treatment of two different energy sources did not seem particularly worrisome to Ottawa when the Arab oil embargo of 1973 and the subsequent rise in the world price of oil provided the incentive for gradual formulation of a national energy policy the main features of which were vigorously opposed by the producing provinces. The process began in 1973 (as was noted in chapter 1) with the imposition of a ceiling on the domestic price of oil and an accompanying export tax, and it led eventually to the announcement of the National Energy Program (November 1980). The 1979 'Intrusions Paper' complained, among other things, that:

non-deductibility (since 1974) of oil and gas revenues for purposes of the federal corporation income tax adversely affected the provinces' ability to tax the resource industries, discouraged oil exploration, and detrimentally affected the provincial governments' attempts to diversify their economies;
price controls over interprovincial and international sale of oil and gas indirectly regulated the flow and production of a provincial natural resource;
the National Energy Board, the activities of which challenged 'the basic principles of provincial resource ownership and management,' changed its regulations 'without provincial input, even though they have had a great impact on the provinces' and the industry's revenues';[19]
the Emergency Supply Act, making provision for meeting a shortage of crude oil, did not involve the provinces in supplying information and in a co-ordinating role;
regarding the 'Canada First' policy on the export of non-renewable resources: 'the Task Force ... although recognizing the federal government's ultimate control over these matters, ... felt that the various provincial responsibilities should be more adequately recognized.'[20]

And so forth. The summary comment is best provided in the words of the report itself: 'Increased federal-provincial consultation in these complex judicial matters would help to eliminate some of the existing tensions relating to energy matters.'[21]

The lesson of this catalogue of complaints seems clear enough. As long as the powers of the federal government were exercised so as to expand levels of resource production and provincial revenues from their exploitation, federal intervention in the interprovincial and international marketing of oil and gas was welcomed by westerners (particularly Albertans). This was evident from their support for the National Energy Policy announced by John Diefenbaker in 1961, which reserved that part of the Canadian market lying west of the Ottawa valley for domestic crude oil and sought to expand Canadian crude oil exports to the United States. When, twelve years later, federal policy turned restrictive and financially burdensome, exercise of traditional instruments of policy now appeared an intrusion into provincial jurisdiction. A regional grievance against the use made of traditional tax and regulatory powers now led to their exercise being presented as a violation, in letter or spirit or both, of the Canadian constitution. The real issue, however – and a vital one for all Canadians – is whether federal regulatory policies consistently, or on balance, subordinate the interests of the less populous regions to those of central Canada.

Broadened Provincial Aims Regarding Economic Development

We have surveyed two reasons why some provincial leaders may perceive a centralizing trend in Canadian federalism. Both have to do with policy initiatives of the federal government: recourse to bilateralism in the context of providing certain services, especially subsidies for regional development, and restrictive or unwelcome exercise of certain regulatory powers. There is also a third reason, though this one has to do with provincial rather than federal policy initiatives.

While the impression that the Canadian federal regime is becoming more centralized derives primarily from the way the provinces are affected by the exercise of federal spending and regulatory powers, a supporting factor is extension of provincial policy aims, especially in the field of economic development. Here, too, it is easy to see how provincial politicians and officials experience frustration when they are unable to exercise powers that they believe are rightfully theirs under the constitution without interference from the federal government. Their policy initiatives have frequently been frustrated, some by judicial invalidation as a result of litigation supported by Ottawa, and some by federal policies having a counter-balancing or neutralizing effect.

Both orders of government showed, during the 1970s and early 1980s, increasing readiness to go to court in an attempt to expand their own powers or to restrict the powers of the other. When the initiative to bring matters before the courts was taken by the provinces their action tended to be symptomatic of failure to resolve disagreements at the political level. The outstanding case, of course, is the reference of the constitutional amendment issue to provincial courts of appeal and from there to the Supreme Court. Another is Newfoundland's reference regarding proprietary rights over offshore resources. In these instances the need for provincial action was blamed on federal unilateralism or intransigence, evidence of its centralism.

An additional subject of provincial grievance has been Ottawa's support for challenges to provincial legislation and/or regulations. Several of the relevant cases – it would be inappropriate to review them individually here – deal with taxation and control of natural resource production or with communications. The flavour of provincial complaints is contained, once again, in the 'Intrusions Papers':

During the last four years [from January 1973 to January 1977] the federal government has attacked the validity of provincial legislation in nine of the approximately ten cases in which provincial legislation has been challenged during this period in the Supreme Court of Canada ... The provinces are concerned over the recent practice by which the federal government has aligned itself as a plaintiff with parties in court cases challenging the constitutionality of provincial resource legislation. It is felt that the co-plaintiff strategy represents an unnecessarily aggressive approach by the federal government to this matter.[22]

There are also instances of federal policies cancelling out provincial policy initiatives or rendering them partially ineffective. Provincial regulatory powers over the economy are evident mainly in the fields of resource production and conservation and to some extent in the field of contract law (which gives the provinces control over intraprovincial trade and industrial relations). The wider range of powers to regulate economic activity, however, is vested in Parliament. Accordingly, a province wishing to stimulate economic development or to shore up declining industries must frequently rely upon discretionary expenditures such as investment subsidies – directly to individual firms in the case of industrial assistance and usually indirectly to several firms in the case of infrastructural support. A major problem with using such policy instruments is that they are inherently expensive, and their effect may easily be overborne by policies of the federal government. Federal expenditures may easily overshadow provincial expenditures; certainly in the aggregate – in the field of industrial assistance – they are much larger. Moreover, reduction in tariff or non-tariff protection for certain industries (reductions that Canada may be forced to accept in multilateral negotiations or may agree to impose in order to expand Canadian exports of other products) may render provincial subsidies totally ineffective. Interest rates set in Ottawa – even if Canada has little latitude to diverge significantly from US rates – can be ruinous for provincial treasuries as well as wiping out the stimulative effect of provincial industrial assistance expenditures.

It is a matter of personal judgment, or instinctual reactions, whether the provinces are trying to decentralize the federation by seeking to extend their control over economic development or whether the federal government is trying to centralize the structure of the federation by challenging or neutralizing the provinces' exercise of their powers. Apparently the provinces, or most of them, see mainly the latter aspect of what is really a trend to expansion of government control over the economy and consequently to more pervasive interaction among governments in framing Canadian economic policy.

(DE)CENTRALIZATION: SIGNIFICANCE

Let us sum up what we have discovered so far. In a classical form of federalism and in a broadly static situation (a given set of policy problems or policy demands; and a given range of government activity), 'centralization' is a double trend: toward expansion of policy responsibilities assumed by the central government and toward contraction of policy responsibilities assumed by the provinces. 'Decentralization' means the opposite. Even in a situation that is simplified (as this one is) by restrictive assumptions, it is not always easy to devise indicators that will unambiguously identify trends toward (de)centralization. The relative importance of various forms of regulation can be assessed only subjectively and only in ordinal terms. If the central government is expanding in one policy field and the provinces in another, the direction of the overall trend – if there is one – may not be at all obvious.

Further difficulties, some pertaining to measurement and some of a conceptual character, crowd in upon us when we take account of various factors that can only artificially be disregarded. 1) There has been, over the past century but perhaps especially since the Second World War, a huge expansion in the role of government. If the more traditional activities of government remain as assigned when the 'federal bargain' was struck, and the newer activities are undertaken mainly by a single order of government (central or regional, as the case may be), it will ·be clear whether the overall tendency is centralizing or decentralizing. However, the typical situation is that both federal and provincial governments assume new policy responsibilities. Accordingly, our impression that there exists a (de)centralizing trend necessarily depends upon a subjective judgment as to which of the new responsibilities are most important. 2) Many policy areas are shared between central and provincial governments, and policy is often formed through interactive processes. The mutual influence that governments have on each others' decisions, and the interplay among policy initiatives (as one order of government neutralizes, complements and extends, or counteracts what the other does), must be taken into account. 3) Over the past fifteen years or so, the problems of economic policy have become increasingly intractable: briefly, the country traversed a period of stagflation, emerging with an apparently uncontrollable deficit, an intolerable rate of unemployment, and a sagging dollar. When governments are manifestly incapable of meeting their policy responsibilities, as conventionally perceived, their failure to do so is easily blamed (especially by themselves) on lack of constitutional power, shortage of financial resources, and/or loss of political independence in wielding the traditional policy instruments. The federal government may then perceive decentralization; the provinces, centralization. It may not be strictly logical to dwell on such perceptions, but when one wants indicators that can bring some order to a confusing topic, the only way to make some sense out of it is to acknowledge that the concept of (de)centralization brings out differences of opinion that objective criteria cannot entirely obviate or resolve.

To put it baldly, '(de)centralization' implies a shift in the locus of policy control in relation to what seem, at the time, the most pressing public issues. In the present climate of opinion, these no longer appear to be provision of major public services (income redistribution, social insurance, education, and health care) but have to do with stimulating and chanelling economic growth. In respect of the economy, sectoral policies and regional development – involving infrastructural support, public and mixed enterprise, investment subsidies, and use of other discretionary policy instruments – for a time acquired the prominence that formerly was occupied by Keynesian schemes for economic management. Electoral pressures and the demands of business coincided in forcing an interventionist policy, which both orders of government committed themselves to implementing. The trend is now toward less intervention and more indirect forms of government control of the economy, but in one sense the situation remains as before: both orders of government are grasping for available policy levers.

It is scarcely surprising, in this situation, that disagreement persists on the (de)centralization question. On the one hand, there are those who emphasize that the federal government has historically had primary responsibility for economic policy and insist that it must continue to do so. It is easy to see why they are worried about what they regard as a dangerous trend toward decentralization of Canada's federal system. On the other hand, there are those who think that while the central government has overall responsibility for economic management or stabilization and for interregional redistribution, the provinces are (as the Quebec Liberal party has put it) 'the primary level of government responsible for the development of their own territories and human resources.'[23] Naturally, when people of this persuasion observe that the federal government controls the more discretionary instruments of economic policy, they decry what they see as unrestrained centralization.

These differences of opinion lead us to pose some very basic questions, much more important than resolution of a terminological or conceptual dispute. These are: 1) what are the appropriate goals of economic policy, 2) how much interventionism should there be, given these goals – but bearing in mind also the constraints that make it difficult for government, and especially the government(s) of a small state in a turbulent world economy, to realize them, and 3) how should the available policy instruments be distributed between, or shared by, the two senior orders of government in Canada? These questions are raised more fully in the last two chapters of this book.

In the mean time, in the next chapter, I address a more immediate question about the political significance of (de)centralization. Underlying a terminological debate that can easily become arcane and may appear arid is a very immediate and pressing political concern. In a centralized state, whether unitary or federal in structure, a national majority can override ('dominate' and 'exploit' are also used) the regions. A more decentralized state, especially one that allots extensive powers and property rights to the regional units on an exclusive (i.e. non-concurrent) basis, offers regional interests protection against national majorities that otherwise might overwhelm them. But it may also offer residents of the wealthier units the advantages of political union without the obligation to share fully its costs.

Behind the (de)centralization issue lies the possible establishment or perpetuation of an asymmetrical or dominant/subordinate relationship among the regions. It is generally presumed that a decentralized state is less capable of imposing regionally discriminatory policies and is therefore less likely to provoke or sustain interregional conflict. Is this so? It's a nice question, one that bears careful examination.

7

(De)centralization and interregional conflict

'It is generally recognized,' wrote the Task Force on Canadian Unity (the Pepin-Robarts task force), 'that substantial gains come from integrating into larger and more complete types of economic association.' The report continued:

Integration allows regions to take advantage of a venerable principle of economics: the division of labour and the specialization of production which goes with it. By operating within an integrated whole, regions can specialize in the production of goods and services in which they have a comparative advantage. At the same time, the possibility of interregional trade permits greater volumes of production, and hence lower costs. The size of the market in which the enterprises of a province, a region, or a state can trade determines the limits of specialization ...

In a nutshell, integration creates a surplus, because the whole is greater than its parts. And the surplus, using the central government as an instrument, can be redistributed so that the strong parts help the weak to the benefit of the whole. At the same time we must recognize that increased economic integration also entails greater sacrifices, or costs ... The cost of integration may be described as essentially social or political... Taking both benefits and costs into account, equilibrium is reached in practice when the advantages in favour of a higher level of integration are counterbalanced by the social and political costs which each region is prepared to tolerate. [1]

This statement articulates with exceptional clarity a particular viewpoint on the subject of economic and political integration. It also implicitly comments on the advantages of federalism and the basis of interregional conflict within federations.

First, the report, while acknowledging that integration imposes constraints on the capacity of regional units to manage their own economies, did not discuss the possibility that integration might entail, for any region, a net economic penalty. Thus it neglected an important feature of orthodox (liberal) economic theory on the subject, and – unlike the earlier Rowell-Sirois report (1940) – did not attempt to evaluate the complaints of those regions in Canada that allege systematic or consistent discrimination against their economic interests.

Second, members of the task force apparently believed that while federalism is a device for balancing gains in material welfare (deriving from economic integration) against losses in provincial autonomy. Economic integration, they suggested, reduces the capacity of regional/provincial communities to implement policies consistent with their own distinctive values and preferences. This presumably explains the inattention of the task force to the existence of values or preferences – other than the value of respecting and supporting diversity – that might be shared by Canadians generally and that a federal political union might help to promote or to realize. The task force did not ask whether there exists in Canada a sense of community broader than an individual province, or each of them severally.

Third, the task force endorsed the traditional scholarly view of federalism that by protecting the autonomy of the constituent parts the unity of the whole may be the more effectively secured. Hence the task force, throughout its report, emphasized the virtue of accommodating cultural diversity and linguistic dualism. These characteristics of the Canadian polity, it said, require decentralization of powers in the fields of social and cultural policy.

It is evident, then, that the task force made certain assumptions about the types of policy dispute that may generate interregional conflict. Implicitly, too, it made assumptions about the factors that give rise to a sense of membership in a political community and engender loyalty toward the state in which it is encompassed. Federalism, for the task force, is a device for achieving certain of the advantages deriving from political integration – the report dwelt on the economic gains to be obtained through union, but other writers, addressing themselves to different circumstances, have stressed the enhanced security that common control of defence and foreign policy may bring – while avoiding the costs entailed in creating a unitary state. This is the classic view of federalism, as expounded (for example) by J.A. Corry:

The great triumph of federalism is that many matters that would cause the sharpest conflict if they were thrown into national politics cause little dissension when dealt with separately in each state. Federalism enables many regional interests and idiosyncracies to have their own way in their own areas without ever facing the necessity of reconciliation with other regional interests. Individuals identify themselves with particular regional interests and find in them a satisfying expression of many facets of their personalities. Federalism is a device for combining unity and diversity in accordance with the requirements of liberal democratic ideals.[2]

Others – for example Richard Simeon, in the passage cited below – have pointed out with equal persuasiveness that:

Federalism is not only a *response* to regionalism, but also ensures that it will continue. It does so in several ways ... It provides an institutional focus for loyalty and identity ... Cleavages which reinforce the territorial division will be highlighted; cleavages which do not do so will either be defined in such a way that they do conform to the pattern, or they will tend to be ignored. There are two reasons for this. At the societal, or mass level, conflicts will tend to be encapsulated at the provincial level. Because provincial governments make the decisions, groups will have to turn to them, will have to respond to provincial policies and to the demands of other groups with which they are in competition at that level. Communication with similar groups in other provinces will therefore be inhibited, and indeed be strategically wasteful ... the federal structure fragments these social forces, and inhibits their mobilization on a national basis. It thus perpetuates the regional difference. [Additionally], at the elite level, federalism has similar effects by conferring leadership on a set of leaders in provincial governments who have [a] vested interest in maintaining and strengthening the salience of the regional dimension.[3]

Federalism, then, is generally portrayed as an institutional device for accommodating interregional conflict, diminishing its intensity by comparison with the levels of conflict that would obtain in a unitary state. The more decentralized state is the less conflict-ridden one. However, it is equally plausible to hold that federalism, or political decentralization, sharpens and may even provoke interregional conflict. Is this a contradiction in the literature? Or are there some circumstances in which the conflict-reducing effect of decentralization predominates, and other circumstances in which the reverse occurs? The latter suggestion seems to offer a promising lead.

CONFLICTS OF TASTE AND OF CLAIM

The most inventive and indeed the most satisfying attempt to identify and delimit the circumstances in which decentralization may reduce interregional conflict is contained in a discussion paper by Jack Mintz and Richard Simeon, entitled 'Conflict of Taste and Conflict of Claim in Federal Countries.' They write:

Differences of taste refer to the preference of regional populations for distinct and variable 'baskets' or 'packages' of public and private goods or services. If regional populations have distinct cultural characteristics, or a distinct socio-economic base, then their preferences for public policy are likely to vary as well. They may, for example, choose to weight economic development more heavily than welfare, to stress different cultural values in an education system, to be more or less egalitarian in social policies ...

Conflict of claim, however, does not depend for its intensity on such cultural differences. It arises where regional populations share values but disagree on the distribution of wealth among them. Conflict of claim ... is based not on differences among but on relations between the regions, and is rooted in competition among them. [It] ... implies that in order for a region to get what it wants, it must gain something from other regions.[4]

Decentralization, suggest Mintz and Simeon, is an 'obvious,' even if not universally applicable, solution to the existence of sharp interregional differences in taste. Ideally, it permits regional majorities to have their way without imposing their preferences on other regions. However, there are some limits to the benefits of decentralization. Some of these limits reflect differences in the fiscal capacities of the various provinces, in which case 'freedom to enact different preferences depends on an element of claim, specifically on some form of equalization.' In other cases a province may be constrained from providing costly public services because the high levels of taxation required to finance them may cause an outflow of capital and the most highly paid categories of labour. Provinces may also be induced, as a result of spillover effects, to harmonize policies even in non-economic fields such as education or income security. Mintz and Simeon conclude: 'Differences of taste are likely to translate quickly into competing claims to the extent that factors are mobile between provinces, that there are unequal resource endowments among them, or that there are large spillovers.' And finally, some conflicts of taste involve goods that by their nature are indivisible; such conflicts cannot be resolved by decentralization. The examples mentioned are 'symbolic questions such as a flag or retention of the monarchy.'[5]

Mintz and Simeon point out that federal theory tends to dwell on conflicts of taste and to neglect those of claim.[6] Their observation is well taken. It explains why Corry and many other writers, including the authors of the Pepin-Robarts report, have regarded federalism – and a fairly decentralized form of federalism at that – as a means of reducing or controlling levels of conflict within a political community. What Mintz and Simeon say about the limitations on the effectiveness of decentralization as a means of reducing conflict also helps explain why the same writers, when dealing with economic issues and intergovernmental fiscal relations, have supported affirmation or extension of central power and have especially stressed the central government's responsibility for ensuring a just interregional distribution of wealth.

In short, the distinction between conflict of taste and conflict of claim identifies some of the assumptions, hitherto only implicit, that are incorporated into much of federal theory and that have lain behind many of the recommendations that have emerged in Canada from time to time for restructuring the federation. For example, it justifies the recommendations not only of the Pepin-Robarts report but also of the Rowell-Sirois report of almost forty years before, although Rowell-Sirois has widely been perceived as centralist and Pepin-Robarts as provincialist in orientation. However, the use made by Mintz and Simeon of the distinction they have introduced is limited – indeed, arguably deficient – in two important respects. One can, I think, incorporate their concepts into a more general typology

A TYPOLOGY OF POLICY DISPUTES

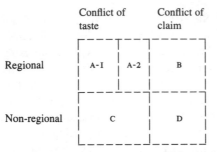

NOTE: Cell A-1 includes taste-related regional policy disputes where regional differentiation in policy is possible; cell A-2 includes taste-related regional policy disputes over non-divisible goods, for example symbols pertaining to the nation as a whole (flag, monarchy).

of forms of political conflict and use this more inclusive typology to perceive some of the longer-term consequences of (de)centralization, which they did not discuss. If one does so, one can evaluate as well as explain the position taken by, for example, the Pepin-Robarts task force. Its conclusions, and, I would argue, those of Mintz and Simeon as well, appear rather shaky when the analysis is broadened beyond the limits that have so far confined the discussion.

A first step toward broadening the analysis is to extend the Mintz-Simeon typology of policy disputes (forms of conflict) to make reference also to non-regional issues. Although only regional disputes are of direct concern to us in this chapter (as was so also with Mintz and Simeon), our subject requires us to be attentive to the ways in which institutional reform can change a regional conflict into a non-regional one, or vice versa. A 'purely' regional dispute, as defined below, may perhaps be resolved through decentralization: the Mintz-Simeon categories alert us to the situations where this is so and to those where it is not. Conversely, one supposes, centralization might create controversies where none existed before. These situations may be represented by constructing a simple matrix (see figure).

What Mintz and Simeon have pointed out is simply that many but not all of those regional issues arising out of conflict of taste – the issues located in the top half of the matrix – are resolvable through decentralization. Some of the issues concern public goods of a non-divisible nature, like national symbols; in the matrix, these are located in cell A-2. Thus the only policy disputes resolvable through decentralization are located in cell A-1 although even here financial considerations or spillover effects may make decentralization only an imperfect solution.

In response, I think one should recognize that even in the best of circumstances issues can scarcely be expected to vanish altogether as a result of decentralization.

At best, most regional issues simply reappear in non-regional guise – not an insignificant achievement, since some conflicts may (as Corry thought likely) be much less disruptive if confined to the regional level. If this were the only phenomenon to consider in discussing the effects of constitutional (de)centralization, we could safely ignore the bottom half of the matrix. However, I think it is incumbent upon thoughtful observers to consider a more general and more complex question: whether the institutional structure (federal/non-federal; centralized/decentralized) is relevant to the categorization of issues as regional/ non-regional, or indeed as taste-related or claim-related. Mintz and Simeon asked, in effect, whether constitutional change could make certain issues evaporate; one should ask also whether it may not transform the character of certain issues, eliminate some, and create others. In terms of the matrix: Which issues fit into which cells? Are constitutional arrangements relevant to this? Are some issues factitious in the sense that they exist because of the constitution and would not arise at all under a different institutional structure?

One implication of putting these questions is that our analysis addresses an important issue concerning conflicts of claim, an issue that Mintz and Simeon did not consider. They pointed out that conflicts of claim are not resolvable through decentralization. Ought one to infer that the degree of centralization (however measured) is irrelevant to the intensity of conflicts of an economic character, neither diminishing nor raising the salience of the regional aspect of controversies over economic development and the distribution and redistribution of wealth?

There is another major respect in which the Mintz-Simeon analysis deserves to be extended. Their inquiry is limited to the short term, that is, to an exposition of possible responses to a given and therefore static situation. For example, they note that interregional conflicts of claim cannot arise except where there already exists a sense of community within the component states of the federation (why otherwise would region be relevant to a discussion of the distribution of wealth?); but they do not discuss the extent to which policy or policy controversies affect the strength of personal identification with the region, that is, on the growing or waning strength of regionalism. Moreover, in defining 'conflict of claim' they refer only to the distribution of a given quantity of wealth, not to policies that may affect levels of production (wealth-creation) in the future.

One cannot take for granted that the structure of a political regime is in any important degree responsible for long-term changes in the strength of regionalism or the condition of the economy and its place in relation to other national economies. Nonetheless these are clearly important questions for us. The matter of regionalism is self-evidently at the centre of our subject of inquiry; and a large part of the argument in favour of federalism is (as the Pepin-Robarts report made clear) that it offers a long-term economic benefit that would be unavailable to states that had rejected any significant degree of political integration. Admittedly, increases in wealth do not necessarily diminish the intensity of disputes over its distribution; but, to the extent that federalism is perceived to bring economic benefit, interregional conflicts of claim are more easily subject to at least partial resolution through bargaining, regardless of the institutional context in which it occurs. It is important to take this into account in our analysis. Conversely, it would be interesting to know whether or not, if irreconcilable conflicts of claim were to result in the dissolution of a national state (federal or unitary), dismemberment would obviate the basis for conflicts of claim among its former members or would merely transfer them to the arena of international politics, where the poor are notoriously impotent in making good their claims against the rich.

The distinction between conflicts of taste and claim is useful. Indeed, I think it is necessarily basic to any attempt to explore the relationship between the structure of federal regimes and the severity of interregional conflict. However, to make the most of the concepts invented by Mintz and Simeon, their analysis must be extended in two ways: by constructing a more inclusive typology of policy disputes and by using it as a framework within which to construct a theory of the dynamics of interregional conflict in a federal state.

WHEN ARE CONFLICTS REGIONAL?

The 'pure case' of a regional issue would be one in which opinion in one part of the country was unanimous and was in conflict with unanimously held opinion in another part of the country. (We would presumably ignore those who have no opinion on the question.) Conversely, the pure case of a non-regional issue would be one in which opinion was divided in the same proportions everywhere in the country. Needless to say, even in the latter case, intensity of feeling on the issue might be high: the level of political conflict implied in or generated by the issue could conceivably provoke disorder or even contribute to revolution; but the conflict would not be of a regional nature.

Obviously, in 'real life' there is no such thing as a purely regional or a purely non-regional issue: these are ideal types or (as I would prefer) the limiting cases where a particular feature of every 'real-life' political conflict is imagined to be exaggerated to its logical extreme. Such distortion, far from obliterating nuance, warns the observer how much nuance he loses by classifying political issues (as surely we all do tend do) according to a regional/non-regional dichotomy. What one really wants to know is to what extent, on any given issue, territory correlates with attitudes – and, to the extent it does so, whether the correlation occurs because territory largely determines attitudes, because politically relevant groups (e.g. occupational, ethnic) are unevenly distributed among regions, or because the structure of our institutions and the behaviour of public people give 'region' a degree of visibility that it would not otherwise have, or even create new issues of a regional character.

Territory Determines Attitudes

Let us try to imagine circumstances in which a 'real-life' Canadian political controversy approximates the limiting case of a purely regional issue. Naturally, the conditions that would eliminate non-regional aspects will be somewhat contrived– but the issue itself will be familiar to almost every Canadian with any interest in public affairs: it is the 'Canadian content' rules for television stations licensed under the Canadian Radio-Television and Telecommunications Commission (CRTC).

Let us suppose, to begin with, that everyone wants to be able to watch American television. Those who live close to the US border ('southerners') can all get their favourite programs simply by switching to a nearby US station. However, some of them want also to be able to watch a different kind of show, quintessentially Canadian. Canadian content rules create conditions favourable to this kind of programming, which otherwise would not exist. Therefore, southerners are either indifferent to the imposition of Canadian content rules or support them. However, those who live outside the zone where they can receive US TV signals ('northerners'), can't get as much US programming as they want if the CRTC imposes Canadian content rules. All northerners who have an opinion on the issue therefore oppose them.

Under these assumptions, plus the very strong assumption that no other factors are relevant, the controversy is a pure case of a regional issue. Of those who care about it at all, none of the advocates is a northerner; all are southerners. Indeed, within each region, opinion is remarkably homogeneous: southerners, if not indifferent, are nationalist; northerners are anti-nationalist. It is even the case that northerners who move south become indifferent or nationalist, while most southerners who move north become anti-nationalist. Region not only correlates with attitudes on the question, it largely determines them.

Are there actual policy disputes in Canada that partially resemble our artificially simplified portrayal of the Canadian content rules controversy? (The test here is that when people move to another region their preferences and opinions also tend to change.) There is no practical way to answer this question conclusively, but it is possible to think of a few issues where interests (we avoid the trickier question of attitudes) do reflect residence and where political debate appears to recognize this. Consider, for example, the following cases:

locational policies, i.e. those affecting the location of economic activity: government procurement, provision of transportation infrastructure (location of ports, rail lines, etc), and direct job-creation activities such as investment subsidies granted on the basis of location of capital installations;
other regionally discriminatory policies such as establishment of a shorter qualifying period for unemployment insurance in the Atlantic region (an area of high unemployment); and

deregulation of passenger air services, an action expected to reduce fares between major cities but probably raise fares and/or reduce quality of service everywhere else.

To this list could probably be added an additional item, the offering of favourable tax-and-subsidy treatment to specific industries that form the main economic base of particular areas. Indeed, some regions are wholly dependent upon a specific industry or even a specific firm, as is often the case with mining or forestry. Although policies may be defined in relation to the industry and not in relation to their location, the effect is sometimes the same for certain parts of the country. Even residents not directly in the employ of the industry are dependent upon it and its workers, for example, as retailers, restaurateurs, teachers, health care workers, or contractors.

Regional dependence on a single industry is, however, less common than it once was. As a consequence, some policies that were formerly at the heart of interregional conflict in Canada are now less clearly regional in their incidence than previously they were. Let us consider two examples: transportation of prairie grains and the protection of secondary manufacturing through the tariff.

In the days when the prairie region was almost wholly dependent upon the export of wheat, regulation of rates for carrying grain was a policy that approximated the ideal type of a purely regional issue. In 1897 a legislated rate was established for transportation of prairie grains to port terminals (the Crow's Nest Pass rate); until 1984 the rate was, except for a brief period during and after the First World War, maintained at the same level. This policy imposed substantial costs on the railways and required subsidization of spur lines by the federal government; with persistent cost inflation, maintenance of a rate established eighty years earlier became increasingly anomalous. However, until the 1980s any attempt to tamper with 'The Crow' was ruled out by the intensity of regional (prairie) feeling on the matter, since the legislated rate, in addition to providing substantial financial benefits to the producer, quickly acquired great symbolic significance for the entire region. It became almost the sole visible compensation to the prairies for the costs imposed by the protective tariff and other 'national policies' devised (as the west saw it) to support the economy of central Canada.

The emotions attaching to 'The Crow' persist in some parts of the prairie region, especially in Saskatchewan; but – and this is a telling indicator of changed economic relations among Canada's regions – the policy eventually lost its unanimous support in the prairie region. The reasons it did so are complex and cannot be fully set out here, but a few points are worth noting. First, during the 1970s the federal government allowed, perhaps deliberately, the western rail transportation system to deteriorate to the point where it was evidently inadequate to carry grain to the ports in the desired quantities. Provincial governments alleviated the situation by purchasing rolling stock; but the policy of neglect demonstrated the shortcomings of a pricing arrangement that gave the railways a negative incentive to serve the needs of the producer. It also weakened provincial governments' support for the Crow, since they found themselves forced to pick up some of the costs of the deterioration of the system. Second, the railways were forced to compensate for their losses in carrying grain by charging higher prices for other goods, and it eventually came to be understood that the Crow was a significant factor holding back diversification of western agriculture and, more generally, helping to perpetuate the traditional structure of the prairie economy, with its heavy dependence on grains production. As long as it was cheap to send grains to market but costly to export other products from the region, 'downstream' or processing activities would be discouraged (for example, feedlots for cattle would be located in the east). As non-farm groups and indeed all those not directly engaged in producing or selling grains began to perceive how the Crow was hurting them, support grew for its abolition. Simple abandonment appeared too drastic, but when a federal task force recommended its replacement by a 'Crow benefit' or compensating cash subsidy, the idea proved politically saleable. The irony was that the form of the subsidy – its payment not to the producer as the task force had recommended, but to the railways – was determined more by the reaction of the Quebec caucus, reflecting the interests of Quebec farmers, than by opinion in the prairie west.[7]

Trade policy is another case of an issue once understood largely in regional terms but now much less so. The erection of a protective tariff was an essential ingredient of an import substitution strategy[8] to develop a manufacturing industry, located mainly in central Canada. Its costs have been borne by consumers and also, to an indeterminate extent, by producers of export goods. Although the majority of consumers have always lived in the industrial areas, and therefore these areas have borne a large part of the costs of protection, it has generally been argued that those central Canadians not directly employed in the protected sector have still benefited from the tariff because of the spread, or linkage, effects of manufacturing activity. For example, those in service industries have profited because they have had more customers. By contrast, primary producers oriented to the export market have had to pay higher prices for goods entering into their costs of production; and additionally they have had, as consumers, to pay more for clothing and other items. Since most of them live outside the industrial areas, it has been easy to perceive the tariff issue in regional terms; and this has indeed generally been the case.

The trade policy issue is now, however, much more complex than earlier controversies over the protective tariff. Partly this is because tariffs have declined in importance relative to other trade barriers, and current debates focus on a broader range of concerns for which the catchword is 'free trade'; but the main factor is structural economic change. Some of the most heavily protected manufacturing activities are now located outside of central Canada, notably on the prairies; one consequence of this has been to make the government of Manitoba very cautious and somewhat ambivalent about the idea of negotiating a trade agreement with the United States. The key change, though, is that there are now growing up both in Ontario and Quebec a set of industrial and related financial interests oriented to world markets and committed to reciprocal reduction in international trade barriers. For them, Canadian tariffs and other protectionist devices such as subsidies are at best a bargaining chip to be traded in for improved access to foreign markets. At worst, tariffs and subsidies are a factor raising their production costs and an embarrassment in their dealings with foreign business interests and foreign governments.[9] While both the Ontario and Quebec governments – especially the former – have expressed fundamental reservations about the prospect of free trade, their position too has been nuanced by strong support for the project emanating from business interests. The issue now appears to divide management and labour as much as, indeed probably more than, regions or provinces.

In short, to the extent that the hoary issues of transportation and trade policy remain regional, they are now so in a second and weaker sense than ones where the relevant groups are actually defined by territory and do not merely correlate with it. This distinction leads us to a second category of issues, the 'regional' character of which is sometimes ambiguous or even dubious.

Territorial Concentration of Politically Relevant Groups

In the two cases we have reviewed, issues that once united large regions in their political preferences and interests subsequently emerged as subjects of controversy within as well as among regions. They have become, like many and perhaps most other 'regional' issues, matters involving groups defined by occupation, ethnicity, or some other non-territorial characteristic; what still gives them a regional aspect is the uneven territorial distribution of such groups across the country.

A large number of issues are similar in this respect to controversies over the Crow rate and trade policy. The bitter disputes of the early to mid-1980s over the National Energy Program are a good example. On the NEP the weight of opinion in producing and non-producing regions was certainly different. The regional aspect of energy policy was correspondingly salient but was always qualified by vigorous controversy within central Canada, where many business interests, some with a direct financial stake in producing firms, actively opposed the thrust of federal policy. Also, even in the heart of the producing regions there were some who stood to gain – or thought they did – from nationalistic policies. In such circumstances a policy not explicitly discriminatory among regions (as, for example, locational policies necessarily are) can be presented both in regional and in non-regional terms.

Opponents of policies of an ambiguously regional character are likely to play up the regional aspect, while supporters may seek to justify them in non-regional terms. Moreover, in these cases the federal government will, if it is astute, seek to identify the beneficiaries of its policies and, by supporting them, to create client-groups in all parts of the country (perhaps especially in regions where the policy is heavily criticized). Thus it may strengthen the coalition of forces that forms its political base. Depending on the success of these endeavours, the policies in question may be perceived among the general public either in regional or in non-regional terms – quite possibly as non-regional in areas where support is strong and, elsewhere, as regionally discriminatory.

Certain issues arising out of conflicts of taste are more properly considered regional than issues reflecting conflicts of claim, even when there is considerable heterogeneity of opinion within each region. The almost inherently regional character of some conflicts of taste is explained by the fact that they have a collective dimension that is generally or perhaps always missing from conflicts of claim.

Demands giving rise to conflicts of claim tend to be group demands only in the sense that many individuals may share the same interest. The group is involved, indeed conceived, only by statistical aggregation. For example, take the case of the production and price controls imposed by CEMA, the Canadian Egg Marketing Agency. The poultry farmer's preference for stable demand and high prices – and hence his support for policies that achieve these aims – is not affected by the size or territorial distribution of his occupation-group; he has an individual interest which, incidentally, others share.

It is quite otherwise with a member of an ethnic or linguistic or religious minority who has absorbed, in the course of his upbringing, a particular set of social values, even if he is unable to articulate what they are and is perhaps unaware of how they differ from those that characterize the majority culture. The values in question prescribe both the extent of individual rights and the institutional structure through which the individual participates in the life of his community. Such cultural attributes may well give rise to political demands; but the character of such demands, as well as the feasibility of realizing them, depends very much on both the number and spatial distribution of people who make them. Accordingly, many conflicts of taste, though in a sense merely the result of a clash among the preferences of individuals, arise only because there exists the possibility of creating a network of social institutions that express and preserve a particular understanding of what man is and of how the individual relates to the community.

The differences in value-systems alluded to here are easily visible in the communal organization of certain dissentient religious sects, such as the Mennonite communities which abjure individual ownership of land and practise an archaic form of agriculture. Such communities can exist, often submitting to considerable hostility and always enduring relative physical hardship, only because they have withdrawn into isolation and make few demands on the larger society. This withdrawal prohibits all forms of change, ruling out the realization of traditional values by adapting forms of social organization to the demands and opportunities of a changing milieu. Local community organization provides the vehicle for perpetuating these values; but the desire to conduct one's life consistently with them does not give rise to political demands on society as a whole.

Such is not the case with communities that are unwilling to make the sacrifices required of those who isolate themselves from the rest of society or wish to develop in their own way rather than to opt for petrifaction. Such communities need to gain control over the entire range of social institutions, at least to the extent that a distinctive institutional structure is necesssary to realize the values they have inherited and may wish to rework or transform. Individual preferences in regard to such matters appear, then, to have a communal dimension that is missing from the set of material interests that may give rise to conflicts of claim.

It is imaginable that community preferences, expressed in certain kinds of conflict of taste, may be realized through nongovernmental institutions. This was to a large extent the case in Quebec prior to the Quiet Revolution of the 1960s. Throughout the 'ancien régime,' as it came disparagingly to be called, the Roman Catholic Church was the dominant social institution, not only in exercising moral and ideological leadership but also in controlling schools, hospitals, and a large part of the social security system. However, if the Church was to do these things, it had to have the support of the state – which it obtained, in the form of financial subsidies and a favourable legislative framework, from the provincial government. The importance of this arrangement explains Quebec's consistent demand that provincial autonomy be respected, even if the powers that the provincial government wished to protect were, in the eyes of critics such as Pierre Trudeau, inadequately used. And more significantly, once the state began to assume many of the functions hitherto performed by the Church, and to take the lead in transforming the institutional framework of Quebec society, demands multiplied for extension of provincial powers and financial reources, transferring both from the federal to the provincial arena.

Thus, in Quebec, the territorial dimension has always been inseparable from preferences arising out of and expressing a distinctive culture. The demands that have given rise to conflicts of taste are those of a community, or at the very least of individuals who are conscious of participating in a community and whose concept of self includes their membership in the community. Not only does territorial concentration facilitate the sharing or propagation of like attitudes; the territorial aspect is integral to the demands being put forward, which derive from a desire to endow the community with a distinctive institutional structure. In this sense certain conflicts of taste are inherently regional. In Quebec the aspirations for separate or distinctive cultural development are inseparable from the demands that have been made for regional autonomy or, recently, for full political independence.

The preceding discussion has shown that issues involving ethnic, occupational, or other groups may be perceived in regional terms when the relevant groups are territorially concentrated. Few would disagree that this is all the more likely to happen in a federal state, where provincial politicians are ready-made spokesmen for regional interests and themselves have an interest in stressing the regional aspect of policy controversies. This happens also when the substance of the issues in dispute does not require territorially distinct responses to people's needs and aspirations. For example, as Richard Simeon remarked, in Canada we tend to treat poverty as a regional problem, requiring fiscal transfers to the poorer provinces – although there are probably more poor people in Toronto or Montreal than in the whole of the Atlantic region.[10]

We should, though, avoid supposing that federalism uniformly exaggerates the regional aspect of political controversies in Canada. Regional interests that do not coincide with provincial boundaries probably receive less attention than they would in a unitary state. The point is conjectural; but it may be illustrated by referring, once again, to our artificially simplified presentation of the controversy over the enforcement of Canadian content rules for television. The regions with interests imagined to be implicated in this issue were 'north' and 'south' and as such cut across provincial boundaries. If every province had about the same proportion of 'northerners' and 'southerners,' no provincial politician would have any incentive to draw attention to the issue and certainly not to present it as a regional one. Indeed, it is likely that the location of provincial boundaries has so conditioned Canadians to think of 'region' in east-west terms that the north-south distinction (at least for southerners) is virtually imperceptible.

The more usual case, however, is that protagonists and antagonists in relation to any issue are distributed in unequal proportions among the provinces. Accordingly, provincial politicians may find it electorally advantageous to make themselves spokesmen for occupational or other groups that are not defined by region but are, for one reason or another, regionally concentrated. The issues of concern to such groups are 'regional' only contingently, because of a particular distribution of the population; but they appear to the public in regional guise. This is the weak sense in which federalism creates regional issues. There is also another, stronger, sense in which this occurs.

'Regional' Issues Reflect Federal Structure

In a federal state some issues appear on the agenda of public debate, cast in terms that bring the regional aspect into special prominence. They become defined in such a way that they engage homogeneous, or nearly homogeneous, territorial interests. Additionally, certain other issues, also implicating a homogeneous territorial interest – issues that simply could not arise within a unitary state – may be created de novo. Both these categories of issue are, by our earlier definition, purely regional; but they may also be held to be factitious, that is, to reflect the institutional structure rather than the composition of the political community and the needs, demands, and aspirations of its members.

To illustrate what I mean, it is convenient to refer again to the case of the Crow rate for the transport of prairie grains. There are different views on the magnitude of the costs that this legislated rate structure imposed on the railways, but at a minimum it may be said that because of the Crow the grains traffic did not contribute to maintenance or other fixed costs. Rates on some other products were held down by competition, as in the instance of steel that was transported from Hamilton to Vancouver (where an alternate water route was available). In still other cases, although the only practical mode of transport was by rail, high transportation costs would have priced the product out of its market: then the shipper and the railways negotiated 'agreed charges' that might be as low as the railways' marginal costs. Thus a large part of the traffic – grain alone accounts for about a quarter of the ton-mile total – could carry only a small proportion of the overhead.

The railways tried to meet their overhead costs by charging higher rates per ton-mile on goods for which there was no competing mode of transport (such as steel to a non-port city like Calgary) and on high-value goods for which the rates were held down neither by regulation nor by market considerations. One result was that transport of industrial products to and from the prairie region was expensive, whereas charges for transporting raw materials and unprocessed goods were low (lower, in the case of grain, than in the United States).

This situation once prompted Alberta Premier Lougheed, speaking for all four western premiers, to declare: 'In our judgment the greatest single impediment standing in the way of the development of Western Canada's full potential is Transportation Freight Rates which discriminates against the West.'[11] One solution to the problem – the one eventually adopted – would have been to increase the charges imposed on bulk goods, including grain. This could have been done by abolishing or revising the Crow and perhaps by providing a provincial subsidy for the carriage of other low-value goods (resource products, from which the provinces draw a royalty). Had the premiers advocated this, however, it would have pitted the interests of the prairie farmer against other interests within the region, a definition of the issue that would have been, at the time, clear suicide for any prairie premier.

What the premiers suggested instead was that the federal government acquire the rail roadbeds and operate them as public utilities. This done, 'the total facility [would become] a public road system,'[12] which would have obviated the need for the grain and raw materials traffic to meet any part of the railways' overhead. Such a solution to the transportation problem would have created effective competition among carriers, improved service, and reduced rates. It would also have been costless to the provincial treasuries.

The western premiers' proposal, if not particularly inventive, was politically astute, because it would have dealt with the transportation problem in a way that avoided controversy between the farm and non-farm interests on the prairies and have imposed the costs mainly on taxpayers outside the region. Now, let the reader decide: is the transcontinental carriage of freight an issue in which the relevant political cleavages are regional? Surely it depends not only on the problem to be resolved but also on the solution envisioned. In a federal state, provincial politicians who want to achieve certain purposes have every incentive to endorse a course of action that defines the issues in regional terms. Conversely, the central government has every reason to focus public debate on proposals that reduce or eliminate the regional aspect of the controversy. If the provinces win what is essentially a public relations battle, creating issues that implicate whole regions and (by the same token) avoid bringing intra-regional cleavages into focus, those issues, while properly regional, may be factitious. How we characterize them no doubt depends mainly on where our own sympathies lie.

Certain other issues do unambiguously reflect the federal structure and are unquestionably regional. The obvious cases are intergovernmental disputes over property rights; taxing powers, revenue sharing, and tax structure; intergovernmental transfer payments; and policies shifting the costs of government from one level to another:

disputes over property rights: ownership of offshore oil and minerals, location of the Quebec-Labrador boundary, fisheries (access to 'northern cod' stocks: Newfoundland versus Nova Scotia), ownership of abandoned rail rights-of-way (federal versus provincial);

taxing powers, revenue sharing, and tax structure: constitutionality of federal export taxes on natural gas and other resource products, constitutionality of provincial taxation of resource production (as direct or indirect taxation),[13] federal and provincial shares of personal and corporate income taxes, deductibility of provincial royalties in calculating federally taxable incomes of resource firms, federal oil and gas production taxes as levied under the the National Energy Program (both of these issues, which relate to taxation of resources industries, affect the sharing of resource rents between federal and provincial governments, if the industry share is held constant);

intergovernmental transfer payments: magnitude of federal grants to the provinces (e.g. fiscal equalization, 'established programs financing,' and cost-sharing for regional development);

policies shifting the costs of government from one level to another: structure of unemployment insurance (period of employment required for eligibility affects provincial welfare costs, as unemployment insurance is federally funded), closure of rail lines (imposes costs on provincial governments, which have to improve roads).

In all the above cases, fiscal resources are transferred from the residents of one province to residents of one or more other provinces, or a fiscal burden is imposed on one set of taxpayers and withdrawn from other taxpayers, according to place of residence. In most instances this effect is produced by transferring resources or costs between orders of government; but in a few of them the territorial aspect of the issue is all the clearer in that the dispute is interprovincial (e.g. the Quebec-Newfoundland dispute over the location of the Labrador boundary). Such disputes, all of which are unambiguously regional, can arise only within a federal state, or in the international arena.

The general conclusion to be drawn from this illustrative survey of forms of interregional conflict is that many of the issues that Canadians usually regard as regional have this character either because the federal system actually creates them or because they are capable of presentation in regional terms, even though they actually implicate occupational, linguistic, or other groups not defined by residence. Many and perhaps most 'regional' issues do not have this character by virtue of the needs, preferences, and aspirations giving rise to them but by virtue of political entrepreneurship. What counts is the actions of public men and women, who formulate proposals for governmental action, inventing, selecting, and amplifying, according to their electoral strategies, the policy demands that they find expedient to inscribe upon the agenda of public debate. The ambiguously regional character of many issues leaves considerable scope for political leaders to affect how the public perceives them and in doing so to deepen interregional conflict or to alleviate its intensity.

The ease with which politicians and others may manipulate the perception of issues as regional/non-regional is all the greater in that many issues combine conflicts of claim and conflicts of taste. Certain conflicts of claim are more easily presented as involving regional interests than are the related conflicts of taste. In other cases, it is the other way around: conflicts of taste seem more regional in character than the conflicts of claim associated with them. In both situations, the ambivalent or compound character of the issues enables public people to present them either in regional or in non-regional terms.

Take, for example, the 1981-85 controversy over whether the education provisions of Quebec's language law (Bill 101) should prevail over the Canadian Charter of Rights and Freedoms. (This is partly a legal question, but I am here referring to its political aspect.) Bill 101 prescribed that as a rule, only those who attended an English-language primary school in Quebec could send their children to English-language schools, whereas the Canadian Charter of Rights extends eligibility to all citizens who received their instruction in English in any part of

Canada. Supporters of the Quebec law insisted that the restriction of individual freedom of choice was necessary to protect the position of the French language, given the assimilationist pressures resulting from francophones' tiny minority position within North America. The primacy of 'collective rights' over 'individual rights' was said to be a matter in which all Quebec francophones had a common interest.

Given the spatial distribution of language groups in Canada, supporters of Bill 101 had little difficulty in arguing that the Charter of Rights (which, alone among the provinces, Quebec refused to endorse) was an outrageous case of English Canada imposing its values and its preferences upon Quebec. The argument had sufficient force that many Quebecers who supported (with the provincial Liberal party) wider individual freedom of choice in language matters than Bill 101 allows none the less categorically rejected external imposition, through the Charter, of the policy they preferred. Thus all parties in the Quebec legislature denounced the infringement of Quebec's constitutional powers by action of the Canadian and British parliaments. Although the Supreme Court of Canada has now ruled that this action did not violate any pre-existing constitutional convention, there was no precedent for a major constitutional amendment affecting the rights and powers of a legislature being passed against the opposition of the government and legislature concerned.

Notwithstanding these facts, both procedurally and substantively the 'English Canada versus Quebec' formulation of the issue is questionable: the parliament that passed the Charter was acting under the impulsion of a government most of whose key ministers were French-speaking Quebecers, and all but three Quebec MPs supported the Charter. To portray the issue in these terms one must explain away the actions of federal Quebec MPs, including the prime minister, by insisting that they in no way represented the interests or views of Quebec. This presentation of the issue also ignores the existence of francophone minorities outside Quebec (who stand to reap substantial benefits from the Charter); and it ignores the fact that public opinion within Quebec itself – even among the francophone majority – has been divided from the start. Thus the issue was simplified if not misrepresented by those who preferred to see Quebec's Bill 101 validated notwithstanding the Charter of Rights. To these people, the issue was (indeed remains) quintessentially a conflict between alternative conceptions of community, a conflict (to employ the words of the Royal Commission on Bilingualism and Biculturalism, some fifteen years earlier) 'between two majorities: that which is a majority in all Canada, and that which is a majority in the entity of Quebec.'[14] They interpreted the conflict, in the specific sense intended by Mintz and Simeon, as a conflict of taste.

The issue was presented quite differently by those who, consistently with individualist rather than communitarian presuppositions, supported the primacy of the Charter of Rights. They insisted that the French language was not in danger in Quebec. Most of them held that the main effect of Bill 101 was to drive out anglophones; some insisted that this was its underlying, if undeclared,. purpose. It was also alleged that the real motive for wanting to 'make Quebec as French as Ontario is English' (a Quebec government slogan) was to create employment opportunities for the francophone middle class, while the considerable economic costs of the policy were borne by the rest of the community.[15] Thus it is possible to argue that the real substance of the controversy within Quebec over its language legislation was not, as it appeared on the surface, a conflict of taste. Rather, the conflict may be said to have been one of claim, and the groups implicated in it may be said to have been occupational as much as they were linguistic. Since the territorial distribution of the two types of group was quite different (indeed, the class beneficiaries were a minority within Quebec, whereas the linguistic beneficiaries were a strong majority), a publicist's success in presenting the issue in regional and communitarian terms depended upon perceptions of the character of the law itself, its effects, and the motives of those who enacted it.

In some situations the regional aspect of policy controversies may be made more visible by highlighting – contrary to the previous case – conflicts of claim that may be associated with conflicts of taste. Say a provincial government opts for certain policies in health services or social security. These are areas in which differences of taste are evident; they are also areas in which the federal government is involved both indirectly (by supporting provincial programs through conditional grants) and with programs of its own. The province, by hypothesis, wants to implement programs of a distinctive character and regards federal policies as an unwelcome intrusion into an area in which the provinces have primary or exclusive responsibility. Its preferences in these fields may therefore be associated with, or give rise to, demands for augmented fiscal resources to implement policies that accord with its own tastes, preferences, or needs. Since, in the absence of an accommodating federal response, all the province's taxpayers have to shoulder a portion of the costs entailed in implementation of distinctive provincial programs, or resulting from provincial refusal to implement a shared-cost program of a design suitable to Ottawa, all residents are similarly affected by the conflict of claim that arises out of differences of taste. Even those whose preferences coincide with the values underlying federal policies find themselves – in that aspect of the policy dispute that engages their financial interests – in the same position as everyone else in the province. The more they see the dispute as a conflict of claim, the more likely they are to perceive it as a regional issue.

The concepts 'conflict of taste' and 'conflict of claim' are abstractions that draw attention to an important feature or aspect of policy controversies but are scarcely more likely to be found in their pure form than are regional and non-regional conflicts. The categories themselves are dichotomous, and it is tempting to shoe-horn actual political issues into them, as within the cells of the matrix presented earlier. But it is wiser to treat each of the four concepts as the logical extension of a particular feature of 'real-life' controversies. Such concepts alert us to the disruptive potential of these controversies, in relation to the existing constitutional order, and they help us to judge the probable effectiveness of various means of managing or controlling conflict. Equally important, they also warn us that the generalizations that we sometimes make about the interrelationship between intensity of political conflict and the structure of a federal system are implicitly based on facile characterizations of the issues that divide the polity.

CONSTITUTIONAL CHANGE AND INTENSITY OF CONFLICT

It will be recalled that Mintz and Simeon suggested that constitutional decentralization, though not practicable in relation to all conflicts of taste, was none the less an 'obvious' solution in most such cases; but that conflicts of claim were not susceptible of any similarly 'efficient' solution.

Their analysis presumed the feasibility of distinguishing fairly sharply the two types of conflict. They did not take account of changes over time in the perception of current issues as being regional or non-regional or as involving differences of taste or of claim. In particular, they did not consider whether changes in the structure of the federation might affect how issues are perceived or the ease with which politicians and others might manipulate the public's perception of the issues. Nor did they consider whether, or how, constitutional change might alter the conditions giving rise to conflicts both of taste and claim, both regional and non-regional. In my view, an inquiry that avoids taking an existing pattern of political demands as given, as if it were unaffected by the structure of the regime (which in turn affects political entrepreneurship), produces arguably different conclusions from those reached by Mintz and Simeon.

It does not seem open to doubt, as Corry and many others have stated, that constitutional decentralization – of powers, of responsibilities, of fiscal resources – removes certain issues from the national political arena, permitting their resolution at the regional (provincial or state) level. Mintz and Simeon have argued that the class of issues resolvable in this way consists of 'divisible' conflicts of taste; for non-divisible conflicts of taste and for conflicts of claim there exists no obvious solution. This appears to be broadly correct, though I would add two comments.

First, there are quite a few non-divisible conflicts of taste, more than Mintz and Simeon appear to realize. Mintz and Simeon refer only to 'symbolic questions such as a flag or retention of the monarchy'[16] and devote only a short paragraph to the subject. Controversies over national symbols are, however, only a small part of the category 'non-divisible conflicts of taste.' It includes many if not all political disputes relating to:

international obligations and diplomacy: supportive or punitive actions toward foreign states, governments-in-exile, and organizations claiming to represent

national groups (e.g. the Palestine Liberation Organization); sanctions against repressive regimes; foreign aid and military assistance; peacekeeping; diplomatic stance toward revolutionary or reactionary regimes;
security issues, external and domestic: size, equipment, and deployment of armed forces; membership in alliances (NATO, NORAD); extent and fulfilment of treaty obligations; weaponry development and testing; arms control; sedition and treason legislation; emergency measures (War Measures Act); and
rights and duties of the citizen.

The last category, the rights and duties of the citizen, is too complex to admit of simple enumeration; it overlaps and extends beyond the other two. The difficulty in discussing the subject is that what 'citizenship' entails depends very much on standards that vary over time and from place to place. Take, for example, the case of personal security, both in the physical sense (as against assault) and in the sense of maintenance of reputation and self-respect (as against slander or defamation). These are matters dealt with in the criminal law and in Canada fall within federal jurisdiction. One might say that implicitly the protection afforded by the criminal law has been treated in Canada as a right indissoluble from the concept of citizenship, a consequence being that the constitution minimizes interprovincial variation in the criminal law. This did not occur in the United States, where, although the protection of individual rights against trespass by other persons was confided to the states (since the criminal law was not listed among the powers of Congress), the citizen's rights against an oppressive government have been enshrined almost from the beginning in the constitution. It is from the public statement of these rights in simple language, in a document familiar to every American schoolchild, that the concept of citizenship in the United States would appear most clearly to derive.

Recently, of course, Canada has followed the American example by including the Charter of Rights and Freedoms in the Constitution Act (1982). Many of its provisions are controversial, especially in Quebec, where not only does there subsist resentment against its striking down a major clause of the language law (see above), but there exists sharp dissent from several other of its provisions. The attack on the 'Canada Bill,' as its detractors call it, is pre-eminently a reflection of conflicts of taste – solvable, according to critics of the Charter, by leaving it up to the provinces to decide whether or not to adhere to it or to apply it. Obviously, however, to its supporters, this would in no way resolve the issue, since it is precisely the uniformity of rights across the country that is at stake. The issue, once seriously posed, became bound up in the concept of citizenship. For those who had already rejected, as applying to themselves, the concept of Canadian citizenship, the Charter was a raw statement of their personal exclusion.

Of all issues that have, historically, polarized Canadians, the conscription controversies of 1917 and 1942-44 are pre-eminent. These were conflicts of taste, though the term seems repulsive in the context of an issue that meant life or death to so many people. The prospect of conscription posed in the most direct possible way, and with the highest stakes, the fundamental question of political philosophy: the relation between the individual and the community and the demands that each may legitimately make upon the other. No one, I think, then suggested that this most anguishing of all issues could be defused by 'letting the provinces handle it.'

There are, then, fundamental issues of public policy that in no significant sense could be said to involve the distribution of national wealth and that cannot be resolved through constitutional decentralization. These are non-divisible conflicts of taste. Issues in this category may, at certain times, be the central ones in a nation's politics. Where, however, demands for a uniform policy are not of the essence, decentralization may sweep otherwise disruptive issues from the agenda of national politics, reducing the level of conflict that they engender. The insight provided by Mintz and Simeon is that the only issues capable of resolution in this way are ones arising out of conflicts of taste.

The Mintz-Simeon thesis, so formulated, may actually be unduly restrictive, because it would appear that certain conflicts of claim, too, may be removed from the national political arena through constitutional decentralization. To appreciate how this may come about, we may consider again the case of freight transport to and from the prairie region, discussed earlier. Evidently, western complaints about transportation would not be satisfied if the federal government were deprived of its present powers in the field, since the western grievances have focused on the inadequate use of existing federal powers. In other words, decentralization would be no solution here. However, the western premiers' ability to cast the issue in terms that reinforced its regional aspect did depend upon the federal government's having the powers and the fiscal resources to expropriate the railbeds. The claim that they put forward could not have been made within a confederal state or, say, a common market that had central institutions with no authority beyond enforcement of the treaty on which it was based.

The general point to be made here is that a claim is groundless in the absence of any means for satisfying it. 'Claim' implies that the claimants think that they may reasonably expect others to recognize an obligation to meet it. Within a federation, especially if central powers are extensive, people in one region may feel that they have a claim to make on residents of other regions precisely because machinery has been set up to achieve a high degree of economic integration and to distribute its benefits fairly. Thus the decentralization of economic powers may reduce the extent or the intensity of interregional conflicts of claim.

All this is speculative; it cannot be otherwise. Still, contemporary political debate in Canada supplies some evidence that people are thinking this way. How else can we interpret proposals that the provinces bear the major responsibility for their own economic development and that the federal government be limited to a co-ordinating and facilitating role? The suggestion is made with increasing frequency that by limiting, if not the formal extent of federal economic powers, then at least their exercise, not only will the provinces be strengthened but so too will the country as a whole, as the claims that each province/ region makes on the others diminish.

The argument can also be put negatively, perhaps as follows. The federal government was originally charged with responsibility for creating and maintaining an economic union and was given the necessary powers. However, it has exercised those powers in a way which, on balance, has been prejudicial to the interests of the primary-producing areas of the country. It does no good to take away only those powers that are used, if inadequately, to compensate these regions for the costs imposed upon them (hence, to go back to the case of transportation, reduction of federal powers is no solution to prairie grievances); but an overall shrinkage in federal capacity to impose discriminatory policies upon the less populous regions would strengthen Canada both economically and politically. It is the reduction of the federal presence in the economy, not a reaffirmation of central leadership, that would diminish interregional conflict. Conceivably an argument such as this could be invoked to support – to take an important example – the recommendations of the Macdonald Commission, as discussed in chapter 9.

What are the counter-arguments, arguments suggesting that constitutional decentralization may increase rather than diminish interregional conflict? I can think of five of them. All take into account the longer-term consequences of a reduction in central powers, responsibilities, and fiscal resources. In this sense they extend beyond the time-horizon implicitly considered by Mintz and Simeon in their discussion of conflicts of taste and claim. For example, conflicts of claim were said to be concerned with the distribution (or more properly, I would say, the redistribution) of wealth; but I think it important to consider also the impact of government on economic development and the initial (pre-tax, pre-transfer) distribution of wealth. We must do this, because interregional conflicts of claim do manifestly revolve also around wealth creation and matters such as availability of employment. This was implicitly recognized in the preceding discussion about the potential for reducing conflicts of claim through decentralization of control over the economy.

One reason why decentralization may, contrary to the argument just presented, increase interregional conflict is that a strong central government may be necessary in order to achieve the potential benefits of economic integration. This argument is a tentative and conditional restatement of the position put forward by the Pepin-Robarts task force, that federalism offers each region gains from trade (because specialization produces an economic 'surplus') but entails costs in that the regions suffer loss of political autonomy. My earlier criticism of the task force's position was not that it was necessarily wrong but that it stated categorically what should only be advanced as a possibility and that it did not take sufficient account of the economic grievances of important regions.

It is widely agreed, even among those economists (the vast majority) who accept the validity of Ricardo's theory of comparative advantage, that membership in a common market or an economic union is not necessarily advantageous for any given region or state. Popular opinion – voiced, for example, by the Pepin-Robarts task force – holds that economic integration offers all participants (regions/states) an economic benefit; but there are circumstances in which it may not. Take, for example, the case of a state with extensive external trade and a domestic economy shaped by the specialization that such a pattern of trade implies: by joining a common market or some tighter form of economic association it will gain access to new markets, but it may lose some of the old ones. New costs may be imposed on its industries by protective trade policies, or it may face additional trade barriers imposed by its traditional trading partners. Thus the negative effects of trade diversion may outweigh the positive effects of trade creation. In addition, as is the case in Canada, the central authorities in the economic union may have and use the power to restrict or to tax certain exports, control the inflow of investment capital, and/or impose heavy taxes on export industries. In short, restrictive policies may constrain the economic development of some and conceivably of all regions. However, one must be cautious not to conclude too readily that a given region would be better off outside the union. The net effect of membership in an economic union, for any region, will depend very largely on the alternative trading arrangements that it could make if it were independent or belonged to a different economic grouping.

It is evident that in some regions of Canada today opinion is widespread that federal economic policies are unfairly restrictive, such that the region concerned is unable to realize the potential benefits that the Canadian economic union has to offer. A few years ago some appeared to have concluded that their regions would be better off on their own. However, this seems at best a guess; and it is equally plausible to argue that only a tightly knit economic union, with a central government possessing and using extensive economic powers, can, in view of Canada's economic geography and the evolving world-economic situation, realize the potential benefits of economic integration for any and all regions. Naturally, whether or not the centralization of economic powers is mutually advantageous to all regions will depend upon the substance of the policies actually implemented; for example, whether the policies described in chapter I as a 'strategy of regional complementarity' are realistically conceived and are effectively translated into action.

In addition to asking whether the potential benefits of economic integration can be achieved without political centralization, it is important to ask whether those benefits can be 'fairly' distributed if there are not extensive central powers. The discussion so far has avoided the question of redistributing wealth interregionally; but one may argue that if the benefits of union flow unequally to the various regions (without actually being negative for any of them), the central government has the responsibility and should therefore have the powers and the resources to redistribute national wealth. In Canada this is done through the tax system and income security payments to individual Canadians, intergovernmental fiscal transfers, various kinds of insurance schemes such as agricultural price stabilization and unemployment insurance, and programs for regional development.

Regionally redistributive policies are virtual hothouses for the culture and nourishment of conflicts of claim; but there can be little doubt that without such redistribution some at least of the recipient provinces would secede. It is not simply that they have become pensioners of the federal government (though some have); but for them the economic rationale of Confederation is that it provides a degree of stability that they could not obtain as independent states. In particular, the resource-based economies of some provinces are vulnerable to wild fluctuations as output, demand, and world prices go up and down. These provinces need to take out an insurance policy, such as is offered by membership in a federation with an economy that is, taken as a unit, more diversified than that of any of its regions. Other provinces appear to have become permanent recipients on a large scale, without prospect of escaping from their unenviable position. This, as Judith Maxwell and Caroline Pestieau have pointed out, poses dangers of its own:

A federation might fail ... if [among other things] the mechanisms for sharing the surplus from integration become a permanent system of income redistribution rather than a stabilization or insurance system. The contributors may begin to question the need to participate if they themselves feel no need to purchase insurance against future economic hardships – such as crop failures, sharp declines in resource prices, and disruptions in traditional markets. They may tend to view the interregional compensation system as an unproductive diversion of their existing wealth rather than as a productive and balanced contribution to the federation. The other side of this coin is that other participants may come to view themselves as perpetual losers and be tempted to withdraw from the federation in order to try to overcome by other means the economic problems that keep them in a state of dependency.[17]

This passage makes clear that the amount of interregional conflict relating to the exercise of economic powers for redistributive purposes is contingent on circumstances that include but are not limited to the policies actually implemented. As various factors – such as technological change, shifting population densities, and evolving patterns of world trade (affecting prices and demand) – modify the impact of economic geography, a once-acceptable set of policies may become intolerable to either donor or recipient regions, or both. In other circumstances redistribution, and therefore the attribution of extensive economic powers and resources to the central government, may be essential to keep interregional conflict to manageable levels. If the latter circumstances are the ones that obtain in Canada today, then constitutional decentralization could intensify already acute interregional conflicts of claim.

Decentralization could, in addition, strengthen existing bonds between provincial governments and their client-groups or client-organizations. It is characteristic of clients that they are dependent upon a patron and therefore have a stake in preserving or extending the patron's authority, prestige, and resources. Alan Cairns has noted[18] that not only do provincial governments – politicians and civil servants – have an interest in expanding their own powers, but that around the provincial governments there have formed encrustations of corporate and other groups with a vested interest in the maintenance and growth of provincial powers. Client interests (my term, not Cairns') from different provinces compete with similar groupings and organizations in other regions, generating pressures for further decentralization and intensifying interregional conflicts of claim.

Decentralization to accommodate conflicts of taste may also have the effect of increasing the severity of conflicts of claim because of the strain that it may place on the system of interregional redistribution. Observers of Canadian politics are well aware that the swelling of the provinces' spending responsibilities over the past two decades has required large increases in federal transfer payments to provincial governments. Transfer payments would be unnecessary if all provinces had a roughly equal fiscal capacity. In such circumstances reduction in federal taxation (for example, a diminution in its share of the personal income tax) would in itself enable every province to augment its revenues in accordance with its expanded needs. This happy situation does not prevail in Canada. Here we experience wide interprovincial differences in fiscal capacity. These, if they are not to result in vast interregional differences in services, require either the centralization of the most expensive functions of government or large federal payments to the provinces in inverse ratio to the size of their respective tax bases. This is accomplished through fiscal equalization and through the design of conditional grants so that the poorer provinces get a proportionally larger federal contribution to program costs.

Inclusion of an equalization feature in shared-cost programs has for more than a decade been offensive to Ontario, which has maintained that redistribution should be done openly within a single program designed for that purpose.[19] However, the dangers of this policy, for those provinces that are heavily dependent upon federal transfers, has become evident in more recent disputes over the design of the equalization formula. These disputes – a copybook example of conflicts of claim – have arisen not because of new steps toward decentralization, but because a widening of fiscal disparities has accentuated the difficulties inherent in fiscal decentralization (i.e. the devolution upon the provinces of both revenue-collection and spending responsibilities).

An awkward feature of the existing equalization formula became evident after 1973, when certain provinces, notably Alberta, began to receive huge increases in revenues from resource production. This automatically, under the then-existing formula, increased the entitlements of all the recipient provinces. In consequence, the government of Ontario began to demand revision of the equalization formula (a demand to which the federal government was more than sympathetic, but which the recipient provinces resisted), since it calculated that Ontario taxpayers contributed about forty cents of every dollar paid out in equalization. The costs borne by Ontario taxpayers were felt to be all the more unjust in that the provinces receiving the extra royalties income did not have to use any of these increased revenues to finance the equalization program.

These events illustrate how easily decentralization of public services, motivated by a desire to accommodate interregional differences in tastes or preferences, may invite intergovernmental wrangling over fiscal arrangements. Decentralization, while reducing interregional conflicts of taste, may generate additional conflicts of claim. It is wrong to focus on the one effect without considering the other.

The interrelationship between conflicts of taste and of claim is further illustrated by Canadian policy relating to income security. For years Quebec, and to some extent certain other provinces, have sought wider control over the whole field of 'social policy' – and of course additional fiscal resources, commensurate with its expanded needs. In spite of these demands, the federal role in income security (pensions, family allowances, unemployment insurance, workmen's compensation, social assistance, and various tax credits) has expanded sharply, especially since the late 1960s. In this area there has been, relatively and absolutely, centralization; by 1978 the federal government was spending about 75 cents of every income security dollar and was raising an even higher percentage of the taxes used to make income security payments.[20] Keith Banting comments:

Transferring responsibility for welfare to the federal government does not necessarily produce programs that are more redistributive between income classes, but it does transform income security into a powerful instrument of redistribution between regions. As long as welfare was primarily a municipal and provincial responsibility, the poorest parts of the country always had the greatest social needs but the fewest resources with which to respond, a problem that became acute during the depression. Centralization, on the other hand, has generated major flows of money from rich to poor regions. National income security programs redistribute inter-regionally because greater proportions of elderly, unemployed and needy people, and children, are found in some regions, and because the revenues to finance those programs are raised disproportionately from different regions. The resulting net inter-regional redistribution through income security is equal to, or greater than that achieved through the more publicized system of equalization grants, and income security payments have become a critical part of the standard of living and the general economy in poor regions.[21]

It takes but little imagination to recognize that any move to return to a decentralized system of income security, in an attempt to satisfy differing regional tastes or preferences, would generate bitter conflicts of claim. Again, Keith Banting:

The only constitutional reform [among those suggested in recent years] with major consequences for income security would be a decision to reverse the centralization of the last half century, and return responsibility for income security to the provincial level. Even here it is important not to overstate the case, since the basic range of programs now in existence and the general principles that govern their operations might not change dramatically. [Still], the overall level of expenditure, the mix of policy instruments utilized in future development, and most important, the distribution of the costs and benefits among Canadians in different regions of the country would certainly be shifted to a new course. But the more profound impact would be on the general economic and political balance of the federation, which would tilt sharply, with the federal government losing much of its fiscal power and one of its few major involvements in the daily lives of individual Canadians. The most important consequences of decentralization in this area would probably be for the political system itself, rather than for the income security policies that it produces.[22]

With this remark, Banting draws our attention to a further (and in this survey, final) reason for thinking that decentralization may ultimately exacerbate interregional conflict. Again, it will depend upon contingencies, and so one cannot be categorical.

Mintz and Simeon have pointed out that subjective conceptions of 'region' are logically prior to the formulation of claims in regional terms: 'Conflict of this sort requires ... that the region or province is considered by its citizens to be a relevant criterion by which to judge the distribution of benefits. It requires some degree of regional or territorial identity and a consequent tendency to assess distributional issues in terms of regionally defined collectivities, rather than non-regional ones such as occupation or religion.'[23] What they do not note is that decentralization (especially, one suspects, in areas subject to conflicts of taste) encourages perception of issues in regional terms. A sense of community is not formed wholly outside the political sphere, with political or constitutional arrangements merely being adapted to pre-existing loyalties and identities. On the contrary, concepts of community and constitutional arrangements evolve in relation to each other. Community is partly a political creation, a sharing of rights established and protected through the polity, and a sharing of obligations for which the polity is again to some extent both instrument and guarantor. Here we return to the concept of citizenship, its rights and duties, and how such a concept may be fostered by a constitutional instrument such as the American Bill of Rights or, potentially, the Canadian Charter of Rights and Freedoms.

Attention to the community-building effects of the concept of citizenship may perhaps explain the prevalence of an apparently intuitive notion according to which there is a minimum of political integration without which subjective conceptions of a national political community cannot survive. This feeling, for it is no more than that, probably has its foundation in implicit recognition that extreme political decentralization not only imperils gains from economic integration, or prevents the central government from doing this or that necessary thing, but is ultimately corrosive of the bonds among Canadians that give legitimacy to the sharing of rights and obligations.

CONCLUSION

The decentralization of constitutional powers, governmental activities, and fiscal resources in a federation has unpredictable effects on the intensity of interregional conflict. In particular, if decentralization is introduced with a view to reducing conflict of taste it may, in doing so, alleviate tensions in the short run but may also generate new conflicts of claim and strengthen regionally focused political identities and loyalties. In the economic sphere, both the short- and the long-term results probably depend upon contingent factors such as economic geography and technological change, as well as upon the substance of policy decisions. All these factors affect the magnitude of the benefits accruing from economic integration and their distribution among regions. Also relevant, though not discussed in this chapter, is the structure of central political institutions and how well they are adapted to reconciling interregional differences of opinion or preventing implementation of decisions that affront the sensibilities or gravely damage the interests of one or more regions.

In spite of these uncertainties, our inquiry into the conditions under which issues are likely to be perceived in regional terms and our exploration of the possibly fragmenting effects of constitutional decentralization do suggest that there is a good case to be made for centralization – though presumably not in all policy areas – as a means of reducing interregional conflict and strengthening the national political community. It is a case that can be made only contingently. One of the necessary conditions for the success of a centralist strategy for the reduction of conflict, both of taste and of claim, is that a political constituency for central policies must be created, including a powerful segment of opinion in all regions.

It is this that is conspicuously lacking in Canada today. Possibly that indicates a failure in leadership. But it is also possible that the regional aspect of political conflict in contemporary Canada is simply too strong to be overcome, or kept within manageable bounds, through adept policy formation, the most brilliant of political strategies, and winning salesmanship. It may be that Canada's perpetual crisis of unity derives from incompatibility of cultures and/or incompatibility of regional economic interests. It may be that a national political community cannot contain two cultures as divergent as those of 'French Quebec' and 'English Canada.' It may be that with changing world-economic conditions, there is no 'surplus,' or net benefit, to be gained from economic union, or that in forming the union one or more regions is inevitably cast in the role of permanent loser: it may be able to obtain a better deal elsewhere, or through independence – or it may judge that the prospects of doing so are good enough to be worth the risk.

However, neither cultural nor economic incompatibility has been demonstrated to exist.

Are the interests and preferences of the Canadian regions so widely divergent that there exists no basis for a national political community? On the cultural side, perhaps there is little that scholarship can do in addressing this question, because what counts is people's feelings; if they think they can't get along, they won't. Still, the last impressive study of Quebec's culture, unfortunately conducted before the Quiet Revolution (the Tremblay report, 1956) concluded that the English-Canadian and French-Canadian cultures, though distinctive, were not mutually antagonistic.[24] Is this view mistaken? Or if this view was once valid, does it no longer hold, now that Quebec has transformed its conception of itself, through a generation of cultural and institutional change?

As a personal aside, I wish to comment that the extent to which values and attitudes are shared among Canadians appears to be strangely underestimated. Herschel Hardin, declaring that 'Canada exists, but is invisible,'[25] wrote a book on this theme. He called it *A Nation Unaware*. In it he suggested that the kernel of Canada's distinctiveness lies in a 'public enterprise culture': an oddly mechanistic description for a culture, perhaps, but the values that (as much as economic exigency) gave rise to public enterprise are important ones.

My own glimpse of cultural similarities among Canadians was afforded by a study that I undertook a few years ago of Canada's universities.[26] It seemed to me then that, for all the real diversity among provinces in the field of higher education – and education is the field par excellence where one expects cultural diversities to find expression – Canadians in every province including Quebec shared basically the same conception of what constitutes a desirable system of higher education, a conception that contrasts interestingly with American and European (including British) models. I looked for diversity, and I found it – but I also found a degree of similarity that surprised me. It made me think that if Canadians dwelt a little less on their cultural differences and thought a little more of the ways in which their values are, if not congruent, then at least compatible, they might arrive at a much more positive evaluation of the non-material benefits of political union – benefits inadequately recognized, for example, in the Pepin-Robarts report.

On the economic side, is there compatibility or incompatibility of regional interests? On this subject we need more scholarly work. Admittedly, Canadians do perennially debate the regional incidence of federal economic policies, attempting to discover the gains and losses to each region resulting from membership in the Canadian economic union – and yet, as Maxwell and Pestieau have written: 'No studies have shown conclusively that a surplus [or net benefit from integration] exists or that Canadians as a group are better off within this federation than they would be under alternate forms of economic association.'[27] Still less has any study shown conclusively that such benefits as there may be are so distributed that every region is better off than it would otherwise be under any other political arrangement available to it. Indeed, no one can ever do so, for the required data (which involve suppositions about alternative arrangements and prediction of future economic behaviour) will never become available. Still, there is a big difference between conclusive demonstration and informed judgment; and I suspect that there is plenty of scope for more of the latter. The way to get it is to take stock of the economic resources of each region (for this purpose there is no harm in equating 'region' with 'province'), to see how and to what extent they are being used now, or might be used under different federal economic policies, and to explore (in a necessarily speculative vein) their potential use under alternative constitutional structures.

8

Economic arguments for
political integration

Let's recapitulate. Chapter 1, which illustrates the relation between politico-constitutional issues and economic ones, is prelude to a more systematic exploration of the same subject in the remainder of the book. It treats concretely, in recent historical context, the theme later developed in a more comprehensive and at times more abstract way. The argument unfolds as follows.

Constitutional arrangements, and specifically the structure of a federal constitution, may have much broader policy significance than was recognized in much public and scholarly debate during the period when, in Canada, constitutional issues were high on the political agenda. The essence of constitutional questions in a federation is not simply which order of government will do a particular thing, or at what cost, or who will bear the cost. The structure of the federation may limit the range of purposes that government (at whatever level) is likely to accomplish: what policy goals will be aimed for, and how effectively they can be met (chapter 2).

However, the effect of federalism on policy is not to be assessed in opposition to other factors explaining policy outputs and outcomes, as one variable among many, each of which has a determinate weight. Rather, the policy impact of federalism is to be understood in conjunction with other factors; its policy significance is always contingent on historical circumstances (chapter 3).

To understand how federalism in Canada has affected policy and will continue to do so, one must have a clear understanding of how federalism works. Does the central government dominate; do provincial governments frustrate national purposes (as seen by the central government)? Concern that these things occur produces demands for disentanglement: each order of government wants a free hand in policy areas for which it considers itself responsible. Such demands are also supported by citizens' desires for efficiency in government and for simplifying their own dealings with government. However, in Canada – as probably in every other federal country – policy responsibilities are shared between orders of government, because jurisdiction is often conferred in terms of instruments that may be used for diverse policy purposes, sometimes co-operatively but sometimes with deliberately neutralizing or counteracting intent. There seems no way of avoiding the potential for intergovernmental conflict inherent in this situation, without putting the federal government in a position to dominate the provinces (chapter 4).

Modes of government interaction in policy formation are diverse; some involve considerable conflict. While much attention has been paid to devising ways of reducing intergovernmental conflict, proponents of reforms aiming to accomplish this have tended to neglect how the projected reforms would alter power relations among governments, which they would surely do (chapter 5).

Interaction between orders of government has modified the working constitution in ways that some observers consider centralizing, while others consider them decentralizing, because (implicitly) different criteria of judgment inform their conclusions. The issue is important, because in a relatively centralized federation those regions lacking influence in politics at the centre are vulnerable to domination or exploitation by the more powerful ones (chapter 6).

Though decentralization of the working constitution is often thought or claimed to reduce levels of interregional conflict, this cause-and-effect relationship cannot validly be asserted to obtain consistently, as a general rule. Political centralization can, under the right conditions, reduce interregional conflict and strengthen the national political community. For this to occur, federal politicians must succeed in creating a strong political constitutency for their policies in all regions, which they will be able to do only when regional cultures and regional economic interests are mutually compatible (chapter 7).

In the remaining two chapters we extend the line of reasoning developed up to the present point, exploring how the structure of the Canadian federal state, the economic role of government, and the intensity of interregional conflict affect – and are affected by – each other. To do this we must first ask (as we do in this chapter) what potential gains there are to be captured through economic integration. To do this we distinguish various stages or levels of integration. Then, in the next and final chapter, we shall turn to more familiar problems: whether the existing constitutional structure in Canada is well adapted to realizing those gains or advantages and in what ways their interregional distribution of the benefits of economic union is affected by politico-constitutional arrangements.

In effect, our aim in the remainder of the book is to formulate an economic-theoretical rationale for Confederation. We shall begin by asking what economic gains, if any, may be derived from reaffirming and perhaps extending the economic powers of the central government in Canada. The question may be inverted: Could the economic benefits that Confederation has to offer be as readily achieved through a relatively loose form of federalism? Indeed, might we not, as a collectivity, reap the advantages obtainable through federalism – and perhaps be more satisfied with the social and cultural policies of our governments – if the range of economic powers exercised at the centre were strictly limited? Perhaps it is not necessary, or at least not for economic reasons, to have a central government with powers any greater than those required to enforce the rules of a common market and to manage a common currency.

It is necessary here to recall the contemporary historical context of our inquiry, as set out at the beginning of this book. From about 1960 onward, at least until the Conservatives came to power in September 1984, the federal government sought increasingly to promote growth and stability, and especially to reduce unemployment, through a set of policies to restructure the Canadian economy. Its initiatives were mainly aimed at strengthening and transforming the manufacturing sector to meet foreign competition in domestic and external markets, although (somewhat inconsistently) it frequently had recourse to various forms of protectionism to sustain failing industries and firms. Nonetheless in a wide variety of concrete measures and policy pronouncements one could detect the emergence of what might be called a third national policy. In one variant of the policy the government seemed ready to make the resource industries subservient to the needs of manufacturing; in another – which ironically received (in a November 1981 budget paper) more comprehensive formulation than the first, but was never followed up in action – the resource industries were to be the main motor of economic development, and manufacturing was to be built up by maximizing its linkages with primary production. Both variants called for an activist or interventionist federal government and required affirming and augmenting its powers over the economy. Both were rooted in, and gave expression to, economic nationalism. The overall policy thrust may therefore be called the interventionist-nationalist option.

The first variant of the third national policy generated a great deal of opposition from most provincial governments, which sought in particular to prevent the federal government from extending its economic powers. More positively, they sought to exercise their own economic powers with a view to strengthening their resource industries. They sought also to diversify their economies by supporting implantation of industries complementary to resource production. Since Quebec increasingly adopted just such a development strategy, finding itself thereby an ally of the provinces traditionally considered to form the hinterland, it became part of a 'provincialist coalition' opposing the extension of federal economic power during the process of constitutional revision. The eight provinces that formed a common front against the federal initiative of 1980-81 thus took an interventionist-provincialist policy stance.

From 1982 onward, and especially after the change in government in 1984, federal policy became much less interventionist, or more liberal. It also became correspondingly less nationalist, or more continentalist. The liberal-continentalist thrust has been most visible in policies toward the oil and gas industry, treatment of foreign investment, and trade relations with the United States. A comprehensive statement of the liberal-continentalist option, and the rationale behind it, is contained in the report of the Royal Commission on the Economic Union and Development Prospects for Canada (the Macdonald Commission), 1985. The Macdonald report[1] recommends facilitating the process of adjustment to changing market conditions and calls on government to support economic development by building up economic infrastructure, especially in lagging or depressed regions. Thus it does not propose a negligible role for government in the economy; but it does urge that, as much as possible, government action be neutral toward specific sectors, industries, and firms and that adjustment assistance be channelled wherever possible to individuals rather than to the firms that employ them. The report, and at least some features of current federal policy, thus contrast with the interventionism that characterized both the emergent third national policy and the policy stance of several provincial governments. Paradoxically, some of the most interventionist provinces endorse negotiation of a free trade agreement with the United States, disregarding the extent to which continentalism and liberalism (prescribing maximum scope for the market in directing economic development) go together.

Clearly, there have been some significant shifts in the direction of economic policy over the past few years. But the options now are the same as they have been for at least a quarter-century: to adopt an interventionist-nationalist, an interventionist-provincialist, or a liberal-continentalist policy thrust. These options will continue to contend with each other and for that matter to coexist uneasily with each other. They do so for two reasons: because, even within a single government, policy inevitably expresses contradictory goals and impulsions and because federal and provincial governments share and contest the field. As a consequence, economic policy objectives, anticipated or supposed benefits of economic union, and constitutional options are closely related to each other.

The nub of the argument in these two final chapters, an argument that attempts to tease out this relationship, is that the interventionist-provincialist and liberal-continentalist theses are linked, logically speaking, to a narrowly stated rationale for economic integration and therefore also for political integration. Conversely, the interventionist-nationalist option – the one favouring a third national policy – fits in with a more inclusive statement of the potential welfare gains from strengthening the economic union.

MARKET INTEGRATION: RATIONALE AND CONSTITUTIONAL IMPLICATIONS

We have already encountered the narrowly stated rationale for economic and political integration in our quotations from the report of the Pepin-Robarts task force (see chapter 7). The task force noted that any expansion of market size permits and encourages firms to specialize their product lines. If firms locate where it is most economically advantageous for them, each region will produce those goods in which it has a comparative advantage. Specialization, at the level of both firm and region, increases economic efficiency and therefore offers gains in output and welfare.[2]

The arguments brought forward by the task force are also highlighted in a number of academic studies of federalism and the Canadian economic union, and they dominate all other considerations in the Macdonald Report. All the works in question are based on principles enunciated two centuries ago by Adam Smith and David Ricardo, which underpin the doctrine of gains through trade. Its liberal or non-interventionist implications are almost universally accepted among economists, most of whom favour the widest possible extension of markets. The consensus among economists is also accepted by many businessmen, as is evidenced by the endorsement of free trade principles by the major Canadian employers' associations.[3] Admittedly, businessmen are generally readier than academic economists to see governments make limited sacrifices in efficiency in order to achieve other goals, such as stability, regional development, or expansion of employment opportunities, particularly when the policies that aim for such goals stabilize or expand sales of their own firms or raise their own profits. Thus, many policy interventions, supported by some business spokesmen and opposed by others, compromise the principle of market allocation. Nonetheless, it is common to cite, as the rationale for maintaining or strengthening the Canadian economic union, a presumed increase in efficiency in allocation of resources, due to increased trade among the regions.

The gains-through-trade doctrine is a necessary part of the argument for the economic association of any two or more political entities. However, taken on its own, the doctrine cannot provide a compelling rationale for any given scheme of integration. It says too much, for its implication is that world free trade, not limited extension of markets through formation of a particular economic association, provides the largest benefits; and it says too little, for it fails to supply any information about the world context that narrows the list of practical options. Even more important for our argument, the gains-through-trade doctrine provides inadequate support for any but the looser forms of economic association. Most of the benefits obtainable through economic specialization can probably be supplied by creation of a customs union, or at best a common market. These are limited, 'negative' forms of economic integration.[4]

The negative economic integration of a group of states is accomplished when they avoid interfering with trade flows among themselves and possibly also prohibit or abjure mutually discriminatory actions that impede the movement of capital and labour. Barriers to trade may be minimized in any of five different forms of integration (the first three 'negative,' the last two 'positive').

In a *free trade area*, members eliminate tariffs and quantitative barriers (quotas) among themselves but retain the right to set their own trade policies toward non-member states. This is the form of economic association that the Macdonald Commission has proposed be created to link Canadian and US markets. Difficulties arise, however, when a low-tariff member state imports goods for immediate re-export or for further processing and subsequent re-export to a high-tariff member state. The expedient typically resorted to in order to circumvent this problem is to devise 'rules of origin' that distinguish domestic from external production. Rules of origin, however, are clumsy and complex. A solution is to move up the scale of integration to a *customs union*, the members of which not only refrain from imposing tariffs and quotas against each others' goods but also establish a common external tariff. This is an important step up the scale of economic integration but may not be enough to satisfy the more ambitious integrationists. The latter may press for the creation of a *common market*, comprising a customs union plus guarantees of the free movement of labour and capital. In other words, creation of a common market extends the interregional or inter-state market in goods to cover also factors of production, thus allocating them (in the absence of market imperfections) to their most efficient uses not only within each region or state but also across the whole grouping of states included within the scheme of integration.

The principle of efficient resource allocation also justifies, though perhaps with less cogency, establishment of more advanced, 'positive,' forms of economic integration. These require co-ordination of economic policies, or their formulation and implementation through a central political authority. Here we distinguish two types: a *monetary union*, which is based on a common market but provides also for a common currency and consequently requires a central bank to manage the currency; and a *general economic union*,[5] consisting of a monetary union in which, additionally, various types of economic policy, e.g. in taxation, industrial assistance, regional development, and transportation, are harmonized or adopted in common.

These last two, relatively advanced forms of economic association may be justified on the same grounds as the more rudimentary ones, namely, that they promote extension and integration of markets. This encourages economic specialization and therefore conduces to efficient use of available resources. A monetary union eliminates the uncertainty and the costs deriving from fluctuations in exchange rates and possible imposition of foreign exchange controls.[6] A general economic union also supports free movement of capital and labour by diminishing or eliminating interstate differences in the regulatory framework for economic activity and reducing discrepancies in level and kind of government services. For example, a common social security network, with portable benefits, facilitates mobility of labour.

The effects of policy co-ordination are real; they intensify market integration. But it may be doubted that the gains are large.[7] Admittedly, quantification of the benefits from market integration is no easy task. For one thing, as noted, the extent of gains through trade accruing to any member state in a free trade area or customs union depends upon what trading arrangements might be available outside it. The efficiency gains resulting from creation of a common market, monetary union, or general economic union are even more difficult to predict on the basis of formal modelling techniques (simulation exercises); but it is likely that each new step taken toward market integration yields more modest benefits than the previous one. Moreover, each of these extra steps toward market integration further restricts the capacity of member states to stimulate and channel development of their own economies. To those who believe that an interventionist policy can augment welfare – a matter much disputed – the benefits obtained by each member state as together they take new steps toward market integration (say, moving up from a customs union to a common market) may well be outweighed by accompanying reduction in political control over the economy.[8]

There is a corollary to the principle that integration of regional or national markets results in an efficiency gain, or a net rise in output, for any given quantity of factors and a given state of technology. The net benefit from integration will be larger to the extent that governments adopt a liberal policy, that is, that they refrain from interfering with operation of the market. This is a key observation, given the intent of our present inquiry, because it implies that only a fairly rudimentary institutional structure is needed to achieve the potential benefits of integration as long as the rationale for integration is not stated more broadly than we have so far done. We shall consider additional arguments later on. In the mean time it is important to note that the principle of efficiency gains through market integration implies the desirability of limiting governmental powers at all levels – central, regional, and local.

It follows that in the 1980 Canadian constitutional debate, the program of the provincialist coalition, which desired to limit federal interventionism in economic affairs, was in this sense consistent with liberal economic theory. However, it was cautious about applying the same principle to provincial activities and powers.[9]

Conversely, when in July 1980 the federal government extolled the virtues of 'securing the Canadian economic union in the constitution' and proclaimed that 'Nothing less [is involved] than ensuring that Canada will remain a country without internal barriers, a country within which people, goods, services and capital will be able to move freely,'[10] it seemed to envision curbing provincial powers while extending federal ones. Specifically, it noted that 'the ability of the federal authority to derogate from common market principles is constrained by the fact that Parliament emanates from a national constituency whose support any federal government must preserve to remain in office. Thus discrimination on the basis of province or region of residence, location, origin and destination in federal laws, regulations and practices must be approved by a majority of the people's representatives in the House of Commons, and may therefore be deemed to be in the national interest.' And, accordingly, it canvassed the idea of 'broadening federal powers so that they may encompass all matters that are necessary for economic integration, thus ensuring that the relevant laws and regulations will apply uniformly throughout Canada, or that the "test" of the public interest will be brought to bear upon derogations from uniformity.'[11]

There was, it is true, some ambiguity in the position put forward in the federal discussion paper, as other passages apparently contemplated constitutional restrictions upon federal as well as upon provincial economic powers. Nonetheless it seems clear that during the discussions of the summer of 1980, both on the federal side and among several of the provinces, there was an evident desire simultaneously to expand their own powers and to limit the exercise of economic powers by the other order of government. Neither side endorsed a constitutional arrangement designed specifically and uniquely to promote efficiency in allocation of resources through the agency of a free market. Nor, later, did the Macdonald Commission propose so limited a role for government. Were this the case it would be sufficient to restrict the provinces' capacity to infringe upon common market principles and to endow a central political authority only with such powers as would enable it to police the common market (if this were not done by joint action of the provinces themselves), to negotiate and enforce commercial arrangements with foreign countries, and to manage a common currency.

POLITICAL UNION: WHY?

Extension of a central authority's economic powers beyond this short list is regarded by some people as irrational and/or undesirable. This view holds that interventionism is the result of special pleading by particular groups (anticipating their ability to bend the state to their own purposes) or betrays hubris – the delusion that one possesses god-like powers – among political elites. Indeed, limitation of central power makes perfect sense, as long as the goal is simply that of extending and integrating markets. Market integration provides an economic rationale for only a very modest degree of political integration.

The term *political integration* is variously defined. Here I use it to mean a process of moving toward co-ordination of policies among independent states and ultimately toward creation of a political union in which previously independent states join together or are absorbed by a powerful neighbour. Important milestones along the way are association by treaty, and then the forming of a new state – confederal, federal, or unitary. The process of political integration may, of course, stop or reverse itself at any of the above-mentioned stages. In speaking of political integration, a direction of movement is indicated, but no final goal or stopping-point is implied.

Political integration may be justified on the grounds that it supports economic integration. There is some latitude for argument here, as one may question, for example, how elaborate or powerful a form of political union is required to make a monetary union work or to achieve the desired degree of policy harmonization. (In Canada, arguments on these questions underlay much of the debate within the Parti québécois regarding the institutional arrangements needed to underpin the desired 'sovereignty-association' arrangements.) The more basic question, however, concerns welfare gains from economic integration, especially positive integration (also called policy integration).[12] This is our main subject in the remainder of this chapter.

While there is no reason to consider the case for political union on economic grounds alone, one's opinion on the range of powers appropriately assigned to or exercised by a central political authority ought to reflect what one thinks the purposes of union are. As noted, the principle of efficiency gains through market integration seems to justify creation of a central political authority possessing only limited economic powers. By this criterion it is mainly important to prevent member-states from discriminating against each others' goods or from impeding mobility of capital and labour. Nonetheless, during the constitutional negotiations of 1980, the federal government laid claim to quite extensive powers to intervene in and to control the economy, and the provinces resisted all restrictions on their own powers. On what grounds, then – if not those supporting market integration – might maintenance and/or extension of federal economic power be sustained?

In answer to this question, I would propose that assignment of taxing, spending, and regulatory powers to a central government may be explained and justified in one or more of the following three ways. First, it may be argued that, as a practical matter and in order to win acceptance for a scheme of integration – or to sustain its legitimacy – certain compromises must be made. For example, one might consider it necessary to make transfer payments to persons or to the governments of member-states, even if these transfers induce inefficiency in allocation of resources. This, as Thomas J. Courchene has argued, they typically do, because they prolong the period of adjustment to changing terms of trade, to technological advancement, to exhaustion or discovery of natural resources, or to changing tastes.[13]

Second, it may be argued that non-economic ('political' or 'social') goals justify attribution of powers to a central government, even if exercise of such powers imposes an economic cost. Thus, various non-economic goals – e.g. defence against external enemies or income transfers in accordance with agreed principles of social justice, particularly when realization of such goals involves redistribution of wealth among regions – may be thought to require a strong political authority at the centre.

Third, it may be argued that economic benefits additional to those achieved through market integration may be obtained through economic union, under which common policies are implemented in areas such as transportation, industrial assistance, labour relations, regulation of financial markets, promotion of and restrictions on operation of cartels, and economic stabilization. In this view, the principle of efficiency gains through market integration supplies only a part of the rationale for establishing an economic union: market integration must be not merely complemented by the pursuit of other economic objectives but limited by them through the agency of a central government endowed with powers to stimulate and direct economic development.

Observe: only the last of these arguments posits an overall increase in output and consumption, given the size of the work-force, as a result of economic union. The other arguments are concerned with redistribution of wealth or with non-economic goals. Since the efficiency criterion (which supports the objective of market integration) cannot justify assigning any but the most limited economic powers to a central government, political union finds economic justification, if at all, only on a double supposition: first, that an interventionist state, governed by people no wiser than those we have the habit of electing, is capable of achieving welfare gains beyond those attainable through market integration alone; and, second, that the desired forms of intervention are more effective if undertaken in common, applying to the economic union as a whole.

These are speculative questions which it is unhelpful to examine in the abstract. It was earlier pointed out that, for any given state, advantages to be derived from membership in a customs union will be contingent upon the trading arrangements available to it; similarly, potential advantages from more inclusive forms of economic association (common market, monetary union, and economic union) also are presumably contingent upon the historical and international context. Let us therefore take a look at the Canadian case, examining in historical context the applicability of arguments both for a customs union (the gains-through-trade doctrine) and for more inclusive forms of economic association.

CONFEDERATION: THE ECONOMIC RATIONALE

The economies of the British North American colonies were based on a combination of subsistence activities (farming, fisheries) and commercial exploitation of natural resources with a view to their sale abroad in raw or barely processed form. Confederation was not, therefore, aimed at the pursuit of efficiency gains from encouraging more specialized production and the division of labour, relative to what had obtained beforehand. Insofar as its objectives were economic, it was a political tool for rehabilitating an already specialized staple-producing economy rendered precarious by Britain's moving to a free trade policy during the 1840s. Another economic objective, which was also an extension of policies that had emerged in Canada during the quarter-century preceding Confederation, was industrialization under tariff protection. Industrialization was attractive because it would expand employment and diversify an economy that concentrated heavily on resource production. In this way industrialization would render the economy less vulnerable to shifts in foreign demand and to the closing-off of established overseas markets, should foreign governments reorient their commercial policies.

With Britain's repeal of the Corn Laws in 1846, the merchants of Montreal ran for cover: first by declaring for annexation to the United States (1849), and then by requesting Britain to negotiate alternative commercial privileges with the Americans. The latter was accomplished with the 1854 Reciprocity Treaty, which guaranteed all five of the eastern North American colonies open access to the United States market in natural products. In return, the Americans were given access to the Atlantic inland fisheries and obtained navigation rights on the St Lawrence. The Montreal merchants hoped, in vain, that the St Lawrence would become the main export route from the interior of the continent to European markets. The treaty did not restrict the parties' right to protect their markets for manufactured goods, a power of which Canada availed itself in the Galt tariff of 1857, contributing to expansion of local manufacturing.

Reciprocity, however, was a short-lived substitute for the comforts of protected dependence upon Britain:

Unfortunately for the peace of mind of the colonies, the change in British imperial policy [introduction of free trade and insistence that the colonies provide for their own defence] coincided with the rise of continental imperialism in the United States. During the fifties and sixties, the [American] far west was rapidly organized into territories ... Settlers were swarming westward and eddying northward towards the domain of the Hudson's Bay Company. This quick advance across the continent was accompanied by hymns to 'manifest destiny' and by repeated, though largely irresponsible demands for the annexation of the British colonies to the north. Even if [the province of] Canada and the Maritimes were not seriously threatened, it became increasingly doubtful whether the United States could be prevented from swallowing the rest of the continent, including the territories of the Hudson's Bay Company and the feeble British settlements on the Pacific Coast.

The American Civil War with its border incidents and its Anglo-American disputes intensified the alarm, and [American] anger at Great Britain ensured that the United States would abrogate the Reciprocity Treaty at the earliest opportunity ... In the early sixties, the era of peaceful political relations and advantageous commercial arrangements with the United States appeared to be definitely over. The political independence of the colonies was insecure and their material prospects were discouraging in the extreme. They had lost their most valuable commercial privileges in the retreat of one empire and they had no hope of countervailing advantages from the threatening advance of another.[14]

It was in a context where more lucrative trading arrangements were closed off, except perhaps under unacceptable political conditions, that the gains-through-trade doctrine provided an important economic rationale for Confederation. Donald Creighton:

Among [the unionists'] expectations, the hope of increased internal trade was perhaps the chief ... 'You in the east,' said George Brown, 'would send us your fish and coals and your West India produce, while we would send you in return the flour and the grain and the meats you now buy in Boston and New York. Our merchants and manufacturers would have a new field before them.' ... Both Galt of Canada and Tilley of New Brunswick prophesied that Confederation would bring expanding opportunities for the manufacturers of their respective provinces, and in Nova Scotia, Lynch answered his own query as to what Nova Scotia proposed to send over the Intercolonial by replying 'our manufactures.'[15]

Confederation was thus, for the British North American colonies, a way of salvaging what they could of an economic structure the precariousness of which was revealed by changes in the commercial policies of Britain and the United States. Indeed, some historians have highlighted the unionist hope that by creating an integrated market comprising some three or four million people, the new federation would have enough bargaining power to force the United States to re-establish reciprocal free trade in non-manufactured goods. That this was unrealistic, as was the fond hope of some Maritimers that they might supply (central) Canada with manufactures, need not concern us. The hopes themselves are enough to explain the colonies' recourse, given their adverse commercial situation, to the expedient of establishing, at the very least, a customs union.

A historical perspective on the economic purposes of Confederation, however, reveals more than an attempt to create an integrated market guaranteed by establishment of a common political authority. A key feature of the Confederation scheme was the intent to promote extensive growth through creation of a state apparatus with powers enabling it actively to participate in and even direct economic development. ('Extensive growth' refers to a process of bringing additional factors of production into use, for example by expanding the work-force through immigration, by geographical expansion in order to exploit hitherto untapped natural resources, and/or by importing foreign capital. It contrasts with 'intensive growth,' a process in which factors already available for use in production are employed more efficiently than in the past.)[16]

A policy of extensive growth appears to have been dictated by several factors, all of which point to the inadequacy of a mere customs union to achieve the purposes for which the federation was formed. Trade between (central) Canada and the Maritime colonies could not be expected to expand significantly until an intercolonial railway was in operation; and it was recognized that the line would not be built without direct government involvement (in the event, as a public works project). The level of tariff protection desired by the Canadians would impose costs upon the Maritime provinces, for which they had to be compensated; similarly, building of the Intercolonial (the main form of compensation for the Maritimes) would impose costs upon the Canadians, for which the agrarian interests of Canada West in turn sought compensation in the form of state-assisted westward expansion. Westward extension of the new Dominion, rapid settlement of the plains region, and construction of a Canadian transcontinental railway were considered necessary to prevent the United States from annexing the Hudson's Bay Company lands.

These are purposes with a political inspiration that cannot be gainsaid; but what we shall want to know is whether a policy of extensive growth, of which the new federation was the instrument, had also an economic rationale. The question involves us in a review of the national policy, comprising tariff protection, active recruitment and rapid settlement of immigrants, and a vast program of railway building assisted by land grants, a legislated monopoly for the Canadian Pacific Railway (CPR), and public guarantees of its debts.

The national policy, which in retrospect supplies the raison d'être of a relatively centralized federation, remains a subject of controversy among historians. We shall examine it: first, as a mercantilist adventure instigated by a self-seeking commercial bourgeoisie (Naylor); second, as a mammoth economic and political failure embarked upon because of over-optimistic estimates of Canada's economic prospects at the time (Dales); and third, as an indispensable instrument of Canada's economic and political development (Innis and Easterbrook).

Confederation and the National Policy: A Mercantilist Adventure

It is well known that Confederation was denounced by its contemporary opponents as 'a Grand Trunk job.' More recently Tom Naylor has suggested that the Baring Brothers, a British firm of investment bankers, may have been the real Fathers of Confederation; according to Naylor, 'Canadian Confederation and the subsequent national policy are an unambiguous example of British mercantilism in action.' This means, as we learn from Naylor's definition of mercantilism, that the national policy was essentially a state-building enterprise, undertaken for private gain:

The system known as mercantilism in Europe consisted of a series of policies aimed at internal economic consolidation and/or expansion. It was the economic counterpart of the political process by which states were integrated and strengthened ... In Britain, mercantilism might be said to have displayed three salient characteristics. (1) The edification of state power was theoretically the ultimate goal, with national wealth supposedly regarded as simply a means to attain it. Economy was held to be subservient to society and society to the state structure. (2) A strong paternalistic state directed the process through regulation of industry and trade, consolidation of the public finances, expansion of the tax base, rationalization of public administration, and the provision of social overhead capital; and all in coalition with a merchant, rather than an industrial, bourgeoisie. (3) Policies were adopted to stimulate industrial development by tariffs and subsidies, and by encouraging an inflow, or blocking an outflow, of skilled labour and capital – capital then largely in the form of bullion.

Naylor's tour de force is the attempted demonstration that national policy tariffs were the work of merchants and the bankers to whom they were allied, rather than of industrial entrepreneurs. He argues that industrialization based on imported technology and management skills is considerably safer for its financial backers than independent domestic entrepreneurship and that Canada's financial-commercial bourgeoisie sponsored a protectionist policy which, in achieving 'industrialization by invitation,' would provide them with low-risk investment opportunities. Naylor concludes: 'Far from being the response of a rising industrial capitalism striving to break down intercolonial tariff walls, Confederation and the national policy were the work of the descendants of the mercantile class which had aligned itself with the Colonial Office in 1837 to crush the indigenous petite bourgeoisie and nascent industrialists.'[17] It is a conclusion that some readers have found unconvincing[18] and to which I myself do not subscribe. Nonetheless, putting aside the question of motive or inspiration, one might reasonably view the national policy as being, like mercantilism in general, 'the economic counterpart of the political process by which states were integrated and strengthened.' As Hugh Aitken has written, commenting on 'defensive expansionism' (a concept that corresponds to 'extensive growth,' with the added connotation that the motive for it was avoidance of absorption into the United States):

Whether the initiative in stating and implementing this policy is to be ascribed to private enterprise or to the state is a question on which opinions will differ. The assertion that the state in the form of the federal government was merely acting as the agent or instrument of private economic interests – the same interests that had worked to achieve Confederation, the sale of the Hudson's Bay Company's lands, and the chartering of a Pacific railroad – could probably be supported. But if the distinction between 'the state' and 'private enterprise' is to be retained (as applied to Canada, the distinction often seems artificial), the weight of the evidence seems to indicate a contrary view.[19]

In other words, where Naylor sees Confederation as an instance of a dominant economic class fashioning political arrangements to suit its interests – in this case mercantile ones – Aitken sees so close a relation between economic and political entrepreneurs that one cannot really sort out whether the economic or the political motives predominated. It is probably fruitless to try to resolve this conundrum. The interesting point is that, for both Naylor and Aitken, economic and political goals were congruent and were implemented through the national policy. Not everyone takes the same view.

The National Policy as a Political and Economic Incubus

To at least one critic of the national policy, government intervention in the economy to promote extensive growth was both wasteful in economic terms and counterproductive in terms of the political objective that it was intended to serve. John Dales[20] has argued that the heavy costs imposed by an overly ambitious program of railway building, by give-aways of public lands, and especially by the protective tariff were incurred because proponents of the national policy held over-optimistic notions of Canada's economic prospects prior to 1900. According to Dales the national policy was, until the turn of the century, incapable of producing the benefits expected from it because circumstances were not yet ripe for rapid growth; after this time, when earlier investments in transportation facilities and industrial infrastructure finally seemed to be paying off, massive government assistance was not really needed to stimulate growth. In the mean time, by forcing the pace of development the federal government had imposed huge costs upon the people of Canada, causing intense resentment among those who were not direct beneficiaries of the national policy. Thus were created powerful, well-founded regional grievances. Dales concludes that the national policy of Macdonald and his successors has been not only unjustifiable in economic terms but – if we take at face value its supposed nation-building intent – politically counterproductive.

Dales does not (to my knowledge) address the question of whether Confederation itself had any economic rationale. Whatever he may have thought on this question, his work supplies no economic rationale – quite the contrary – for the Fathers having endowed the central government with powers to intervene extensively in the functioning of the market:

Sir John A. Macdonald gave us our first national policy, and our first lessons in the irrelevance of economics. Western lands, he argued, must be controlled by the Dominion because provincial land policies 'might be obstructive to immigration,' i.e. provinces might actually try to sell land rather than give it away. Canadian railways, in Macdonald's view, were not to be thought of primarily as business enterprises; they were instruments of national development and served this end by providing both attractive objects of government expenditure and reliable sources of party support. As for the tariff, Macdonald rang all the changes on the protectionist fallacies and promised that his tariff would benefit everyone, the teachings of the dismal science notwithstanding. Macdonald was the first great Canadian non-economist ... [He] has in any event had powerful support from Canadian historians, of both the political and economic persuasions, who have rationalized his national policy and have encouraged Canadians to believe that by disregarding economics they could build a nation that would represent a victory over mere materialism.[21]

The reason why Dales considers it important to understand the character and effects of the national policy is that its overall aims, he says, continued to animate policy-makers into the latter twentieth century. The policy has achieved bigness by sacrificing performance: 'Canadian economic policy – and, what is more important, the economic policy of so many developing nations today [1966] –

aims consistently at maximizing the purse, gross national product, rather than the performance, gross national product per citizen.'[22] The tariff, in particular, has had the effect of increasing the Canadian population by creating a number of jobs in industries that are not competitive internationally and would not, except for the tariff, have located here. As a result of the national policy, absolute GNP is larger than it would be under a more liberal policy, but real income per capita – the key indicator of welfare – is smaller.

An Economic Rationale for the National Policy

H.A. Innis and W.T. Easterbrook offer an interpretation of Canada's economic situation in the Confederation era that differs somewhat not only from Naylor's and Dales', but from Creighton's, cited earlier. Whereas Creighton sees increased internal trade as 'perhaps the chief' expectation of the unionists, Innis and Easterbrook suggest that 'the whole Canadian economy was to be geared, as with the southern United States, to the expanding industrialism of Europe.' They write: 'In the 1840's Canada had elected to continue as an expanding area of commercialism based on export staples rather than to develop a more stable and diversified economy. The colony had embarked upon construction of transportation facilities which committed it to expansion as the only means of meeting their enormous costs.'[23]

The Canada of 1866 was not only suffering from the loss of commercial privileges in Britain and in the United States – as well as being fearful of American jingoism – it had also incurred a huge debt from building canals and railways. These facilities suffered from vast unused capacity as a result of the failure to make the St Lawrence 'the chief continental artery of trade.' Consequently Canada 'was committed to a policy of economic expansion which allowed of no turning back.' An interventionist state was necessary to get Canada out of the difficult situation in which it was placed:

There were staple commodities in abundance, and techniques could be borrowed, but the application of industrial technology to the exploitation of Canada's resources demanded capital expenditures that were enormous for an area so thinly peopled. To the south, the increasingly powerful and competitive United States, a country much more happily endowed by nature, forced the pace far beyond the ability of private enterprise to carry on without substantial state support. As a result, for a century an alliance of business and government has provided a pattern of expansion that goes back to the first penetration of the continent – a pattern unchanged in the emphasis on staples for external markets, but marked by new technical and institutional methods.[24]

I do not think it justified to draw any but the most limited conclusions from this brief and obviously incomplete survey of interpretations of the national policy. However, three facts stand out.

1. The positions taken, respectively, by Innis, Dales, and Naylor differ in the assumptions that they make about the young country's capacity for industrial development in the absence of active state support for extensive growth. Naylor thinks that the mercantilist policies of the new Dominion were responsible for the demise of an otherwise viable manufacturing industry. He argues that prior to Confederation industrial entrepreneurs in Canada and in the Maritime colonies were holding their own against external competition and were restrained mainly by shortage of risk capital. This shortage, he writes, was exacerbated rather than alleviated by a political union the purposes of which were mercantile, not industrial; the federal government created a centralized banking system that absorbed savings made in every corner of the new Dominion, creating pools of capital that financed commercial adventures and the transportation facilities that they required, incidentally ruining hundreds of local industrial entrepreneurs who succumbed to competition for want of capital to finance innovation and expansion. A different policy, involving among other things creation of a banking system on the decentralized American model, would have seen Canada launched upon the road to independent industrialization, hardy and vital because unprotected by tariffs.[25]

Dales, by contrast with Naylor, asserts that the tariff expanded employment in the secondary sector but rendered it less efficient than an unprotected manufacturing industry would have been. Innis, perhaps because he was more keenly aware of Canada's vulnerability to American protectionism and more mindful of the competitive advantages enjoyed by American and British manufacturers (who not only had a head start on their potential Canadian competitors but were assured of access to a much larger domestic market), seems not to have contemplated development of any but small-scale local manufacturing, except with some form of state support.

2. Innis' argument is founded upon the observation that Canadian transportation facilities were under-used. He therefore insists that alleviation of the debt burden imposed by excess capacity required extensive growth. Dales has a completely different point of view. He holds that it is a myth that Canada is or ever has been (relative to the United States) an under-populated country, and he argues that a smaller population would be wealthier per capita. He apparently sees no threat to Canadian sovereignty over the northwestern plains, had they been serviced by American railways. In sum, the nation-building project, central to the scholarly concerns and political values of Innis and his followers, is assumed by Dales to have presented – had they only realized it – no problems requiring the special attention of Canadian policy-makers. As for Naylor, I am unable to draw from his work any inferences on these matters.

3. Innis believed, for the reasons just noted, that prosperity demanded that the state participate actively in economic life. He also assumed that without a national economy, integrated by transportation networks that could be built only with state

assistance, there could be no nation. Nation-building was thus a double-faceted project, equally political and economic. Neither Dales nor Naylor gives any evidence of being impressed with the thought, which was at the core of Innis' work, that *without a national economy there could be no national state – and that without an interventionist state, the Canadian economy would have been in no sense a national one.*

Obviously, it is Innis who, in defending the policies of which Confederation was the political instrument, provides the economic rationale for a relatively centralized form of federal state. To him, the circumstances of the day required an interventionist government, equally for economic and political reasons. Dales and Naylor, though there are significant differences between them, are alike in condemning the national policy; in so doing, they implicitly narrow any possible economic rationale for Confederation to that of securing efficiency gains in the allocation of resources, for which market integration – requiring minimal central powers – is sufficient.

It is striking that, in their criticisms of the national policy, neither Dales nor Naylor makes any allusion to the burden imposed upon state finances and upon the economy in general by unused capacity – an important element in the rationale, according to Innis, for a policy that aimed to bring in large new accretions of capital and labour. Neither Dales nor Naylor refers to the menace of political and economic domination from the south. Possibly Innis and his many disciples have been insufficiently critical of the national policy, being too readily inclined to rationalize the misjudgments and improvisations of the political and economic elites of the day and too indulgent of their sometimes spectacular veniality. However, the revisionist histories presented us by Dales and Naylor pay little if any attention to the external circumstances which, to contemporaries, required state interventionism. They do not recognize, still less refute, the arguments of Innis and his successors.

INTERVENTIONISM AND WELFARE

Our job now is to abstract from the controversies outlined in the preceding section, identifying a set of economic arguments for interventionism. These arguments provide a rationale for at least a limited degree of political control of the economy. But they do not specify at what level – central or regional, federal or provincial – that control should be exercised. As I have repeatedly stressed, arguments on this matter apply only contingently, that is, their applicability in any situation depends on circumstances that may or may not obtain at any given time. In the next (and final) chapter we shall concern ourselves with the contemporary rationale for assigning extensive powers over the economy to the federal government, as we have just done in the context of the latter nineteenth century; but first it is necessary to explore in more general terms the potential benefits of state involvement in the economy. To do so, I try to generalize from the arguments reviewed in the previous section.

It is fairly easy to do this because the present-day policy relevance of a critique of the national policy was much in the minds of Innis, Dales, and Naylor. Innis was the anti-imperialist economic historian, liberal in his political philosophy, but none the less centralist and statist in his sympathies – at least for Canada – because of his antagonism toward American imperialism. Dales urged his readers to acknowledge that the national policy was a failure in both economic and political terms, to reject the historically favoured goal of extensive growth,[26] and to endorse a new policy objective, that of making better use of existing resources. Naylor sought to expose the predations, laziness, and incompetence of Canadian economic elites – then and now – evidently hoping that, by discrediting them and their political toadies, he could help induce Canadians to demand new policies more encouraging of domestic entrepreneurship. In brief, each of the scholars cited here perceived continuities in Canadian economic policy over a period of a century or more; and their evaluation of the policy at its inception was roughly the same as their evaluation of it in the mid- or late twentieth century. By examining the national policy at its origin, they hoped to reveal more clearly the aims, biases, and failures of contemporary economic policy and – explicitly in Dales' case and implicitly in Naylor's – to convince their readers that a different policy would yield better economic performance.

A better economic performance – that is our clue to generalizing from the arguments about the national policy. What does the phrase mean? One assumes that it denotes a contribution (beyond some bench-mark level) to a population's material welfare; but what is welfare, and how may an interventionist policy increase it? We shall examine this question under three headings: expanding consumption possibilities, promoting stability, and avoiding secular unemployment.

Expanding Consumption Possibilities

For Dales there is but one defensible goal of economic policy, and that is to augment real income per capita. Real income is a concept that is capable of considerable extension and refinement, so that ultimately it may be used as a proxy for welfare, covering the consumption of such 'goods' as leisure, unpolluted air, safety on the streets, or even national pride. As conveniently measured, however – and Dales seems content with this – real incomes are merely dollar incomes adjusted for inflation; international comparisons are made by translating one currency into another using the prevailing rate of exchange. (Alternatively, one may base international comparisons on indices of price-levels, in effect calculating a hypothetical exchange rate that would equalize the cost, in different countries, of a standard basket of goods.) 'Real income,' conventionally thought of as nominal income adjusted as described, is an indicator of consumption possibilities for those goods that are sold in the market, especially those traded internationally, valued according to their exchange price.

Real income as conveniently measured[27] has several glaring deficiencies as a measure of consumption possibilities, let alone welfare. It fails to take account of goods not entering into recorded monetary exchange (such as job satisfaction, home-grown vegetables, 'shadow economy' transactions not reported to the tax authorities, and unpaid family labour such as housework). Further, 'public' or 'collective' goods like national defence or a television show – the consumption of which by one person does not exclude their being consumed by others – offer consumption possibilities the magnitude of which is not reflected in estimates of income, monetary or real. Even in the case of marketed private goods, price paid is almost certainly a poor estimate of the consumption value placed upon them by the purchaser (i.e. he might be willing to pay more); and 'spillovers' or 'externalities' may attach to their production or consumption, with the consequence that net benefits to society do not match net benefits to those directly engaged in market transactions pertaining to them. Thus social costs and social benefits get out of whack.

Let us say that we take the view that economic performance is to be equated with per capita consumption possibilities rather than narrowly defined 'real income' per capita (or alternatively that estimates of real income ought to be broadened, taking account of such factors as spillovers, public goods, and non-market valuation). Then the data on which Dales rests his case must be regarded as unreliable. I do not wish to argue that the redefinition of concepts demolishes Dales' thesis. Still, in recognizing the distinction between consumption possibilities and real income as conveniently measured, we have taken the first step toward identifying an economic rationale for interventionist policies and for a constitutional arrangement that facilitates their implementation.

This discovery is in no sense original. Indeed, the sub-discipline of welfare economics concerns itself with the many reasons why allocating resources through the market, even if it maximizes aggregate income, may result in aggregate consumption possibilities that fall short of the level potentially achievable; and it proposes policy norms or guidelines offering greater efficiency in allocation of resources. The many tax, subsidy, and regulatory measures that may compensate for deficiencies of the market as an organizing and allocative device are the special province of welfare economists. Their concepts and analyses are also pertinent to identifying circumstances in which public provision of non-priced goods and services (especially collective goods) works better than reliance upon the private sector, no matter how greatly economic behaviour is hedged about by controls and subsidies.

Welfare economics, however, carries us only a limited distance. It is concerned with the ranking of alternative economic situations (i.e. alternative collections of goods and their distribution): the focus is on the organization of the domestic economy. A large part of the case for interventionism, by contrast, rests upon an analysis of economic exchanges with other countries. The world-economic context is vital; and the case for certain forms of intervention is correspondingly contingent upon the changing place that the country in question occupies within the world economy. An abstract presentation of the case is therefore of only limited value. Bearing this in mind, we shall consider the panoply of developmental and protective devices designed to raise a country's or a region's per capita consumption possibilities, relative to what they would otherwise be, given its situation vis-à-vis other countries or regions.

No country's economic development can be considered wholly in isolation from that of other countries. Foreign markets, foreign sources of supply for production goods (raw materials, semi-manufactures, and machinery), foreign competition in the home market, and foreign capital and technology: all are relevant to the functioning and structure of the domestic economy – more so, obviously, for some countries than for others. It is in the case of small and relatively undeveloped countries that foreign economic relations, and their domestic effects, have received the largest attention; but it is perhaps equally important to consider the evolution of the largest, wealthiest, and most technologically advanced countries in the evolving world-economic context.

External economic relations are, in large part, structured by the operation of market forces. The volume, geographic patterning, and goods-content of foreign trade – as well as international flows of capital, labour, and technology – are to some extent a resultant of economic exchange among private agents (individuals and firms). However, some of the markets most relevant to the international division of labour are highly oligopolistic or monopsonistic (characterized by a single dominant purchaser). The imperfectly competitive character of these markets is by no means a matter of indifference to governments, which in some cases work to compensate for or neutralize the adverse effects of the exercise of market power by multinational firms or international cartels. In other cases, governments are directly involved in establishing cartels or in securing conditions favourable to the foreign operations of home-based multinationals. It is not uncommon for governments to become economic agents in their own right, by establishing public corporations and by contracting for the sale and purchase of goods and services, either as members of cartels or as brokers for domestic firms.

There would be no excuse for belabouring such obvious matters were it not for the fact that many discussions of the benefits of liberalizing the conduct of international trade and adopting an open door policy toward foreign investment ignore them. A major part of the case for government interventionism, directed toward raising domestic consumption possibilities, derives from the prevalence of imperfections in the structure and operation of world markets.[28] Government responses to market imperfections include the following four types.

1. To mobilize domestic savings for investment purposes, or to secure foreign investment, governments may – as they have in Canada, at both federal and provincial levels – underwrite risks, guarantee access to resources (often on a monopoly basis), and assist development through provision of infrastructure such as transportation facilities or services such as geological surveys or manpower training. 'Forced growth' policies may of course serve merely to reveal the credulity of government or its incompetence in business,[29] but in some cases government's assistance or even direct participation may be required to launch economically viable development projects that the private sector is unwilling or unable to undertake on its own. The argument applies particularly in cases where, for one reason or another, it is preferred not to rely upon foreign capital and the projects in question are beyond the capacity of the domestic financial system.

2. Among the most notoriously imperfect markets is the market in technology. This fact has led governments to try to stimulate technological innovation and entrepreneurship, sometimes by encouraging importation and adaptation of foreign technology and sometimes by supporting or itself conducting industrial research and development.

3. Where policies to maintain or enhance business competition are ineffective or impractical, recourse is generally had to government regulation or to public enterprise. If the firms exercising monopoly power are foreign-controlled, however, regulation may be ineffective, particularly if the firm(s) involved have financial resources exceeding those of the public treasury of the host country. Regulation may also be ineffective, even where the industry is not monopolistic or oligopolistic, in preventing abuses such as transfer pricing, inefficient sourcing of production goods and business services, and parent controls on production and marketing decisions of the subsidiary.[30] It may be impossible in some cases to devise effective governmental responses to situations such as these, but evidently they motivate governments to monitor and where possible control operations of foreign multinationals, to require that domestic investors be given the opportunity to buy shares in their subsidiaries, or to insist that domestic firms be offered participation in joint ventures. For similar reasons governments may themselves become involved in consortia or in mixed enterprises with one or more governmental appointees on the board of directors. Preventive action may also be taken. Thus, where it is feared that an open-door policy on foreign investment will result in foreign-controlled firms acquiring 'undue' market power, and it is thought that foreign funds and know-how can be dispensed with, restrictions may be imposed on foreign investment (especially takeovers) and/or special assistance may be offered to domestically owned firms to invest in the industry.

4. Of course, governments do not act merely defensively in world markets for goods, capital, and technology. Where conditions are favourable, they may attempt to augment and exploit the market power of domestic industry by promoting establishment of export cartels, marketing boards, or state trading

companies. They may also act to establish opportunities (or create privileges) for domestic firms in their foreign operations. In rarer cases an attempt may be made to establish monopsony power, either alone or in combination with other countries, by creating import cartels.

These instances of market imperfections, which government involvement in the economy may attempt to compensate for, to minimize, or to create – whichever action favours the domestic economy – do not of course establish a presumption in favour of widespread intervention. In some cases intervention may be ineffective or counter-productive in respect of raising consumption possibilities. In acknowledging this, one merely underlines a fact of great importance: that for any given country the potential advantage of an interventionist policy necessarily depends upon the circumstances in which, at that time, it finds itself – as suggested, for example, by the foregoing list of factors impelling governments to become involved in external economic relations.

In sum: welfare is increased to the extent that consumption possibilities are raised. Market integration contributes to this goal, but so, potentially, do interventionist policies. The reasons for this, insofar as domestic economic exchanges are concerned, are evident from the principles of welfare economics. Other reasons pertain to the exercise of market power in international economic exchange, where with some regularity governments try to reduce the vulnerability of domestic producers/consumers to foreign-based economic actors. Then again, when circumstances permit, governments may assist domestic producers in exercising a degree of monopoly power in world markets. Where such interventions are successful, consumption possibilities for the domestic population are raised. This brief survey of what governments may do to raise consumption possibilities, however, far from exhausts the subject of how an economically active government may increase welfare.

Promoting Stability

So far we have said nothing about time. Our discussion of potential benefits of an interventionist policy has made no mention of the fact that resources may lie idle during a downturn or that people may be thrown out of work as the economy adjusts to changes in relative prices or as shifts in demand patterns occur.

Some sources of economic instability may be of domestic origin, reflecting dips and swings in the business cycle, technological innovation, resource discoveries or exhaustion, and novelties in taste. It is, I think, everywhere agreed that in the face of destabilizing events such as these, appropriate forms of government intervention in the economy will ensure more efficient use of resources and therefore higher levels of production and larger consumption possibilities. Of course the joker here is the word 'appropriate,' since there is no end of argument as to the combination of fiscal and monetary instruments that will be most effective in minimizing unemployment and stabilizing prices; and consensus is also notoriously lacking on the mix of cushioning and adjustment-inducing devices that will reduce the distress so often associated with the decline of particular industries and regions. Among those persons directly injured by such trends, protectionism in all its Promethean forms is loudly and quite consistently called for, while among liberal economists it is urged that gentle adjustment merely prolongs the pain, that market-enhancing policies are superior to market-retarding ones, and so forth. Prudence demands that I leave such controversies to the professionals; and I shall say nothing more about those forms of intervention that are designed to respond to demand and supply 'shocks' of internal origin or to smooth out the business cycle.

Destabilizing events of foreign origin are more interesting to us because they may motivate a policy that actually inverts the arguments derived from the gains-through-trade doctrine. Governments may undertake to structure or restructure the economy to diminish its vulnerability to external shocks. With this objective, they may aim for diversification, forgoing immediate and possibly short-term advantages from specialization within the international economy. Disregarding the tenets of international trade theory, according to which trade creation and the exploitation of comparative advantages raise production per capita (and therefore consumption possibilities), governments may aim to stabilize incomes over time by imposing barriers to trade: tariffs, import quotas, production and export subsidies, and export taxes and licences. The incentive for having recourse to such measures is, of course, much intensified by fears – justified or otherwise – that profitable trading arrangements may be closed off by changes in the commercial policy of foreign governments. Even if political action of this kind is not an apparent danger, it may make good sense to avoid building up an economy that is heavily reliant upon the export of a few products, particularly if the products in question are subject to wide fluctuations in demand and/or price. For example, it will be recalled that, in the case of Canada's national policy, one of the key motives was precisely to reduce the vulnerability of the domestic economy to violent fluctuations in the world price of its staple exports.

I do not mean to assert that trade restrictions aiming at diversification of the economy will necessarily have the effect intended or, even if they do, that the cost will be as small as economic nationalists suppose. These are matters which, in Canada, fuel continuing controversy. At best, average economic performance over time will rise because fewer resources (labour, capital, and land) lie idle during an economic downturn. Some sacrifice in incomes during boom times may, in other words, be more than compensated for by moderation of recessions, resulting in fuller use of resources over time. At worst, attempts at diversification may entail sacrifices in periods of upswing, succeeding only in establishing industries that go belly-up in a recession and thus exacerbate boom-and-bust patterns of economic activity. In between these 'best' and 'worst' scenarios, diversification may involve some sacrifice in real incomes, averaged over the business cycle while, in subjective terms, more than compensating for this by achieving greater stability. An analogy here might be the purchase of an insurance policy: in the aggregate, policy-holders reduce their consumption of material goods in order to buy security, or peace of mind. When nations 'purchase' diminished vulnerability to external shocks, the benefit thereby obtained does not show up in the national accounts but is scarcely the less real for not being measured or measurable. Thus governments that succeed in stabilizing the economy, or in rendering economic activity less sensitive to fluctuations in foreign demand and world prices, arguably help to raise aggregate welfare.

Avoiding Secular Unemployment

One of the foundation stones of neoclassical economic theory is that economies tend to operate at or near full employment. Though of course everyone recognizes that people are temporarily thrown out of work in an economic downturn, neoclassical economists hold that over the longer haul unemployment is not a problem. Since Keynes' day, this postulate has been doubted and debated. For those who hold to the neoclassical (or as Keynes had it, the classical) view, governments need be concerned about unemployment only in the sense that they may have a responsibility to smooth out the business cycle and to ease the processes of adjustment to changing conditions; for the dissenters, one of the primary objects of economic policy is to minimize or avoid secular unemployment. A government that succeeds in doing so obviously promotes economic welfare.

This is not the place to tackle directly a problem that has been at the core of contemporary controversies in economic theory. Still, one way of looking at the possible role for government in dealing with secular unemployment is to return to Dales' critique of the national policy. He makes the interesting suggestion that the tariff has increased population and national income while lowering income per capita. He posits that, 'while the *direction* of international migration is determined largely by international differences in the standard of living, the volume and timing of such migration is probably dependent mainly on international differences in the level of 'job opportunities', and especially on the state of the labour market in the country of intended destination.'[31] One infers that he believes the tariff has created job opportunities in manufacturing without reducing them (or not by much) in other sectors; but unfortunately I cannot find in Dales' work any explicit discussion of the net employment effects of protectionism. We shall have to reason the matter out for ourselves.

It is plausible to suppose that employment in the primary sector is limited by, on the one hand, the supply of available resources (agricultural land, forests, mines, and energy) and, on the other, by the extent of world demand at any given price. More intensive application of labour may add somewhat to aggregate production, but beyond a certain point the marginal productivity of labour may be presumed to drop sharply. As a result, it will not be possible significantly to expand the primary sector work-force (employed or self-employed) in return for a moderate drop in average income per worker. If, moreover, we presume that employment opportunities in the tertiary or service sector depend mainly on the size of the primary and secondary sectors, and construction activity also reflects developments elsewhere in the economy, the key to estimating total employment opportunities is the number of jobs available in manufacturing.

Employment opportunities in manufacturing may vary considerably with the wage level, as compared with wages abroad. For a country – Japan, say – possessing few natural resources, with exports consisting mainly or exclusively of manufactured goods, one would expect the exchange rate to vary inversely with the level of money wages, with the result that its manufactures remain competitive both in the domestic market and internationally. By contrast, a country that is richly endowed with natural resources, and that exports considerable quantities of resource products in raw or semi-processed form, may have an exchange rate that is buoyed up by these exports (and indeed also by the influx of foreign capital, if resource development is financed through external borrowing or foreign direct investment). Its manufactures may not, accordingly, be internationally competitive unless wage rates in manufacturing are far below those prevailing in the primary and tertiary sectors – an unlikely situation, for political as well as for market reasons. In other words, the very strength of the resources sector may make manufacturing unviable, unless protected. Economists call this 'the Dutch disease,' because the phenomenon was noted in the Netherlands following discovery of natural gas in its territorial waters; gas production improved its balance of payments, raising the exchange value of the guilder, causing hardship for its manufacturing industry.

In circumstances where the exchange rate is buoyed up by resource exports and/or the influx of foreign investment, a protectionist policy may expand employment opportunities in the economy as a whole. To primary-sector jobs of more or less fixed number, and to construction and service-sector jobs associated with resource production, would be added a certain number of manufacturing jobs. The employment opportunities available in manufacturing would, however, be limited by the fact that manufacturing would be restricted to serving the domestic market in those goods producible at home, behind the barriers created by tariffs, subsidies, and other protectionist devices.

The economic model sketched out in the preceding paragraphs may represent Canada's situation through much of its history. Of course the model is too crude to fit precisely. Some processing of natural resources has always occurred, and artisanal or small-scale manufacturing has always existed to serve markets where 'natural' protection (arising, for example, out of transportation costs) affords opportunities for it. Moreover, not only is some manufacturing import-competitive without tariff protection, but some firms produce for external markets. The question is whether we have less employment in the export industries because the tariff protects some other industries geared only to the domestic market.

Manufacturing is not an either/or proposition; and it is therefore necessary to consider employment effects of tariff and non-tariff barriers, bearing in mind their impact on firms other than those that need protection if they are to survive. Here we should note that protectionism creates revenues for the protected industry and that these revenues may be used up in various ways. They may permit manufacturers to offer higher wages (without which they might be unable to recruit a stable or reliable work-force: thus the higher wage may be a condition of the existence of the industry). Some portion of the extra revenues enjoyed by the industry may inflate profits, attracting capital to the industry and away from other possible employments. Another portion may be absorbed in inefficient use of labour and/or production goods. Across the economy as a whole, the net employment effects would equal increases in manufacturing employment due to exclusion of foreign products and perhaps due also to wasteful use of labour in industries serving the domestic market, minus potential manufacturing and non-manufacturing employment forgone as otherwise competitive industries incur cost increases and lose export markets and/or as foreign barriers to trade are raised against them in retaliation.

Of course, it is the net employment effects of protectionism we are interested in. In a country with a large export-oriented resource sector, especially if the domestic market is small and if potential or actual trading partners have raised tariff and other barriers against its manufactures, the manufacturing sector may well be non-viable unless supported by tariffs and/or by subsidies and other non-tariff barriers. In these circumstances, policies to shore up declining industries or to stimulate growth of new ones that otherwise would be incapable of establishing themselves are likely to have positive net effects on employment. If these effects are large enough, the policies in question – even taking into account their negative real income effects for consumers and for workers in other industries – will succeed in raising incomes across the population as a whole as otherwise idle workers fill the jobs created for them.

This suggestion is at variance with Dales' analysis of per capita income effects of the national policy. The clarity of his argument makes it easy to identify the reason. Our model takes population size as given; Dales' model does not. On the contrary, he takes account of a fact that is certainly pertinent to an evaluation of the historical effects of protectionism in Canada, namely that for decades federal policy encouraged heavy immigration from Europe. It did so both to populate the western plains and to supply manpower for tariff-protected industries. Notwithstanding this welcoming policy, the availability of higher wages in the United States has encouraged, through much of Canada's history, a steady stream of emigration, especially of skilled workers and professionals, with the result that net migration has often been only very slightly positive and has sometimes been negative. In short, the presuppositions of Dales's argument include a condition of 'excess demand for labour,' that is, labour shortages in relation to supply at current wage-rates. Canada's national policies determined that such labour shortages should be met in part by immigration and not wholly through a rise in wages.[32] By contrast, the situation we are modelling is one where there is or might be considerable unemployment, given existing or desired population size. This is more apposite in Canada's present situation, since immigration policy has become much more restrictive, and even so secular unemployment (i.e. the long-term rate) has risen steadily during the post–Second World War period.

Dales, presuming ceaseless population flows both in and out of the country, did not consider the question of whether job-creating policies would be necessary to prevent unemployment, given existing population size. Conceivably, he would endorse employment-shrinking policies so long as, by encouraging emigration, they raised per capita incomes; but he seems not to have faced this issue, remarking instead that if protectionism diminished, 'gross emigration would be smaller [than at time of writing, 1966] and gross immigration smaller still.'[33] In other words, Dales contemplated population growth at a rate less rapid than had previously obtained but not at a rate less rapid than natural increase would achieve. He foresaw, in these circumstances, a rising demand for labour that would be held in check by increases in wage rates. Had he presumed declining demand for labour relative to the size of the work-force, he would either have had explicitly to endorse emigration as a device for raising welfare – an attitude that I suspect relatively few Canadians would share – or he would have had to treat the national policy, given its employment-creating effects, as arguably a device for raising rather than lowering per capita incomes. (He did not do this, presumably because circumstances did not require him to consider the problem.) Or there is another possibility: he might have argued that the earlier employment-creating effects of the national policy existed because of special conditions obtaining in the late nineteenth century and during the first half of the twentieth and that changes in Canada's position in the world economy since the Second World War have transformed protectionism, in the present international context, into an employment-reducing policy.

CONCLUSION: ECONOMIC ARGUMENTS FOR POLITICAL INTEGRATION

Political integration is accomplished through various devices: by treaty providing for association of independent states and by political union – confederal, federal, or unitary. Since political decentralization facilitates accommodation of differences of taste, a presumption exists in favour of the minimal degree of political integration consistent with intended goals. These may be intrinsically political or expressive of community solidarity and community values; that is the case when union is required for purposes of defence, to implement a preferred public philosophy, or (consistently with a certain concept of citizenship) to establish some uniformity of individual entitlement and obligation vis-à-vis the collectivity. Realization of economic goals may also be prominent among the reasons for political integration.

In the latter case, it is common to argue that extension of markets increases efficiency in allocation of resources. This argument, however, supports only a very limited degree of political integration; if allocative efficiency is the nub of the case, its logic is to restrict the capacity of government, at whatever level, to interfere with and distort operation of markets. In Canada there has been a tendency to support reaffirmation or even extension of federal powers over the economy by referring to the benefits to be obtained through market integration. This is loading too much freight on an argument that is basically limited to supporting negative economic integration.

Positive integration, involving policy co-ordination or centralized policy control, can be justified only on the basis of arguments that support a degree of political control of the economy and demonstrate that, in the circumstances prevailing at the time, requisite forms of intervention in the economy are most effectively undertaken at the centre.

In Canada, the work of some economic historians – Innis and his school – does precisely these things, at least in the context of the mid or late nineteenth century. Other Canadian economic historians (Dales, Naylor) disagree. As we review this scholarly controversy, partly in light of some of the propositions worked out in the sub-discipline of welfare economics, it becomes evident that an interventionist state may be justified on any or all of the following grounds: that it increases consumption possibilities, that it increases stability, and that it helps reduce or avoid secular unemployment.

Even if one accepts that in the circumstances of the late nineteenth century an interventionist state was required, justifying a relatively centralized form of federalism, it is possible to hold that this is no longer true today. For example, the Macdonald Commission, the report of which will be discussed in the next (concluding) chapter, affirms that economic performance would improve if governments were less prone to exercise discretionary powers over the economy. A contrary argument, which we shall also be reviewing, affirms that in today's world trading environment, and given the internationalization of production processes and capital flows, only a new partnership of government and business can effectively support realization of Canada's economic goals, raising consumption possibilities, reducing vulnerability to external shocks, and counteracting tendencies to secular unemployment. It is this argument, calling (though not necessarily in so many words) for a third national policy, that supports the idea of a federation in which the central government exercises extensive powers over the economy.

9

Economic policy,
politics, and
the constitution

The National Policy of 1879 has played itself out.

Macdonald Commission[1]

This, the concluding chapter of my study, explores the interplay among economic policy, politics, and the constitution. It does so with reference to three major policy orientations:

a liberal or market-reinforcing policy, which necessarily (in the Canadian context) has strong continentalist implications;
a provincially oriented and provincially directed policy, or one that proposes minimal interference in the market by the central government while prescribing provincial interventionism to channel and promote economic development of the regions ('as the regions strengthen, the country strengthens'); and
a policy in which the central government takes the lead in shaping national and regional economic development, subject to constraints imposed by the market and by foreign governments, with the provincial governments playing a complementary and supporting role.

Obviously, if the central government is to play the leading role in devising and implementing a national policy, or overall development strategy for Canada, extensive federal powers over the economy are required. For those who are persuaded that such a national policy is desirable, the question arises whether the existing range of federal powers is adequate to the purpose. Also: can federal politicians mobilize the requisite political support for a preferred development strategy? And what impact would the attempt to devise and implement a national policy have on the Canadian political system? The pertinence of these questions is obvious in the case of an interventionist-nationalist policy orientation, but similar questions also arise with reference to the liberal-continentalist and the interventionist-provincialist orientations. Hence it is useful, as is done in this chapter, to block out the political and constitutional preconditions of each of the three policy orientations we have identified and also to explore their political and constitutional consequences.

THE LIBERAL-CONTINENTALIST OPTION

The liberal-continentalist option calls for minimal government interference in the market as a mechanism for allocating economic resources. Its supporters insist that government should limit itself to those forms of intervention that are strictly neutral in relation to various sectors, industries, and firms – and therefore also in relation to the regions. This option holds pride of place in Canada today, in the sense that much political rhetoric voices it, some policies are clearly inspired by it, most business opinion is ranged in its favour, and intellectually it is supported by an overwhelming majority of the economics profession. It has received comprehensive formulation, and qualified endorsement, in the report of the Macdonald Commission: the report, while making some gestures toward the interventionist-provincialist position, adopts mainly a liberal-continentalist line. Its principal recommendations have the persuasive quality that come from the internal coherence of the supporting arguments. Thus our own examination of the liberal-continentalist option is conveniently based on a review of the Macdonald report.

The most striking feature of the report is not the single recommendation for a Canadian-US free trade agreement (coupled with the assertion that the original, protectionist national policy has 'played itself out') but the conviction that Canada would be much better off without a national policy at all. The market must be given free rein to shape Canadian economic development:

Most Canadians are naturally inclined to believe that our federal and provincial governments ought to be able to co-ordinate their activities so as to give our industries the competitive edge they need to compete effectively both in domestic and in international markets. That degree of co-ordination might take place in a rational world, but, in its extreme form, it would also constitute a basic denial of the genius of the market economy. To select those areas in which we presume ourselves to have a comparative advantage over other countries is to assume that governments are as able as markets, if not more so, to judge the rapid changes taking place globally in consumer demands and production processes. This is an assumption that belies experience.[2]

In other words, the commission concluded that it is counterproductive to attempt to control or direct economic development, even if the intent is to identify the direction in which market forces are leading the country and to work for the restructuring of the economy accordingly. The commissioners believed that it is better not to try to guess where the market is headed; the best policy is to expose Canadian industry to the discipline of the international market-place, while reducing to a minimum all impediments to adaptation and adjustment. Economic resources – labour, capital, and natural resources – will be most efficiently allocated if government opens up the frontiers, liberalizing capital flows and trade, both in services and in goods. In a nutshell: 'Free trade is the main instrument in this Commission's approach to industrial policy.'[3]

However, government should not, according to the commission, simply expose Canadian industry to the chill winds of international competition and then stand aside. Government has responsibility for devising and implementing an industrial policy the aims of which are to achieve 'enhanced productivity growth and a stronger competitive position.' While these objectives may be supported by establishing 'a steadier framework for private decision making and investment policy,' government must actively facilitate redeployment of the resources of declining industries into 'more productive industrial enterprises.' The clearest instance of this is probably the TAAP, or 'Transitional Adjustment Assistance Program,' a proposed mechanism for developing employment-related skills and for promoting labour-force mobility. Its key feature is that it would be geared to the needs of employees in declining industries, not to firms; indeed, entitlements would be based on displaced individuals' willingness to undertake adaptive behaviour; it would be more a trampoline than a cushion. The same overall thrust is evident in all major components of industrial policy. Regional development programs, education and training, labour-management relations policy, the taxation system, and the treatment of foreign investment are all to be geared to support resource allocation through the market. The guiding principle is that government should step in only in cases of 'market failure,' that is, when the market would misallocate resources because society's cost-benefit ratios differ from private ones: 'It is only in the case of very serious market failings that intervention is likely to be at all helpful ... Intervention should be considered only if it is likely to improve the allocation of resources.' However, this is not laissez-faire, because (one infers) market failure is a not uncommon phenomenon. This justifies the commissioners in asserting that they 'do not favour a strictly hands-off approach' but merely 'a more neutral policy.'[4]

The more neutral policy favoured by the commission has strongly continentalist implications that are not only acknowledged in the report but encapsulated in the recommendation that has received widest attention, the proposal for negotiating a free trade agreement with the United States. 'The principle of comparative advantage,' the commission wrote, 'must be the primary determinant of our position in the international division of labour. Commissioners advocate a greater reliance on international market forces to determine the evolution of the economy in the future than has been true in the past.'[5] And because Canada relies so heavily on the United States as an outlet for Canadian goods and as a source of investment funds and technology, first priority must be given to stabilizing our economic relations with the United States through a free trade agreement and a mainly open-border policy on foreign investment. Thus the commission acknowledged the obvious: that the first consequence of liberalization is North American economic integration, or continentalism.

Some essential constitutional and political preconditions of the liberal-continentalist option appear to be lacking. Because taxing and spending powers are largely concurrent in Canada, it is very difficult to restrict or restrain the role of government in the economy. Suppose, for example, that the federal minister of finance were to decide that the size of the public sector, at 48 per cent of GNP, is too great. Even assuming that he could crimp federal expenditures, he could do nothing to stop the provinces from expanding theirs; only a co-ordinated federal-provincial policy could realize the desired objective. The same is true for more specific types of expenditure: government procurement, investment subsidies (grants or loans), public or mixed enterprise (equity participation), transportation or other development expenditures, and investment in public utilities such as generation of electrical power. All these forms of expenditure can be and typically are used by both federal and provincial orders of government to stimulate development or expansion of certain industries and to bail out faltering firms. If what is desired is a market-enhancing or non-targeted industrial policy, both orders of government must somehow be persuaded to restrain themselves from playing favourites with the public purse and also to avoid regulatory activities and 'tax expenditures' having similar effect. While the constitution gives the federal government exclusive power to regulate interprovincial and international trade and commerce, and thus restricts the range of regulatory activities undertaken by the provinces, it scarcely limits provincial discretionary spending or tax expenditures. Thus under the constitution neither the federal government nor the courts can do much to stop the provinces from altering the market allocation of economic resources.

This fact received a limited degree of public attention in the late 1970s and early 1980s in the context of the 'Canadian common market' debate. Interprovincial barriers to the movement of goods, services, capital, and labour were decried by some businessmen and quite a few economists and were the subject of a 1980 federal position paper entitled *Securing the Canadian Economic Union in the Constitution*. By the mid-1980s concern over fragmentation of the Canadian market had declined somewhat, at least in government and among economists, who now estimated that the costs of internal barriers were slight. Their attention had already shifted to the international scene; concern now focused on the danger that the provinces might interfere with the project for US free trade. It became urgent to consider how the provinces could be restrained from erecting non-tariff barriers to trade and interfering with the operation of capital markets, on both of which subjects American negotiators could be expected to seek assurances. No significant progress has been made on this subject, where wishful thinking has been much more in evidence than clear reasoning. It has been known since the Labour Conventions case in 1937 that the federal government lacks the power to enforce treaties in areas of provincial jurisdiction, though it alone may negotiate and enter into them. Provincial powers cannot be overridden simply by making an international agreement in an area of provincial jurisdiction.[6]

The Macdonald Commission, recognizing this, proposed that the provinces be fully involved in negotiating a trade agreement, supposing that if they were party to the process from the beginning they would agree to be bound by the results. The premiers, all of whom, except Ontario's David Peterson, have ranged themselves in favour of an agreement, have strongly given this impression; federal spokesmen have avoided the issue, while assuring the provinces that they will be fully consulted. No government spokesman, to my knowledge, has publicly addressed the problem of what will happen if an agreement is negotiated that one or more of the larger provinces rejects as failing to achieve essential objectives or as entailing unacceptable restrictions on the province's exercise of its economic powers. This, in my opinion, is the most likely outcome, if an agreement is negotiated at all. There is simply no available mechanism to constrain a province to observe the terms of a treaty or other agreement to which it does not willingly assent. A province could give effect to a treaty through legislation, but no constitutional mechanism is available to force it to pass the legislation or to refrain from amending, nullifying, or perhaps simply disregarding it in the future (say, after a change in government, or a change in heart).

The Macdonald Commission has put forward the suggestion that, eventually, there might be a constitutional amendment establishing a mechanism for ratifying and enforcing treaties that infringe upon provincial powers.[7] The suggestion was that the general formula for constitutional amendments might be applied to such treaties: approval by Parliament and by the legislatures of two-thirds of the provinces covering at least one-half of the population. (Assent once given could not subsequently be withdrawn by a province, though presumably the government of Canada would retain the power to denounce a treaty, which it would be likely to do only after obtaining approval of Parliament.) Where this formula would differ from the one now applying to most constitutional amendments is that a non-agreeing province would not be able to avail itself of the opting-out provision in section 38 of the 1982 Constitution Act, according to which an amendment infringing upon the legislative powers or prejudicially affecting the proprietary rights of the province is without effect if the legislature so resolves. A treaty-implementation clause such as was proposed – for some indefinite future time – by the Macdonald Commission would indeed establish the necessary mechanism for ensuring its enforcement. However, the ratification procedure would be difficult successfully to invoke. Moreover, to create it would require unanimity, since it would be tantamount to changing the amending formula itself. It is hard to imagine circumstances in which the provinces would agree to forgo the guarantees they fought so hard to have written into the 1982 Constitution Act.

The conclusion seems inescapable: an essential constitutional precondition of the liberal-continentalist option for economic policy is missing. The constitution sets up obstacles, probably insurmountable, to curbing or constraining provincial activities that impinge upon market allocation of economic resources. Unless there is a constitutional amendment, eleven governments, not one, must become convinced that market allocation of economic resources works best and must adhere to this principle. This, then, raises a new question: if the political will is strong enough, might not constitutional impediments be overcome? Here we enter upon highly speculative ground, but the possibility does seem remote. The Macdonald Commission carefully avoids claiming that its policy prescriptions would raise employment, and it does not discuss the desirability of diversifying the industrial structure in order to improve stability (reduce Canada's vulnerability to external shocks). Its recommendations make few concessions to the fact that public tolerance of government inaction in the face of severe economic problems is very low. Moreover, when we consider the international aspect of economic liberalism, and specifically the proposal for US free trade, the opposition of the labour movement is palpable. Thus it is hard to imagine circumstances in which political support for liberal-continentalism reaches the proportions needed to overwhelm constitutional obstacles. Nonetheless, should there occur a dramatic, irresistible increase in public support for market-oriented policies, it might become legitimate for the central government to start cudgelling non-co-operating provinces. It could do this by making all fiscal transfers discretionary and by withholding them from recalcitrant provinces. More generally, it might start linking together a number of federal-provincial issues that hitherto have been regarded as distinct. This is, however, something that could happen only if public opinion threw its weight solidly behind the gutting of provincial powers.

For these reasons even a moderately consistent policy of economic liberalism, with its attendant continentalism, appears unlikely. A more credible scenario could be continentalism together with those elements of economic liberalism, or neo-conservativism, obtaining in the United States. Both federal and provincial governments may be induced to align their policies with American ones. Indeed, a logic of policy harmonization may come into play when a small state ('B') lives in the economic shadow of a large neighbour ('A'), if A decides that its own rules define the norms of 'fair trade' (as appears increasingly to be the case with the United States). On the one hand, B may be induced to avoid policies that favour domestic producers, since those policies may be futile: they may be used by A to justify its imposing countervailing duties or otherwise engaging in forms of contingent protectionism if B's producers do not limit their ambitions to their domestic market. On the other hand, B may also be induced to avoid policies that impose costs on domestic producers if A does not impose similar costs on its own firms: thus may arise a tendency for B to mimic A not only in the overall level but also in the form of taxation, regulation, and industrial assistance policies. How powerful this logic is or may become in the Canadian-US case we have yet to learn. Perhaps the most ominous thing about this situation, which threatens Canada's economic independence, is that the logic of policy harmonization can be compelling even in the absence of any formal trade agreement. Indeed – though one hears nothing of this in the Canadian debate over free trade – it is conceivable that a trade agreement might, by defining permissible forms of government intervention in the economy (in both countries), actually augment rather than diminish Canadian policy-makers' freedom of manoeuvre.

These speculations are partly about factors that may induce Canadian governments to adopt a strongly continentalist policy orientation and a certain degree of economic liberalism, but they are also about political and (in a broad sense) constitutional implications of these policy tendencies. Formal constitutional powers are hollow when they cannot practically be exercised, whether because fiscal resources are lacking, as occurs with some of the provinces, or because an external agent wields de facto control. Canada's close economic relationship with the United States may, if and as that country becomes more protectionist, limit the real scope of the trade and commerce power, of the several clauses of the constitution relating to banking and finance, of the property and civil rights clause, of taxing powers, and of the various powers relating to design of social policy. Whether the constraints are likely to be more pervasive in relation to federal or provincial areas of jurisdiction is difficult to say and perhaps may not matter. But it is certainly time that Canadians started to think a lot harder and more systematically about the real scope of their political and economic independence, quite apart from the question of US free trade and the more traditional 'sovereignty' issues pertaining to military alliances, navigation in the Arctic seas, and the extraterritorial application of US law.

To conclude this section: if Canadian economic policy moves toward economic liberalism or neoconservatism, the likely cause would be that US protectionism, in combination with fiscal constraint – itself traceable in part to inability to impose taxes 'too high' above US levels – prod us in this direction. We are less likely to choose it for ourselves, through the internal dynamic of the Canadian political process. To say this is not to suggest that 'downsizing the public sector' or curbing government economic regulation has insignificant appeal in Canada, for that manifestly is not the case. However, state interventionism has a powerful tradition behind it in Canada, and even those governments that most frequently declare their commitment to the free enterprise economy complement and support private-sector activities with a view to expanding consumption possibilities, increasing stability, and creating jobs. Since a policy of non-intervention cannot be implemented except by joint resolve of federal and provincial governments, any overall shrinking of the economic role of the state seems unlikely to occur except as a result of, and to the extent required by, budgetary deficits and external pressure. Within these constraints, the overall thrust of economic policy is likely to be interventionist. Whether primary responsibility for economic development policies is assumed by the provinces or by the federal government is, in this situation, a vital question.

THE INTERVENTIONIST-PROVINCIALIST OPTION

The Macdonald Commissioners came close to inverting a principle that was supposed to guide their work, namely that: 'The Government of Canada has the primary responsibility for managing the national economy, for encouraging reasonably balanced economic growth among the various regions of the country and for ensuring that fiscal disparities among provinces are reduced, while at the same time the provincial governments also have important responsibilities in the development and carrying out of economic and social policy.'[8]

It is instructive to compare this statement, drawn from the commission's terms of reference, with the four-fold role that it prescribed for the federal government: to be primarily responsible for Canada's presence in the international world, to be the advocate and catalyst for effective functioning of the economic union, to be primarily responsible for stabilization policy, and to be primarily responsible for redistribution between regions and provinces, between social and economic interests, and among individual citizens. The commission also emphasized that the federal role in all these areas is not exclusive and suggested that 'federal activity in management of the economy does not preclude provincial involvement; ... [it] can set a tone, establish priorities and promote new ideas or approaches, ... can provide economic leadership that alters the climate of ideas within which both orders of government act, ... [and] can act as a catalyst and innovator without designing and delivering programs.' In a nutshell: 'The federal task is to provide a unified national framework for private economic activity and provincial activities to encourage economic development.' In other words, the framework is federal, the context is continental, and the agents are private industry and the provincial governments. Insofar as it is appropriate for government to alter the play of market forces, it would appear that the provinces are to have the active role.[9]

The most telling insight on this question probably comes from examining what the commission had to say about regional development, a policy objective to which it ascribes considerable importance. The topic is introduced with the remark that 'there may be [is?] a short-term trade-off between regional development and national income, [but] there need not be in the long run. To the extent that regions underemploy resources, those resources are not contributing their full potential to national output. The national economy will be stronger to the extent that each region develops its potential.' (Interestingly, the distinction between short-run and long-run considerations, and the derivative argument for developmental policies, did not intrude upon the commissioners' thought processes in the context of the operation of the international economy, where trade liberalization was the dominant policy prescription. It is thus ironic, to say the least, that the report states: 'The federal government has been unable to form a satisfactory link between its regional development responsibilities and its broader role in managing our national economy.')[10]

After a back-and-forth argument that nicely illustrates the conundrums with which regional development policies must deal, the commissioners conclude that 'Our national government's responsibility should be to work to remove differences in labour productivity across regions and any factors that impair the efficient operation of regional labour markets,' a recommendation that brings regional development under the rubric of governmental responsibility 'to correct for market failures of whatever origin.' This limited form of regional development policy was judged desirable in that it would even out productivity levels across the land and therefore even out wages; but the commissioners acknowledged that it would not serve to buoy up employment in regions where the labour-saving bias in productivity improvement is strong and the scope for capturing new markets weak.[11]

Apparently the federal government should do nothing to affect interregional or interprovincial migration patterns:

It is at this point that Commissioners introduce a sharp distinction between federal and provincial functions in regional economic development. The federal government, we wish to suggest, should not involve itself directly in regional job creation. Its responsibilities end with its commitment to overcome regional productivity gaps and labour-market imperfections ... Provincial governments and their electorates typically want more than this from economic policies. Specifically, they have absolute employment targets as well ... Community preservation, to the extent that people want it, is ultimately the responsibility of citizens and of their local and provincial governments. The federal government must not stand in the way of achieving that goal, in the sense that its economic and social policies must not consistently discriminate against particular groups, but neither need it devote resources directly to meet that goal. Provinces, however, must have access to such funds and be free to use them in this manner if they so desire.[12]

In this context, the report recommends that provinces receiving equalization payments should also receive Regional Economic Development Grants from the federal government and that the total federal financial commitment to regional development should increase significantly over the next few years. While the federal government would have a hand, through a set of Economic and Regional Development Agreements, in designing the programs thus funded,[13] it would appear that the commissioners thought that the lead role should be assumed by the provinces.

Perhaps the commissioners thought that with an increased federal financial commitment to regional development, the poorer provinces might be enabled to stimulate and channel the growth of their economies, in roughly the manner that some of the resource-rich provinces have attempted to do. In reflecting on this, we should consider the cases of Alberta and Saskatchewan, as analysed by John Richards and Larry Pratt, in their book *Prairie Capitalism*.[14]

Richards and Pratt have traced how control over resources – stemming from provincial legislative powers and from provincial ownership of crown lands, of mines, and of energy resources – has enabled Saskatchewan and Alberta to play a significant role in overall economic development. The tradition of prairie populism, with its habits of self-reliance and its grievances against the dominance of eastern financial and manufacturing interests, predisposed these provinces to action; but the factor that, more than any other, led to the emergence of an indigenous, state-supported entrepreneurship was experience in controlling resource development. Regulation with a view to conservation of the resource base, which had the support of private-sector interests, eventually gave these governments the expertise and the self-confidence to challenge these same private-sector interests for a larger share of economic rents (or above-normal rates of return to investment) and eventually to foster indigenous entrepreneurship, whether through public enterprise (Saskatchewan) or through 'state-induced and subsidized industrialization' managed by the private sector (Alberta).[15]

The objectives of the interventionist economic policies analysed by Richards and Pratt have been roughly those identified in the preceding chapter. The conservation of resources and the restructuring of royalty systems and corporate taxation have been aimed at augmenting net provincial product, or per capita real incomes, enabling those provinces to offer a high standard of public services at lower rates of taxation than would otherwise have been possible. Another aim, perhaps of even greater importance, has been to diversify the provincial economy in order to reduce its vulnerability to the fluctuations in demand and prices to which a resource-based economy – especially one heavily reliant upon a single commodity – is inevitably exposed. The strategy here has been to develop new resource industries and especially to process (as much as possible) resources within the province, close to source. Thus both Alberta and Saskatchewan have worked hard to expand the manufacturing and service sectors, diversifying an economy originally based on agriculture, both expanding job opportunities and reducing swings in the level of employment.

One of the most interesting features of the argument presented by Richards and Pratt is their emphasis on the efficacy of provincial government action in defending the interests of hinterland areas against exploitation by metropolitan interests, whether those of central Canada or those located in the United States. In this respect they forthrightly challenge the political centralism that has been predominant among Canadian economic nationalists, especially those of socialist persuasion. Within such circles it has commonly been thought that federalism, by fragmenting political power, has weakened Canada's capacity to defend its interests against American domination and exploitation. Richards and Pratt's study of post-war Alberta and Saskatchewan led them to assert that the 'left-nationalist' school has 'underestimated the entrepreneurial role, past and present, of the provincial state in English Canada, ... [has drawn] unwarranted generalizations that economic specialization upon staple products inevitably implied political dependency of that region upon the "metropolis" to which it exported, and finally, [has] generally underestimated the autonomy of the state in Canada, notably in its relationship to foreign capital.' They add, later:

We find no confirmation of the thesis that provinces heavily dependent on the exploitation and sale of staples are thereby placed in a permanent position of political dependency vis-à-vis external capital ... Within the context of a changing balance of bargaining power, conflicts arise among the provinces, federal government, and the international firm over the distribution of rents, pricing, and rates of development; or over the regional impact of the investor's operation. What begins as a relatively simple and highly unequal, often exploitative relationship evolves into a much more complex pattern of relations as the provincial government moves up a learning curve of skills and negotiating expertise and the foreign company faces the steady erosion of its monopoly power.[16]

While Richards and Pratt clearly state, 'We have forsworn any temptation to extend this analysis to the other western provinces, let alone to all ten,' there do appear to be analogues in some of the other provinces. H.V. Nelles has written of 'the politics of development' in turn-of-the-century Ontario, in which the province successfully sought to create a 'manufacturing condition' based on resource exploitation, especially where the resources in question were publicly controlled (minerals, lumber, and pulpwood from crown lands; water for hydroelectric power). British Columbia has followed a similar strategy, involving massive state support for gigantic development projects (electricity, coal), though one may doubt whether its policies have asserted or even seriously sought to achieve indigenous control over resource development, in opposition to external interests, or whether diversification has been much in mind. The case of Newfoundland is much clearer, at least as regards intent, though its bargaining power over external agents – whether foreign capital or central Canadian interests – has been slight.[17]

Perhaps the copybook example of province-led development, however, is Quebec, which appears today to be the most entrepreneurial of the provinces. There a territorial interest in resisting dependency and outgrowing a 'rentier mentality' (one of Richards and Pratt's favourite phrases) has been conjoined with the interest of the francophone population in outgrowing its inferior economic status in relation to the anglophones. The province's development strategy rests partly on resource exploitation, particularly hydroelectricity, and partly on state-supported development of the manufacturing and service sectors, stressing a high degree of indigenous financial control and technological innovation. While it is quite possible to interpret some of these policies as 'investments in ethnicity'[18] promotion of francophone interests appears to win public acceptance as a goal that is congruent with broader social goals: job creation (and not just for the professional and managerial classes), economic stability, and the raising of income levels or consumption possibilities.

We now have enough information to return to our main subject: the preconditions for the interventionist-provincialist policy stance, as well as the political and constitutional consequences of this option. On the matter of preconditions the key observation to make is that the provinces probably do have adequate constitutional powers to play the lead role in economic development if political conditions and financial resources permit. This, I think, is one of the lessons of the analysis by Richards and Pratt, in spite of their study being limited to two provinces. Although (writing in the late 1970s) they pointed to some possible constitutional obstacles to provincial control over resource development, amendments made to the Constitution Act in 1982 have extended provincial powers in this area. These powers are limited by provisions designed to retain and affirm Ottawa's exclusive jurisdiction over international trade and to preserve the economic union (a province cannot discriminate in favour of its own residents or resident firms, either in terms of price or access to supplies); however, subject to these important qualifications, and to the federal government's capacity to capture a share of resource rents through taxation, the provinces do have adequate powers to implement an economic development strategy based on resource production.

A wide range of constitutional provisions is relevant here: the proprietary rights vested in the provinces (though these have, in some cases, been sold to the private sector); regulatory powers in relation to resources; and several other powers not directly bearing on resources or resource management. Most of these powers overlap with federal powers. The provinces not only have broad taxing and spending powers, they also have extensive powers in relation to key financial institutions and processes (trust companies and credit unions, insurance, and securities regulation), competition policy, transportation, including (by delegation) interprovincial trucking, industrial relations, environmental issues, agriculture, occupational safety, and land use. Because these powers mesh with areas of federal jurisdiction, as described in chapters 4 and 5, the provinces do not have sole authority in these fields, but if federal policies do not conflict with provincial ones – and even more, if federal policy leaves the provinces with the lead role – the constitutional preconditions for an interventionist-provincialist policy thrust are indeed in place.

What about the political preconditions? Richards and Pratt, who of course took pains to acknowledge the importance of having a rich resource base as well as the constitutional powers to control resource development, parted company with the economic determinists in stressing how much 'politics matters.' They wrote: 'Since the Second World War the central problem of development in Saskatchewan and Alberta has been whether or not the governments of these provinces could, with the passage of years and the appearance of a favourable political climate, mobilize the requisite will, expertise, and power to break with their inglorious rentier traditions. In turn, their ability to do this has depended crucially on the outcome of political debates and conflicts.' Here they were referring to political debates and conflicts internal to the provinces in question, where the emergence of an urban middle class and its rise to a politically controlling position was seen as an essential step toward acquiring any significant degree of indigenous control over economic development. As long as the provinces remained dominantly agrarian they could neither mobilize the skills needed for challenging established economic elites in central Canada and in the United States nor outgrow the populism that animated the farmers' movements while limiting the mental horizons of their leaders.[19]

Agreed. However, the political debates and conflicts that must be won if the provinces are to play the lead role in promoting and controlling economic development (that is, if the interventionist-provincialist option is to hold sway) are not merely internal to the provinces individually, and especially not to the resource-rich provinces alone. Given the extent of overlapping powers over the economy, political debates in the federal arena and therefore across the country as a whole are relevant. Richards and Pratt were concerned with the economic development of two hinterland provinces with interests that conflicted both with those of foreign capital and with those of central Canada, as promoted through the actions of the federal government.

In my opinion, even for the two provinces in question, Richards and Pratt did not sufficiently appreciate the federal government's ability to frustrate and to counter provincial development policies and therefore did not reflect upon the factors shaping federal policies. They assumed, as they had some warrant to do in the context of the late 1970s and would have had even more reason to do in the early 1980s, a straightforwardly adversarial relationship between Ottawa and the two provincial governments of concern to them. One of the tasks that they set themselves was to determine how effectively provincial governments could assert provincial interests in the context of such an adversarial relationship. Clearly some federal policies were restrictive and, from a prairie perspective, predatory; these policies were the target of provincial action, based on ownership and partial regulatory control over resources, to counteract and neutralize them.

The National Energy Program demonstrated that the federal government has regulatory and taxing powers adequate to counterbalance and partially to override provincial policies over economic development, even in the resources sector, provided that it considers that circumstances justify its doing so and provided that it has the requisite political strength and will. The powers in question were left intact by the resources clause (section 92A) of the Constitution Act, inserted in

1982. In effect, the federal government must be willing to follow a policy of non-interference in relation to provincial development strategies, if the provinces are to wrest control from external economic elites and generally to play the active role that the Macdonald Commission was willing to concede them. Thus the constitutional prerequisites of the interventionist-provincialist option shade off (as typically happens across the whole range of constitutional powers) into the political ones. Public opinion across the whole country, and the attitudes of political leaders in every province and from every region, are important.

In this connection we may observe that political support for provincially directed development strategies may be limited by several considerations. First, resource-based development strategies are broadly unhelpful for those regions or provinces without resource endowments rich enough to generate substantial economic rents or for which the resources sector (production of raw materials, and primary manufacturing) is counterbalanced or outweighed by strength of secondary manufacturing and the tertiary sector. Thus its appeal, while not limited to resource-rich provinces, is strongest there and falls away elsewhere. Second, provinces with resource-based economies remain vulnerable to shifts in international market conditions and to shifts in policy in the United States and other major trading nations or blocs and thus cannot by their own actions significantly diminish the economic instability that characterizes hinterland regions. To the extent that a resource-dependent province is worried about the instability of its economy, it may welcome 'safety-net' policies implemented by Ottawa.

Third, when resource development generates high rents, and especially when the province is successful in claiming a substantial share of the rents, diversification is difficult and may not be achievable at all because the very prosperity of the resources sector militates against the development of unrelated activities. This is illustrated by Alberta's recent experience, where the oil and gas boom intensified rather than diminished the province's reliance on the petroleum industry, in spite of efforts of the provincial government to the contrary. The high wages and the real estate booms that typically accompany headlong growth in the resources sector apparently increase the cost of general industrial development.

Fourth and finally – and flowing from the three considerations just referred to – the experience of boom and bust may lead people even in the most resource-rich provinces to view themselves as dependent upon the policies of foreign governments over the decisions of which they can have no impact other than by bargaining. In boom times it may be attractive to barter, as Alberta did, US access to resources against its own access to US markets for industrial products,[20] but when resource prices slump, alleviation of economic distress can come only from stabilizing policies of the Canadian federal government. This way of viewing the issues appears to have made relatively little headway in Alberta, though it is not absent among independent petroleum producers (the small firms); in Saskatchewan it may be more prevalent.

In sum, while in those provinces that are best able to rely upon their resource wealth the interventionist-provincialist policy orientation may have wide support, the intensity of that support may fluctuate with resource prices; elsewhere, the federal government may find encouragement for implementing policies that limit the scope or effectiveness of provincial development strategies. It therefore remains an open question whether, across time and across the regions, there is or will develop an adequate political base for a sector-neutral federal policy that is deliberately adhered to so that the provinces may actively engage, within the framework of federal policy and international trading rules, in policies to channel and direct their own economic development. In other words the political preconditions for the interventionist-provincialist option may not obtain.

The constitutional and political implications of the interventionist-provincialist option are difficult to predict but do deserve at least brief discussion. The first point to make is that powers left unexercised eventually become a dead letter. Legitimacy and political support are needed to wield even those policy instruments that from the legal-constitutional point of view a government possesses. If, over time, the federal government were to refrain from using certain powers conferred upon it by the Constitution Act, limiting itself to the sector-neutral 'framework' policies prescribed by the Macdonald Commission, the powers themselves would atrophy like disused muscles.

For those who would like to see government play a less active role in the economy than it has done in the past, this may be an attractive prospect, but it may entail dangers unsuspected by those whose mental habits have been formed more by economics than by political economy. The Macdonald Commissioners evidently allowed themselves to be persuaded by such people. Thus the political risks entailed by the policies that they recommended appear not to have been recognized (or at least not taken seriously) by the commission, which largely neglected to investigate the political context of economic policy formation. The commissioners evidently did not consider that curtailing the economic role of the federal government, while conceding a more active role to the provinces, might weaken it politically; and they did not stop to think that a politically weakened federal government might be ineffectual in meeting the responsibilities that they did prescribe for it: to mediate between 'the international world' and domestic economic and political life (negotiate and ratify treaties, co-ordinate federal and provincial activities abroad, and manage the domestic adjustments that follow from international acitvities),[21] to preserve the economic union, to stabilize the economy, and to redistribute wealth interregionally and otherwise (always, in conjunction with the provinces).

The commissioners' neglect of the political ramifications of their assignment of policy roles is a major flaw in the report. They clearly knew that the public had expectations of government, and supported a degree of government involvement in the economy, that they themselves chose to reject. Their rejection was categorical for the federal government and qualified for the provinces. (Perhaps, though, they did not really expect the provinces to be much more interventionist than the federal government, since the provinces' activities would be constrained by the hoped-for trade agreement with the United States, one by-product of which would be to force Canadians to observe more faithfully the principles of the domestic economic union.) The approach that they recommended, whether justified or not by contemporary economic theory, sidestepped the question of political legitimacy in a context where government, especially the federal government, would in effect be telling the electorate that its expectations were inflated and unreasonable.

A federal government that followed the commission's recommendations could scarcely avoid appearing unconcerned about problems that people experience every day. Unemployment is the persistent, classic, painful case. The commission regarded it as 'largely a cyclical problem ... best resolved through the traditional tools of demand-management policy, [although] complementary industrial and related adjustment policies could help to accelerate the creation of new jobs.' Surely it is a sign of political naïveté that the commission proposed adjustment-facilitating policies for Ottawa and (regional) development – employment-generating – policies for the provinces. Even within the context of a strictly economic analysis, it is puzzling that the commission steadfastly refused to follow the trail blazed by John Dales, when he explored employment effects of the tariff. It would have been useful if the commission, rather than ignoring Dales' work, had built upon it, undertaking a broad inquiry into the employment effects of protectionism in general, including subsidies, as well as non-protectionist forms of industrial policy or development policy.[22]

But the commissioners were evidently not thinking along these lines. Perhaps the most striking illustration of the boundaries that they established for themselves is that, while declaring that the old national policy had played itself out, they did not even discuss whether the historic role of the state in capital formation was now superfluous (or, conceivably, had been a mistake from the start). Although the terms of reference specifically instructed the commission to examine Canada's capital requirements – perhaps re-examining the estimates of the Major Projects Task Force, that $440 billion would be needed for resource development by the year 2000, and generating additional estimates for manufacturing and other sectors of the economy – the report makes no attempt to do these things. It suggests only that 'the main immediate concern ... is whether investment will recover quickly and sufficiently from its present cyclically weak level. If it does not, governments may need to induce more investment.'[23]

Once again, the statement illustrates the commission's rejection of the idea that the federal government should have anything to do with structuring the economy, whether the goal is to raise levels of employment, to reduce vulnerability to external economic 'shocks' (in prices, volume of demand, and availability of supplies), or to improve Canadians' standard of living. It wrote of the federal government's responsibility for 'mediating' Canada's relationships with the rest of the world rather than of its responsibility for asserting and defending Canadian economic interests against those of foreign countries, where the state has made itself the partner of business enterprise. Perhaps most strangely, it endorsed the principle of regional development, mainly through provincial initiatives supported by federal grants, but not a program of national economic development. Surely it is politically unrealistic to suppose that Ottawa could do for stagnating regions, by bankrolling provincial programs, what it abjures for the whole country.

It may be seriously doubted whether a federal government that accepts no responsibility for overall economic development, other than through framework policies, and (in the name of flexibility or speedy adjustment) refuses to underwrite the risks inherent in resource-intensive regional growth could legitimately mount programs to redistribute wealth interregionally. In the circumstances, such policies could scarcely be interpreted by the donor regions as anything but plunder. Politically, redistribution is likely to be much more acceptable, and indeed to have positive appeal, in conjunction with other policies having broad nation-building objectives, namely:

to support and encourage national economic development and, within this context, to aim for regionally balanced growth and in particular to support the development of those provinces disfavoured by poor resource endowments or locational factors; *to reduce* Canadians' vulnerability to shifts in policies of foreign governments or to changes in world-market conditions, not only 'on average,' but in all regions; *to assert and defend* the economic interests of Canada and its regions vis-à-vis other countries; and, in this three-fold context, *to support* the provision of public services on a broadly comparable level across the whole country.

These are policy responsibilities that only the federal government can shoulder. They call for a much more interventionist state than the Macdonald Commissioners were willing to contemplate. In short, they call for a national policy.

THE INTERVENTIONIST-NATIONALIST OPTION

The task of designing and implementing a national policy suited to the late twentieth century is a high-risk enterprise. However, Canada will be impelled to it if the alternatives, the liberal-continentalist option and the interventionist-provincialist option, are judged impractical or undesirable or both. The constitutional or the political preconditions for these options may not obtain, or indeed both may be lacking. Moreover, either their political or their constitutional implications (or both) may be unacceptable, given Canadian attitudes and values and the behaviour of foreign governments, particularly the United States. If these two options lose their lustre, a new phase of economic nationalism, in which the federal government takes the lead in shaping economic development while the provincial governments play a complementary and supporting role, may be born. Its inherent risks and disadvantages have recently steered Canada in a continentalist direction, but if this policy thrust loses momentum (or even more, if it fails spectacularly) the idea of a national policy may suddenly look attractive again.

An essential starting point for any useful discussion of this subject must be recognition that the old (or first) national policy has indeed, as the Macdonald Commission has urged, played itself out. Its characteristics were that government (especially the federal government) worked actively in tandem with both domestic capital and foreign investors to force the pace of growth in export-oriented resource sectors, for example by building transportation systems capable of handling high volumes of raw or semi-processed commodities, while also implementing a protectionist trade policy to build up and support a high-cost manufacturing sector oriented to the domestic market.

Both aspects of this policy have now become outmoded. First, the resource base is too weak, relative to some other countries, to sustain an economy the principal characteristic of which is the export of staple products. Second, it is no longer tolerable to have manufacturing and service sectors oriented almost exclusively to the domestic market. It is increasingly difficult, as a result of tariff reductions under the GATT, to follow a protectionist policy, and the costs of attempting to do so are probably rising with the growing sophistication of technology and the emergence of low-wage, high-quality producers of manufactures around the globe. There appears to be general agreement, except in the ranks of the threatened industries, that to try to preserve the sort of manufacturing industry built up under tariff protection is not a viable or certainly not an acceptable policy for Canada.

That major structural changes in the Canadian economy are needed and indeed cannot be avoided is not in doubt, but opinions clearly differ on the desirable role for government in promoting adjustment. The 'strict neutrality' prescription, for example as presented in the Macdonald report, is based on the presumption that businessmen are the people best equipped to size up economic opportunities and to exercise judgment about the ventures that make a good risk. Governments have a poor record at trying to second-guess the market, and when the state gets involved in large-scale ventures for economic development, the price of miscalculation runs high. (Development costs both in resource projects and in major manufacturing enterprises, aerospace for example, can easily reach into the billions.) Moreover, the argument continues, the potential for wasteful capital expenditure is higher for publicly backed projects than for ones financed uniquely from private sources, partly because cost control may be less stringent and partly because decisions may well be made with political objectives in mind as much as with the goal of obtaining a return on the investment.

The case for a more interventionist policy stance rests not on denial that these criticisms are valid but on the claim that other relevant factors are uniformly underplayed or ignored by those who hymn the virtues of the market. Proponents of an industrial strategy or a targeted industrial policy tend to frame their arguments to address problems concretely experienced by a specific national economy. In other words, the case for direct government involvement in structuring the economy is almost necessarily contingent upon the circumstances prevailing at the time and bearing upon the country in question. This is not to say that the arguments are uninformed by theory, only that the theory implicitly or explicitly lying behind them stresses the significance of structural and behavioural factors that most conventional economic analysis neglects. For example, Richard G. Harris writes, in a study for the Macdonald Commission (the recommendations of which the report explicitly rejects):

In addressing the issues of global competition and Canadian economic development, it is my opinion that the strict paradigm of neoclassical trade theory is not useful or accurate in its description for a substantial part of world trade and investment patterns ... The foundations for the 'alternative view' of the market system put forward in this study lie in recognition of the importance of market structures, including the many markets that are oligopolistic or monopolistic, and the importance of certain market failures in explaining trade, investment and their impact on the Canadian economy ... The main conclusion [of the study] is that a coherent industrial policy for Canada based on selected and limited forms of government action is crucial to sustaining long-term growth and employment while keeping the social risks of such a policy within acceptable limits.[24]

A non-targeted policy such as that subsequently proposed by the Macdonald Commission is not, according to Harris, adequate in the present context, which requires both development of new high-technology industries and state-promoted 'disinvestment ... in the case of Canadian industries which are already developed but cannot compete without protection from low-wage competition from abroad.' First, it is not politically realistic to suppose that organized labour or indeed the relevant provincial government would allow plant closures to occur if there are not, at the same time, positive and obvious steps being taken to put something else in their place: 'Failure to propose positive adjustment policies will only result in defensive protectionist policies which are the worst form of response.' Second, Canada has a small open economy in a world where leading industrial nations are engaging in technological competition. Outcomes will be heavily influenced by various forms of government subsidy; to ignore this fact and (as neoclassical trade theory does) the role of oligopolistic multinational firms in determining world trade patterns, especially non-market or intra-firm trade, is absurd. Thus, 'An active industrial policy is the optimal policy for a small country in response to the imposition of similar policies by other industrial nations,' especially in the context of declining employment opportunities in the primary sector and in traditional manufacturing industries.[25]

The Macdonald Commission proposed an industrial policy, too, but what Harris puts forward is considerably more far-reaching. For him, as in conventional usage, an industrial policy is 'some type of intervention in the market system which is not based on any of the standard arguments of market failure or public goods that economists like to resort to.' Substantively, Harris recommends (in addition to appropriate tax policies, manpower training, and other framework policies) the use of subsidies allocated on a discretionary, firm-by-firm basis to assist in resource development, to help weak or declining industries meet foreign competition, to promote creation or expansion of high-technology industries, and to influence location decisions. These suggestions will be familiar to readers of works on industrial strategy and economic nationalism.[26] However, there are two things that make Harris' study (so far as I know) unique. One is the systematic exposition of the justifying arguments in the context of contemporary economic theory, such that they are likely to gain the respect of the economics profession even if they do not convince many of its practitioners. The second is that his policy recommendations are avowedly non-protectionist; where most people have treated interventionism and free trade as policy alternatives, the whole thrust of Harris' study is to explore how they can be made complementary to each other and to show why indeed they must be. For him, any industrial policy not set in the context of open international competition and a welcoming stance to foreign capital (requiring 'national treatment' for foreign-owned firms) would be sub-optimal and indeed self-defeating.

The suggestion that Canada adopt a non-protectionist industrial policy raises an interesting set of political and constitutional as well as economic questions. A brief review of five related questions follows, concluding this book.

1. *Can protectionism be avoided; can a Canadian-us free trade agreement be combined with an interventionist or targeted industrial policy?* The goals of economic policy are to promote growth in average real income (i.e. to raise aggregate consumption possibilities), to achieve stability, and to minimize unemployment. Some would add: to bring about a consensually acceptable distribution of income – though this could also be classified as a political or social objective, rather than a strictly economic one.[27] There is a case to be made that at least some degree or certain forms of protectionism are necessary in order to diversify the economy (diversification presumably contributing to stability) and to buoy up employment; moreover, when people are out of work aggregate production and therefore average incomes will be lower than would be achieved under full employment. The economic and political issue here is essentially whether, or how quickly, unemployed resources can be transferred to alternative and more productive uses under a positive industrial policy (i.e. with an appropriate mix of prodding and assistance by government.) As Harris argues,

neoclassical theory underestimates how long adjustment is likely to take in the absence of an industrial policy, because it neglects to consider the role of the firm as an organization within which non-market transactions occur. In any case, adjustment always causes pain; the losses to workers whose skills are specific to the firm and industry will be irretrievable. It is therefore inevitable, for a variety of principled and pragmatic reasons, that the efficacy of a positive industrial policy, relative to protectionism, should become a subject of political controversy. The political appeal of protectionism may be irresistible.[28]

It may also prove impossible to combine, as Harris would like to do, free trade and an industrial policy of the kind that he envisions. A policy that is 'positive' or adjustment-promoting to Canadians may easily be viewed in the United States as negative or protectionist, in other words, as reducing competition in the domestic market and competing unfairly in foreign ones. This incongruence of perception on the two sides of the border may be great enough to wreck the negotiations. However, it may be possible to reach agreement on acceptable forms of government intervention in the economy. The United States, while vastly larger and more technologically advanced than Canada, also has basic industries that face severe competition from low-wage countries and may want to retain control over policy instruments that Canada too regards as essential to its national interests. There is probably not a single country in the world today that does not attempt to shield itself in some degree from the international environment, to support its manufacturing industry, to underwrite business risks or intervene to help firms weather a crisis, and to favour domestic over foreign capital.

On all sides, states preach the virtues of liberalizing trade and stabilizing the international economic order but cheat on both. This unedifying situation creates obstacles to both bilateral and multilateral trade negotiations but also impels states to undertake them. All can recognize that some forms of protection are more costly than others, both to the home country and to its trading partners. From this angle, what is needed, domestically, is resolve to achieve the politically unavoidable degree of protection in the least-cost form; internationally, states must work toward conventional definitions of 'protectionism' (inadmissible) and 'positive measures' (acceptable). To say so, of course, merely blocks out a large section of the agenda for international negotiation, perhaps first in the Canadian-US context and later in a multilateral one, refining and extending the present GATT subsidies code. Thus, while in a strict sense it may be impossible to combine free trade and an industrial policy, to adopt this as a goal may be a sensible, indeed the only defensible, course of action.

2. *In what senses, if at all, should an industrial policy be nationalist?* The policy thrust we are now discussing I have labelled interventionist-nationalist, mainly in order to distinguish it from an option in which the provinces, together with the private sector, are the active players within a federally established framework. In other words, the label was chosen to emphasize that the policy option now being

discussed is one in which the primary responsibility for an industrial policy is to lie with the federal government, while the provinces play a complementary and supporting role. However, the label also evokes the idea of economic nationalism, or the assertion and defence of Canadian economic interests vis-à-vis those of other countries. Not only the question of federal leadership but also the hoary issue of public policies toward foreign capital and the newer but related issue of Canadian investment abroad or the establishment of Canadian-based multinationals deserve our attention.

The case for federal leadership in formulating and implementing an industrial policy has already been stated in the context of our discussion of the interventionist-provincialist option. There it was argued that federal policies for the interregional redistribution of wealth are likely to be supported by public opinion to the extent that they are set in the context of other policies having broad nation-building objectives. One such objective is to support and encourage national economic development, aiming for regionally balanced growth. This necessarily is the fundamental goal of an industrial policy, a governmental response to situations inadequately portrayed by neoclassical models. There would be no logic in proposing that the federal government act as if the world were a neoclassical one, while the provinces are responsible for coping with problems cast up by the fact that it is not.

Other objectives, rounding out the fundamental one of promoting economic development nationally and regionally, are to reduce Canadians' vulnerability to external 'shocks', to compensate where possible for the disadvantages of smallness in an international economic system dominated by major players (i.e. by the giant multinationals and, on the governmental side, by powerful entities such as the United States, the European Community, and Japan), and to support the provision of public services on a broadly comparable level across the whole country. These are goals that the provinces may have little incentive to strive for or, if they do, are poorly placed to achieve. Such goals call for positive integration – formulation of common or co-ordinated policies among the provinces – necessarily under federal leadership if not always under federal direction.

Part of the rationale for an industrial policy, at least in Canada's case, is to minimize the disadvantages of smallness. From this perspective, an industrial policy cannot but be nationalist. This raises an interesting question: can an industrial policy be nationalist without being punitive or discriminatory toward foreign enterprise? I think it is recognized by all thoughtful participants in the 'foreign ownership' debate that foreign investment involves more than importation of capital. It typically also brings management skills and technology and may enhance access to foreign markets; but sometimes it inhibits exports, discourages development of new technologies or their adaptation to Canadian needs, and (since the apex of corporate hierarchies is located abroad) results in the outflow of managerial talent. Intrafirm transactions may be advantageous to Canada or may impose costs on this country through 'transfer pricing' (the purchase of management services or technology by Canadian subsidiaries at an inflated fee or the sale of goods produced by the subsidiary at prices below those probably obtainable in a market transaction). Employment effects may be positive or negative, depending on whether the subsidiary purchases its inputs domestically or abroad.[29]

This complex mix of advantages and disadvantages has made the foreign ownership issue a controversial one, with many Canadians adopting an ambivalent position; policy has wobbled. The main institutional response, the Foreign Investment Review Agency (FIRA – now called Investment Canada, to emphasize a more positive attitude toward foreign investment), was assigned responsibility for 'screening' foreign investment projects including takeovers and mergers, approving those considered to provide a net benefit to Canada and imposing, where judged appropriate, conditions on operation of the firms in question. FIRA's critics, who were many, complained that it was illegitimate to adopt a policy stance toward firms on the basis of ownership or control; and the United States has complained sharply – in the context both of FIRA's operations and of policies such as the National Energy Program – about infringements of the principle of 'national treatment' for foreign firms. It probably is, as the critics have urged, self-defeating as well as unfair to accept foreign investment but to insist that foreign-owned or foreign-controlled firms operate under different rules from those applying to Canadian ones.

It is also hard, however, to justify, in the context of an industrial policy implemented in part through negotiated agreements with individual firms, the principle that government should be completely blind to ownership. To the extent that firms become instruments of national policy, it would be illogical to place foreign firms on a par with domestic ones. It has been common practice, perhaps especially at the provincial level and most obviously in Quebec, to create public corporations to achieve public purposes precisely because no 'indigenous' firm was available.

Quebec's former minister of finance, Jacques Parizeau, has long favoured the resale of public corporations to Quebec entrepreneurs, saying that the public-private distinction is far less important than the geographical locus of control – within what network of industrial and financial interests (and personal ties) decisions are taken. While in Parizeau's view stimulative and control-exercising bodies such as the Caisse de Depot, the Société Génerale de Financement, and the Société de Développement Industriel must remain part of the state apparatus, operating companies (except for ones central to the province's development strategy, such as Hydro Québec) are more appropriately situated in Quebec's private sector. There is clearly a (Quebec) nationalist thrust behind this thinking; it would be completely bizarre in the context of Quebec's industrial policies to suggest that the locus of ownership and control should be irrelevant to the dealings between government agencies and the private sector. But that is not to say that externally controlled or externally owned firms should be discriminated against or made to operate at a disadvantage to indigenous ones. Similarly, it would be inappropriate to argue that it is punitive or discriminatory that the Quebec Stock Savings Plan offers tax breaks to those who invest in small and medium-sized Quebec enterprises but not to investors in major Canadian firms or multinationals.

What is needed – in the Canadian just as in the Quebec context – is a policy or an integrated set of policies that offer support to domestic capital without infringing the principle of national treatment for foreign-based firms. As with the distinction between protectionism and a positive industrial policy, there is a fine line to be walked here; definitions are subjective; and conventionally acceptable practices can be identified only through an iterative process of governmental experimentation, invention, and, from the private sector and other governments, response.

3. *Is an industrial policy of the sort contemplated here feasibly implemented within the present Canadian constitution?* A policy that is non-protectionist and non-discriminatory toward foreign capital necessarily relies heavily on government incentives, a mixture of taxes and tax expenditures[30] that is constitutionally equally available to federal and provincial governments. Other relevant subjects are competition policy; banking and the regulation of non-bank financial institutions and of securities markets; product standard laws; environmental protection policies; control of both renewable and non-renewable resource production and marketing; and labour law. As earlier chapters have shown, all these are areas in which both orders of government have either concurrent or exclusive powers that can be used to complement or to counteract policy initiatives at the other level. In several areas, notably competition policy and policies toward financial institutions, conventions have arisen about respective federal and provincial roles that could be challenged by new policy initiatives, especially federal ones. In other words, significant changes in de facto constitutional responsibilities could be brought about without formal amendment.

At present both orders of government engage in a wide range of activities lying within the scope of an industrial policy, though frequently these activities are only weakly co-ordinated even within individual governments. Perhaps what is most at issue is whether the federal system permits coherence if the central government should decide to take the initiative. Interprovincial co-operation does have potential for some policy co-ordination, but the reasons earlier identified for Ottawa's playing the key role are, to my way of thinking, conclusive. The main question, then, is whether the provinces can be recruited as willing partners in a joint enterprise, both federal-provincial and public-private. If the two orders of government are adversaries, the federal authorities have (in most cases) the superior range of constitutional powers, but their capacity to draw upon these powers to override provincial action is necessarily limited by public opinion. Moreover, public tolerance for federal-provincial infighting has worn thin, and, while a cause célèbre could rally regional opinion in support of provincial powers, co-operative action is far preferred and, by any disinterested appraisal, far preferable. Thus an inquiry into preconditions for the interventionist-nationalist option needs to focus more on the political angle than on the 'black-letter' law of the constitution.

4. *Does the idea of a national industrial policy have enough public support to make the interventionist-nationalist option practical?* Obviously, this question cannot be answered except in the context of a specific set of policies or a development strategy implicit in them. Perhaps, then, the better question to ask is: *Is it possible to design a national industrial policy that the provinces could be persuaded to help implement through a set of complementary policies?* To do so is a delicate balancing act. Sectoral and regional interests that are in conflict when issues are taken one at a time must be reconciled through a process that combines them within a single package acceptable across the country. Many people are sceptical that such a package can be put together or that, if the attempt is made, the results can be anything but a rationalization of the regional interests of south-central Canada, especially southern Ontario. Past experience would seem to justify this point of view; the history of the national policy of 1879, as well as recent attempts to revive the concept in a new form, do much to explain the strong degree of support for a neutral, framework-type federal policy together with some degree of provincial interventionism, as endorsed by the Macdonald Commission.

Previous sections of this chapter have, however, identified important respects in which the constitutional and political preconditions for the liberal-continentalist and interventionist-provincialist options appear to be lacking and have identified the shortcomings of these options in terms of their probable political and constitutional consequences. These failings point to the necessity of making an effort to rehabilitate and reconstruct the concept of a national policy on a new basis that is regionally non-discriminatory. Given the regional diversity of the Canadian economy and the strength of provincially focused political loyalties (which in the case of Quebec are bound up in a still-persisting ethnic nationalism), the task of devising a politically feasible interventionist-nationalist policy is daunting; but there seems to be no option but to try.

The 'new' policy would necessarily look familiar in several respects. It would have to protect, develop, and enhance the renewable resource base: forests, agricultural land, and fisheries. It would continue to support major projects in the non-renewable resources sector, and perhaps in hydroelectricity development. It would acknowledge continued federal responsibility for aspects of manpower training and income security, ideally (as the Macdonald Commission has proposed) redesigning them with a view to facilitating industrial adjustment. Public subsidy or provision of infrastructure, as in the case of transportation systems, would continue.

Even within these traditional elements of federal policy there is considerable room for innovation; but the main strategic choice, suggesting new policy directions, would be to design a minimally protectionist industrial policy and to complement it with a policy that underwrites – to the extent that the fiscal resources of the federal government allow – the risks involved in resource development. The net regional impact would be to remove the central Canadian bias of recent policies. This would be done partly by reducing the cost (both to government and to the consumer) of policies to strengthen the manufacturing and service sectors and partly by stabilizing the economies of those areas heavily dependent upon a narrow resource base. Of course these things will not be easy to do. They are inherently difficult, in the problem-solving or policy design sense; and, in addition, one cannot sensibly ask any elected government to turn its back on the most populous region of the country. Thus the new policies must serve the interests of central Canada no less well than did the old ones but not in a way that subordinates the interests of the rest of the country to those of southern Ontario and Quebec.

An industrial policy, implemented through a combination of tax measures, public expenditures, and regulation, cannot be costless, but if it succeeds in reducing unemployment it will pay for itself through reduced social expenditures. Moreover, only if there are strong manufacturing and service sectors can the federal government put into place an effective insurance policy for the resource industries. If the federal government makes clear that these are the goals it is aiming for, an industrial policy credibly adapted toward these ends would have ample support among the public, among relevant interest organizations, and among provincial governments.

5. *If a minimally protectionist, regionally non-discriminatory industrial policy is devised, what effect would its implementation have on the Canadian federal system?* Even an industrial policy enjoying widespread support would necessarily contain elements that produce dissatisfaction. The compromises and counter-balancing features built into it would have to be worked out through the patterns of federal-provincial interaction that are already familiar to Canadians. While one would hope for less of the aggressive unilateralism, or policy-making by a process of thrust and riposte,[29] than has often occurred in the past, it would be vain to expect that federal-provincial agreement could always be accomplished simply by talking things out. Bargaining processes take place within a context of power relations, which in the case at hand are configured by the constitutional allocation of powers, by the fiscal resources available to the various governments, and by patterns of public opinion. Successful implementation of an industrial policy under federal leadership would require astute management by Ottawa of its relations with the provinces, with careful attention being paid to factors capable of strengthening its strategic position.

In the process of implementing national policies for economic development, there would inevitably occur changes in the de facto roles of federal and provincial governments, presumably without formal changes in the constitution. The direction of change would be toward expansion of federal power, or at least toward extension of the federal government's capacity to shape policies jointly implemented with the provinces. This would not, as some provincial spokesmen have alleged is the historical pattern, turn the provinces into administrative agencies of the federal government, because they would have sufficient bargaining power to affect the overall policy design. The guarantee of this is their retention of important constitutional powers, enabling them to counteract or to diminish the effectiveness of federal initiatives if their substance or direction is unacceptable. Thus the federal government has incentives to accommodate the provinces, as they have reason to co-operate with the federal government in a joint enterprise for national and regional development. Such an enterprise is a far stronger basis for Canadian unity than mere avoidance of conflict, and its undertaking would do much to strengthen the fabric of the nation.

Notes

CHAPTER ONE: PROVINCIAL ALLIANCES

1 The policy or policies designated by this phrase are identified later in this chapter. The term is not used in the sense in which it has been employed (unfortunately, in my opinion, since it falsely implies an analogy with the original national policy) by Donald V. Smiley. See his 'A Dangerous Deed: The Constitution Act, 1982' in Keith Banting and Richard Simeon, *And No One Cheered: Federalism, Democracy and the Constitution Act* (Toronto: Methuen 1983).
2 See Royal Commission on the Economic Union and Development Prospects for Canada, *Report*, 3 vols (Ottawa: Minister of Supply and Services 1985).
3 W.A. Mackintosh, 'Economic Factors in Canadian History' [1923], in W.T. Easterbrook and M.H. Watkins eds, *Approaches to Canadian Economic History* (Toronto: Macmillan 1978), 15
4 B.S. Kierstead, 'National Policy,' in Alexander Brady and F.R. Scott eds, *Canada after the War* (Toronto: Macmillan 1943), 19
5 V.C. Fowke, 'The National Policy – Old and New' [1952], in Easterbrook and Watkins, *Approaches*, 247ff
6 Donald V. Smiley, 'Canada and the Quest for a National Policy,' *Canadian Journal of Political Science*, 8:1 (March 1975), 55-6
7 *Ibid.*, 58-9
8 *Ibid.*, 55
9 *Ibid.*, 56
10 A high price not only provides more incentive to find new pools but also justifies the use of more sophisticated recovery techniques, which increase production from earlier discoveries. The percentage of oil that is recoverable from a known reservoir depends very much on the geological characteristics of that particular field. It is therefore difficult to generalize about the productive capacity of oil fields. However, in an 'average' field, simple pumping and pressure maintenance methods may extract about 30 per cent of the oil actually contained in the porous rock, which is like

a hard sponge. The use of solvents, heat, etc (tertiary or enhanced recovery schemes, some now only in the experimental stage) may in some cases nearly double this percentage. But tertiary methods are costly. Thus the eventual output from a reservoir will depend to a large degree on the current price of oil.

11 I am grateful to Craig Flood for this suggestion.

12 For a description, see John Richards and Larry Pratt, *Prairie Capitalism: Power and Influence in the New West* (Toronto: McClelland and Stewart 1979), chapters 7 and 9.

13 The PQ's economic development strategy was set out in two documents published under the authority of Bernard Landry, Ministre d'Etat au Développement économique: *Bâtir le Québec, Enoncé de politique économique, synthèse, orientations, et actions* (1979) and *Le Virage technologique, Bâtir le Québec, Phase 2: Programme d'action économique 1982-1986* (1982).

14 *Bâtir le Québec*, 125

15 For an insiders' account of these events, see Roy Romanow, John Whyte, and Howard Leeson, *Canada ... Notwithstanding: The Making of the Constitution 1976-1982* (Toronto: Carswell/Methuen 1984).

16 Government of Canada, *Economic Development for Canada in the 1980s* [budget paper], November 1981, 2

17 *Ibid.*

18 *Ibid.*, 5

19 Macdonald report, III, 562, 562-3, 563

20 *Ibid.*, I, xii, 50

21 *Ibid.*, I, 60; III, 133; II, 617

22 Peter M. Leslie, 'The State of the Federation 1985,' in Peter M. Leslie ed, *Canada: The State of the Federation* (Kingston, Ontario: Institute of Intergovernmental Relations 1985), 14-15

CHAPTER TWO: WHY THE CONSTITUTION MATTERS

1 Frederick J. Fletcher, 'Public Attitudes and Alternative Futures,' in Richard Simeon ed, *Must Canada Fail?* (Montreal: McGill-Queen's University Press 1977), 36

2 Albert Breton and Anthony Scott, *The Economic Constitution of Federal States* (Toronto: University of Toronto Press 1978), 262

3 *Ibid.*, 39-41. Anthony Scott, 'An Economic Approach to the Federal Structure,' in *Options: Proceedings of the Conference on the Future of the Canadian Federation* (Toronto: University of Toronto 1977)

4 Scott, 'An Economic Approach,' 268

5 Peter Lougheed, 'Address by Premier Peter Lougheed at the Progressive Conservative Conference on March 26, 1977 – MacDonald Hotel (Edmonton)' (press release)

6 Harold L. Wilensky, *The Welfare State and Equality* (Berkeley: University of California Press 1975), 52

7 Donald C. Creighton, *The Commercial Empire of the St. Lawrence* (Toronto: Macmillan 1935). The substance of this sentence is considerably expanded in chapter 8 of this book.

CHAPTER THREE: EXPLAINING PUBLIC POLICY

1 Marcel Proust, *The Remembrance of Things Past. Swann's Way. Part Two*, trans C.K. Scott Moncrieff (London: Chatto and Windus 1951), 68-9
2 Ernest Nagel, *The Structure of Science, Problems in the Logic of Scientific Explanation* (New York: Harcourt-Brace and World [1961]), 30-2, 547-51
3 The academic literature on policy formation and factors relevant to it is voluminous, and I do not intend to embark upon a general review. The following are useful critical surveys: Richard Simeon, 'Studying Public Policy,' *Canadian Journal of Political Science*, 9:4 (December 1976), 548-80; R.F.I. Smith, 'Public Policy and Political Choice,' *Australian Journal of Public Administration*, 36:3 (Sept. 1977), 258-73; Roy A. Speckhard, 'Public Policy Studies: Coming to Terms with Reality,' *Polity*, 14:3 (Spring 1982), 501-17; A.P. Pross, 'From System to Serendipity – The Practice and Study of Public Policy in the Trudeau Years,' *Canadian Public Administration*, 25:4, 520-44. My intention here is much less ambitious than these authors'. The present chapter may be considered (apart from its political character, to which I have already confessed) a response to the not uncommon tendency among Canadians to attribute policy failures to the complications of working a federal constitution.
4 C. Wright Mills, *The Power Elite* (New York: Oxford University Press 1959)
5 Pierre Elliot Trudeau, 'The Practice and Theory of Federalism,' in his *Federalism and the French Canadians* (Toronto: Macmillan 1968), 124-50
6 Donald V. Smiley, 'An Outsider's Observations of Federal-Provincial Relations among Consenting Adults,' in Richard Simeon ed, *Confrontation and Collaboration – Intergovernmental Relations in Canada Today* (Toronto: Institute of Public Administration of Canada 1979), 108-9
7 Alan C. Cairns, 'The Governments and Societies of Canadian Federalism,' in *Canadian Journal of Political Science*, 10:4 (December 1977), 696-725
8 Garth Stevenson, 'Federalism and the Political Economy of the Canadian State,' in Leo Panitch ed, *The Canadian State: Political Economy and Political Power* (Toronto: University of Toronto Press 1977), 71-100
9 J.A. Corry, 'Constitutional Trends and Federalism,' in A.R.M. Lower, F.R. Scott, et al, *Evolving Canadian Federalism* (Durham, NC: Duke University Press 1958), 95-125
10 David M. Cameron, 'Whither Canadian Federalism? The Challenge of Regional Diversity and Maturity,' in J. Peter Meekison ed, *Canadian Federalism: Myth or Reality*, 3rd edition (Toronto: Methuen 1977), 304-24
11 Cairns, 'Governments and Societies of Canadian Federalism'

CHAPTER FOUR: ENTANGLEMENT

1 Albert Breton and Anthony Scott, *The Economic Constitution of Federal States* (Toronto: University of Toronto Press 1978). For a discussion, see chapter 2 (above).
2 Donald V. Smiley, *Canada in Question: Federalism in the Eighties*, 3rd edition (Toronto: McGraw-Hill Ryerson 1980), 91-119
3 The allusion here is to K.C. Wheare, who writes: 'Does a system of government

embody predominantly a division of powers between general and regional authorities, each of which, in its own sphere, is co-ordinate with the others and independent of them? If so, that government is federal.' See his *Federal Government*, 4th edition (London: Oxford University Press 1963), 33.

4 J.A. Corry, 'Constitutional Trends and Federalism,' in A.R.M. Lower, F.R. Scott, et al, *Evolving Canadian Federalism* (Durham, NC: Duke University Press 1958), 95-125

5 Paul Weiler, *In the Last Resort* (Toronto: Carswell 1974), 167

6 Canada, Senate, *Report Pursuant to Resolution of the Senate to the Honourable the Speaker by the Parliamentary Counsel Relating to the Enactment of the British North America Act, 1867* ... Parliamentary Counsel of the Senate, William F. O'Connor (Ottawa: Queen's Printer 1961 [1940]), 48-9, 48

7 William R. Lederman, 'Classification of Laws and the British North America Act,' in William R. Lederman ed, *The Courts and the Canadian Constitution* (Toronto: McClelland and Stewart 1964), 184-5

8 Canada, Privy Council Office, *Constitutional Conference Proceedings*, Third Meeting, Ottawa, 8-10 December 1969, 83-5

9 Lederman, 'Classification of Laws,' 190

10 Weiler, *In the Last Resort*, 168

11 *Ibid.*, 173, 177

12 William R. Lederman, 'The Concurrent Operation of Federal and Provincial Laws in Canada,' in Lederman ed, *The Courts and the Canadian Constitution*, 201

13 *Ibid.*, 207-10

14 *Canada Supreme Court Reports*, 1976, v. 2, 452, 458

15 Donald V. Smiley, *Canada in Question*, 49-52

16 *Revised Statutes of Canada 1970*, v. 5, chapter M-8, s. 4 (pp. 5025-6). David C. Hawkes and Bruce Pollard, 'The Medicare Debate in Canada: The Politics of the New Federalism,' *Publius: The Journal of Federalism*, 14:3 (Summer 1984), 183-98

17 William R. Lederman, 'The Constitution: A Basis for Bargaining' [1976], in W.R. Lederman, *Continuing Canadian Constitutional Dilemmas* (Toronto: Butterworths 1981), 366-73

CHAPTER FIVE: GOVERNMENT INTERACTION

1 The literature on the processes of government interaction in policy formation is growing apace. Some of it focuses on styles of interaction and the wide range of factors affecting the behaviour of negotiators of interprovincial agreements; the outstanding example is Richard Simeon, *Federal-Provincial Diplomacy* (Toronto: University of Toronto Press 1972). Early examples of other studies are those of R.M. Burns (Institute of Intergovernmental Relations, Queen's University [R.M. Burns], *Report: Intergovernmental Liaison on Fiscal and Intergovernmental Matters* [Ottawa: Queen's Printer 1969]) and Gérard Veilleux (*Les Rélations inter-gouvernementales au Canada, 1867-1967; les mécanismes de coopération* [Montreal: Les Presses de l'Université de Montréal 1971]. For an update and summary, see 'The Evolution of Machinery for Intergovernmental Relations,' in Richard Simeon ed, *Confrontation and Collaboration: Intergovernmental Relations in Canada Today*

[Toronto: Institute of Public Administration of Canada 1979].) Burns and Veilleux deal with availability of suitable machinery for intergovernmental liaison, frequency of meetings, and the increasing complexity of informal communication networks among officials.

Much of this burgeoning literature reflects the authors' concern with the impact of decision-making processes on substantive policy outcomes. Individual studies dwell on specific aspects of the topic. Thus Douglas Brown and Julia Eastman with Ian Robinson, *The Limits of Consultation: A Debate among Ottawa, the Provinces and the Private Sector on an Industrial Strategy*, Discussion paper of the Institute of Intergovernmental Relations, Queen's University, Prepared for the Science Council of Canada (Ottawa: Science Council of Canada 1981), have focused on the degree of co-ordination that governments are capable of achieving in formation of economic policy. Anthony Careless, *Initiative and Response: The Adaptation of Canadian Federalism to Regional Economic Development* (Montreal: Institute of Public Administration of Canada and McGill-Queen's University Press 1977), and Donald J. Savoie, *Federal-Provincial Collaboration: The Canada–New Brunswick General Development Agreement* (Montreal: Institute of Public Administration of Canada and McGill-Queen's University Press 1981), have both treated in detail an aspect of the same subject, focusing on relations among officials in the formulation of regional development policy. An interesting complement and corrective to these studies is provided by Allan Tupper, *Public Money in the Private Sector: Industrial Assistance Policy and Canadian Federalism*, Queen's Studies on the Future of the Canadian Communities (Kingston, Ontario: Institute of Intergovernmental Relations, Queen's University 1982), who surveys industrial assistance policies and the conflicts (interprovincial as well as federal-provincial) that they frequently engender. Timothy B. Woolstencroft, 'Organizing Intergovernmental Relations,' Discussion Paper 12 (Kingston, Ontario: Institute of Intergovernmental Relations, Queen's University 1982), effectively countering a hypothesis put forward by Donald V. Smiley, 'An Outsider's Observations of Federal-Provincial Relations among Consenting Adults,' in Richard Simeon ed, *Confrontation and Collaboration*, 113-14, suggests that creation of ministries or other agencies for overseeing intergovernmental affairs may promote harmony and effective collaborative action among governments. Albert Breton and Anthony Scott, *The Economic Constitution of Federal States* (Toronto: University of Toronto Press 1978) raise the question of the administrative costs entailed by the need to co-ordinate the actions of several governments. And Smiley, 'An Outsider's Observations,' and Alan C. Cairns, 'The Other Crisis of Canadian Federalism,' *Canadian Public Administration*, 22:2 (Summer 1979), 184-5, picking up on the concerns of many parliamentarians over the past two decades and more, have explored the relation between 'executive federalism' and the capacity of the electorate, through Parliament and provincial legislatures, to exercise democratic control over government decisions.

2 S.E. Finer, *Comparative Government* (London: Allen Lane The Penguin Press 1970), 7-8
3 R.D. Brown, 'The Fight over Resource Profits,' *Canadian Tax Journal*, 22 (1974), 317
4 *Ibid.*, 321
5 Alan C. Cairns, 'The Governments and Societies of Canadian Federalism,' in

Canadian Journal of Political Science, 10:4 (December 1977), 695-726; Richard Simeon, 'Regionalism and Canadian Political Institutions,' in J. Peter Meekison ed, *Canadian Federalism: Myth or Reality*, 3rd edition (Toronto: Methuen 1977), 292-304

6 H. Ian Macdonald, 'Economic Policy: Can We Manage the Economy Any More?,' *Canadian Public Policy*, 2:4 (Autumn 1976), 554

7 Canada, Federal-Provincial Relations Office, *Federal-Provincial Programs and Activities: A Descriptive Inventory 1984-1985* (Ottawa: Minister of Supply and Services 1985)

8 For a review of the act, see Grace Skogstad, 'The Farm Products Marketing Agencies Act: A Case Study of Agricultural Policy,' *Canadian Public Policy*, 6:1 (Winter 1980), 89-100.

9 Gunter Kisker, 'Unitarian and Cooperative Federalism: A Changing Concept of Federalism in Western Germany?,' mimeo, presented to a Twinned Workshop on Federalism, sponsored by the Canadian Political Science Association and the European Consortium for Political Research, Queen's University, August 1977

10 G. Campbell Sharman, 'The Courts and the Governmental Process in Canada,' unpublished PH D thesis, Queen's University, 1972. Note, for example, at 213: 'The judiciary has been moulded to reflect regional diversity through the dominant role that the provincial executive plays in controlling access to the judicial process over a wide range of social activity. This has resulted in a large measure of congruence between the operation of the courts and the priorities of the provincial government. This extends not only over the legislative jurisdictions of the provinces, but also over much of the criminal law, the legislative responsibility of the central government.'

11 See John D. Whyte, 'Federal-Provincial Tensions in the Administration of Justice,' in Peter M. Leslie ed, *Canada: The State of the Federation* (Kingston, Ontario: Institute of Intergovernmental Relations 1985), 173-91.

12 W.R. Lederman, 'The Concurrent Operation of Federal and Provincial Laws in Canada,' *McGill Law Journal*, 9 (1962-3), 185-99, especially 192

13 Nicholas R. Sidor, *Consumer Policy in the Canadian Federal State* (Kingston, Ontario: Institute of Intergovernmental Relations 1984), 34-8, 56-62

14 Gerhard Lehmbruch, 'Party and Federation in Germany: A Developmental Dilemma,' in *Government and Opposition*, 13:2 (Spring 1978), 170-1

15 Gordon Robertson, 'The Role of Interministerial Conferences in the Decision-Making Process,' in Simeon ed, *Confrontation and Collaboration*, 78-88

16 Canada, [Privy Council Office?], *The Constitutional Amendment Bill, Text and Explanatory Notes* (Ottawa: Queen's Printer 1978), 21-32. Canada, Task Force on Canadian Unity, *A Future Together: Observations and Recommendations* ([Ottawa]: Minister of Supply and Services 1979), 96-9. British Columbia, *British Columbia's Constitutional Proposals, Reform of the Canadian Senate* (Paper No. 3), September 1978; Ontario, [Premier's Office], *First Report of the Advisory Committee on Confederation*, April 1978; Canadian Bar Association, Committee on the Constitution, *Towards a New Canada* ([Toronto?]: Canadian Bar Foundation 1978); Quebec Liberal Party, Constitutional Committee, *A New Canadian Federation* (Montreal: Quebec Liberal Party 1980)

17 *Canadian Forum*, 34 (December 1954), 196-7

18 M.J.C. Vile, *The Structure of American Federalism* (London: Oxford University Press 1961), 190
19 Richard Simeon, *Federal-Provincial Diplomacy: The Making of Recent Policy in Canada* (Toronto: University of Toronto Press 1972), 304
20 The term is attributed to Karl Loewenstein. See Alan C. Cairns, 'From Interstate to Intrastate Federalism in Canada,' Institute Discussion Paper 5, Institute of Inter-governmental Relations, Queen's University, 1979, 3 and passim.
21 Some readers may quarrel with this. They might note, for example, that the Quebec Liberal party's Beige Book entitled *A New Canadian Federation* (1980) proposed a clause guaranteeing free circulation of goods and capital, and the Canadian Bar Association's Committee on the Constitution (*Towards a New Canada*, 1978) not only proposed a rather stronger common market clause but also endorsed extension of federal powers in specific economic fields, such as competition policy and regulation of financial markets.

A Future Together (1979), the main report of the Task Force on Canadian Unity, contains (84-94) a rather complex statement on the division of powers that is not (contrary to a commonly held perception) uniformly decentralist in its implications. 'We have concluded,' the task force wrote, 'that there is need for a clarification and adjustment in the distribution of powers to reduce ... sources of friction and to fit more adequately the contemporary socio-economic, technological, cultural, and political realities of Canada' (85). But when it came to describing 'the essential role' for each of the two orders of government, the task force adhered quite closely to existing notions of where policy responsibilities lie. In its enumeration of the areas in which the provinces should have 'exclusive (or occasionally concurrent) jurisdiction,' the report was slightly more specific than when it listed the areas in which the central government should have 'overriding responsibility.'
22 Cairns, 'From Interstate to Intrastate Federalism in Canada,' 11
23 Gordon Robertson, 'Un sénat élu: Notre meilleur espoir d'une véritable réforme,' mimeo, presented to a colloque 'La loi constitutionnelle 1982: Un an après,' Château Frontenac, Québec, 26 March 1983
24 Cairns, 'From Interstate to Intrastate Federalism in Canada,' 21
25 Canada, Task Force on Canadian Unity, *A Future Together*, 93; Quebec Liberal Party, *A New Canadian Federation*, 66

CHAPTER SIX: (DE)CENTRALIZATION

1 Claude Morin, *Quebec versus Ottawa: The Struggle for Self-Government 1960-72* (Toronto: University of Toronto Press 1973), 134
2 Jean Chrétien, speech to the Vancouver Board of Trade, reprinted in the *Whig-Standard* (Kingston, Ontario), 28 August 1981
3 K.C. Wheare, *Federal Government*, 4th edition (London: Oxford University Press 1963)
4 Morin, *Quebec versus Ottawa*, 149, 161-2
5 W.H. Riker, 'Federalism,' in F.L. Greenstein and N.W. Polsby eds, *Handbook of Political Science* (Reading, Mass.: Addison-Wesley 1975), V, 132-3. Canadian Bar Association, Committee on the Constitution, *Towards a New Canada* ([Toronto?]: Canadian Bar Foundation 1978), 64-5

6 Richard M. Bird, *Financing Canadian Government: A Quantitative Overview* (Toronto: Canadian Tax Foundation 1979), 64

7 *Ibid.*, 67

8 M.J. Trebilcock, J.R.S. Prichard, T.J. Courchene, and J. Whalley eds, *Federalism and the Canadian Economic Union* (Toronto: University of Toronto Press for the Ontario Economic Council 1983); A.E. Safarian, *Canadian Federalism and Economic Integration*, Constitutional Study Prepared for the Government of Canada (Ottawa: Information Canada 1974); Garth Stevenson, *Unfulfilled Union* (Toronto: Macmillan 1979); R.E. Haack, D.R. Hughes, and R.G. Shapiro, *The Splintered Market: Barriers to Interprovincial Trade in Canadian Agriculture* (Ottawa: Canadian Institute for Economic Policy 1981).

On quantitative impact, see John Whalley, 'Induced Distortions of Interprovincial Activity: An Overview of the Issues,' in Trebilcock et al eds, *Federalism and the Canadian Economic Union*, 161-200. See also Royal Commission on the Economic Union and Development Prospects for Canada, *Report* (Ottawa: Minister of Supply and Services 1985), III, 120; but contrast the commission's remark: 'Some intervenors claimed that it sometimes seemed easier to develop foreign markets than those in Canada ... Research to date does not tell us whether existing barriers have kept firms smaller and less efficient than they would otherwise have been, although logic suggests that to some extent this must indeed be so' (III, 134). In other words, estimates have failed to consider the dynamic effects of interprovincial barriers, which surely is the nub of the matter. For more on this issue, see chapter 9, note 6, below.

Jean Chrétien, *Securing the Canadian Economic Union in the Constitution*, Discussion Paper published by the Government of Canada ([Ottawa]: Minister of Supply and Services 1980), Annex A.

For an interesting exposition of interprovincial conflicts arising from procurement policies, see Allan Tupper, *Public Money in the Private Sector* (Kingston, Ontario: Institute of Intergovernmental Relations, Queen's University 1982).

9 Edwin R. Black, *Divided Loyalties: Canadian Concepts of Federalism* (Montreal: McGill-Queen's University Press 1975), 83

10 Donald J. Savoie, *Federal-Provincial Collaboration: The Canada–New Brunswick General Development Agreement* (Montreal: Institute of Public Administration of Canada and McGill-Queen's University Press 1981), 4, 17, 160-1

11 For a brief description, see Donald J. Savoie, *Regional Economic Development: Canada's Search for Solutions* (Toronto: University of Toronto Press 1986), 80-6. I am grateful to David Hawkes for insights on the working relationships between orders of government in relation to the ERDAS.

12 Savoie, *Federal-Provincial Collaboration*, 57

13 Anthony Careless, *Initiative and Response: The Adaptation of Canadian Federalism to Regional Economic Development* (Montreal: Institute of Public Administration of Canada and McGill-Queen's University Press 1977), 195-6

14 Western Premiers, Task Force on Constitutional Trends, *Third Report*, 1979, 10

15 *Ibid.*, 10

16 This is a judgment not on their importance, only on their bearing on this particular part of the argument. Some of the 19 have to do with duplication of provincial services; some are revenue or property disputes or grievances about federal actions placing a

potential financial burden on the provincial treasury; and some have to do with administration of justice (jurisdiction of the Federal Court of Canada relative to that of provincial high courts and courts of appeal, prosecutorial authority, and federal involvement in court challenges to the scope of provincial powers under the constitution).

17 Western Premiers, *Third Report*, 26, 27
18 A.E. Dal Grauer, 'The Export of Electricity from Canada,' in R.M. Clark ed, *Canadian Issues: Essays in Honour of Henry F. Angus* (Toronto: University of Toronto Press 1961), 248-85; Neil A. Swainson, *Conflict over the Columbia: The Canadian Background to an Historic Treaty* (Montreal: McGill-Queen's University Press 1979), 31-2, 193-4, 204-52, 310-15
19 Western Premiers, *Third Report*, 17
20 *Ibid.*, 18
21 *Ibid.*, 17
22 *Ibid.*
23 Quebec Liberal Party, Constitutional Committee, *A New Canadian Federation* (Montreal: Quebec Liberal Party, 1980), 63

CHAPTER SEVEN: (DE)CENTRALIZATION AND INTERREGIONAL CONFLICT

1 Canada, Task Force on Canadian Unity, *A Future Together: Observations and Recommendations* ([Ottawa]: Minister of Supply and Services 1979), 67, 69-70
2 James Alexander Corry, *Democratic Government and Politics*, 2nd edition (Toronto: University of Toronto Press 1951), 591
3 Richard Simeon, 'Regionalism and Canadian Political Institutions,' in J. Peter Meekison ed, *Canadian Federalism: Myth or Reality*, 3rd edition (Toronto: Methuen 1977), 301
4 Jack Mintz and Richard Simeon, 'Conflict of Taste and Conflict of Claim in Federal Countries,' Institute Discussion Paper 13 (Kingston, Ontario: Institute of Inter-governmental Relations 1982), 2, 4-5
5 *Ibid.*, 25-7
6 *Ibid.*, 1
7 For a good account of these events and an analysis of the political forces relevant to the outcome, see Bruce Pollard, *The Year in Review 1983: Intergovernmental Relations in Canada* (Kingston, Ontario: Institute of Intergovernmental Relations 1984), 105-22.
8 Glen Williams, *Not for Export: Toward a Political Economy of Canada's Arrested Industrialization* (Toronto: McClelland and Stewart, 1983). See especially chapter 2.
9 Raymond Hudon, 'De la gérance de l'intégration continentale au redéploiement de l'économie canadienne: Politiques économiques et constitutionnelles des années soixante dix au Canada,' PH D thesis, Queen's University, 1981
10 Conversation with the author
11 'Statement by Premier Lougheed,' Presented to the Western Economic Opportunities Conference, Calgary, 25 July 1973
12 *Transportation*, a position paper jointly submitted by the premiers of Saskatchewan,

British Columbia, Manitoba, and Alberta to the Western Economic Opportunities Conference, Calgary, 24-26 July 1973

13 This issue arose in the Canadian Industrial Gas and Oil Limited (CIGOL) case, 1978, in which the Supreme Court ruled that Saskatchewan production taxes were indirect and consequently *ultra vires*. Critics of the decision wondered why, if the tax was indirect (i.e. ultimately paid by persons other than the firm[s] from which it was collected), the Supreme Court ordered Saskatchewan to reimburse CIGOL.

14 [Canada], Royal Commission on Bilingualism and Biculturalism, *A Preliminary Report* (Ottawa: Queen's Printer 1965), 135

15 Albert Breton, 'The Economics of Nationalism,' *Journal of Political Economy*, 72 (1964), 376-86

16 Mintz and Simeon, 'Conflict of Taste,' 27

17 Judith Maxwell and Caroline Pestieau, *Economic Realities of Contemporary Confederation* (Montreal: C.D. Howe Research Institute 1980), 15

18 Alan C. Cairns, 'The Governments and Societies of Canadian Federalism,' *Canadian Journal of Political Science*, 10:4 (December 1977)

19 Ontario Budget, 31 March 1970, 65, 74, 79

20 Keith Banting, *The Welfare State and Canadian Federalism* (Kingston and Montreal: McGill-Queen's University Press 1982), 54-7

21 *Ibid.*, 175-6

22 *Ibid.*, 179

23 Mintz and Simeon, 'Conflict of Taste,' 5

24 David Kwavnick ed, *The Tremblay Report* (Toronto: McClelland and Stewart 1973), 32, 58

25 Herschel Hardin, *A Nation Unaware: The Canadian Economic Culture* (Vancouver: J.J. Douglas Ltd. 1974), 9

26 Peter M. Leslie, *Canadian Universities 1980 and Beyond: Structure, Enrolments, and Finance* (Ottawa: Association of Universities and Colleges of Canada 1980)

27 Maxwell and Pestieau, 'Economic Realities,' 22

CHAPTER EIGHT: ECONOMIC ARGUMENTS

1 Canada, Royal Commission on the Economic Union and Development Prospects for Canada, Report, 3 vols. (Ottawa: Minister of Supply and Services 1985)

2 Canada, Task Force on Canadian Unity, *A Future Together: Observations and Recommendations* ([Ottawa]: Minister of Supply and Services 1979), 67

3 The Business Council on National Issues, the Canadian Manufacturers' Association, and the Canadian Chamber of Commerce have all issued statements supporting negotiation of a free trade agreement with the United States. See Peter M. Leslie, 'The State of the Federation 1985,' in Peter M. Leslie ed, *Canada: The State of the Federation 1985* (Kingston, Ontario: Institute of Intergovernmental Relations 1985), 14.

4 The distinction that I make here between negative and positive integration follows that introduced by J. Tinbergen. See his *International Economic Integration* (Amsterdam: Elsevier 1954), 117-22.

5 The typology employed here is an adaptation of Balassa's classic list of five

consecutive stages of economic integration: free trade area, customs union, common market, economic union, and total economic integration. In this typology, an economic union is a common market 'with some degree of harmonization of economic policies, in order to remove discrimination that was due to disparities in these policies'; and total economic integration implies policy-making by a central political authority. See Bela Balassa, *The Theory of Economic Integration* (Homewood, Ill.: R.D. Irwin 1961), 2.

6 This argument for monetary union is important to the degree that the currencies of each member state are not tied to a medium of exchange over which the members have no control: gold, or US dollars, or a composite like SDRs (Special Drawing Rights at the International Monetary Fund). Otherwise, the justification for monetary union is derived not from reduction of market imperfections but from arguments supporting state intervention in the economy, e.g. for purposes of stabilization (control of inflation and maintenance of high employment rates).

7 I am grateful to Bernard Bonin and to Ivan Bernier for discussions on this subject.

8 The point is not that integration produces economic benefits against which must be weighed a political or social cost. Rather, on the economic side alone, benefits of market integration (more efficient allocation of resources) may to some extent be counterbalanced by the loss of advantages that might be achieved through various forms of government intervention in the market. In other words, the theory of negative or market integration is of limited application. See Jacques Pelkmans, 'Economic Theories of Integration Revisited,' *Journal of Common Market Studies*, 18:4 (June 1980), 333-54.

9 In the course of constitutional negotiations during the summer of 1980, there was considerable provincial opposition to strengthening the terms of section 121 of the BNA Act, which stipulates that each province's goods shall be 'admitted freely' into each of the other provinces. The federal government sought to extend this clause to cover also services and capital, whose free movement would consequently be enforceable through the courts. Several provinces objected to this. However, they showed themselves much more receptive to such a 'common market clause' if a political enforcement mechanism were to be established. Alternative enforcement mechanisms also discussed were an interprovincial council and a reconstituted second chamber with provincial delegates. The principle of non-discrimination was reportedly agreed upon by all governments, provided there was a flexible enforcement mechanism, having authority to permit derogations from common market principles.

10 Jean Chrétien, *Securing the Canadian Economic Union in the Constitution*, Discussion paper published by the Government of Canada ([Ottawa]: Minister of Supply and Services 1980)

11 *Ibid.*, 24, 29

12 Pelkmans, 'Economic Theories of Integration Revisited,' 334-5

13 Thomas J. Courchene, 'Avenues of Adjustment: The Transfer System and Regional Disparities,' in Douglas Auld et al, *Canadian Federation at the Crossroads: The Search for a Federal-Provincial Balance* (Vancouver: Fraser Institute 1978), 145-86

14 Canada, Royal Commission on Dominion-Provincial Relations, *Report*, Book 1, *Canada: 1867-1939* (Ottawa: Queen's Printer 1954 [1940]), 20

15 Donald Creighton, *British North America at Confederation*, Study Prepared for the Royal Commission on Dominion-Provincial Relations (Ottawa: Queen's Printer 1963 [1940?]), 45

16 John Dales, *The Protective Tariff in Canada's Development* (Toronto: University of Toronto Press 1966), 154-5

17 Tom Naylor, 'The Rise and Fall of the Third Commercial Empire of the St. Lawrence,' in Gary Teeple ed, *Capitalism and the National Question in Canada* (Toronto: University of Toronto Press 1972), 15, 14, 13-14, 16

18 Glen Williams, 'The National Policy Tariffs: Industrial Underdevelopment through Import Substitution,' *Canadian Journal of Political Science*, 12:2 (June 1979), 333-68

19 Hugh G.J. Aitken, 'Defensive Expansionism: The State and Economic Growth in Canada,' in W.T. Easterbrook and M.H. Watkins eds, *Approaches to Canadian Economic History* (Toronto: McClelland and Stewart 1967 [1959]), 209

20 John Dales, *The Protective Tariff*

21 *Ibid.*, 144

22 *Ibid.*

23 H.A. Innis and W.T. Easterbrook, 'Fundamental and Historic Elements,' in John J. Deutsch et al eds, *The Canadian Economy: Selected Readings* (Toronto: Macmillan 1961), 368, 367

24 *Ibid.*,367, 364

25 Tom Naylor, *The History of Canadian Business 1867-1914*, I (Toronto: Lorimer 1975), 20-59

26 Dales, *The Protective Tariff*, 158

27 I have borrowed this phrase from E.J. Mishan, *Introduction to Political Economy* (London: Hutchinson 1982).

28 This point is discussed in chapter 9, below. Its theoretical foundation is set out in Richard G. Harris, *Trade, Industrial Policy, and International Competition*, volume 13 of the research studies for the Royal Commission on the Economic Union and Development Prospects for Canada (Toronto: University of Toronto Press 1985).

29 Philip Mathias, *Forced Growth* (Toronto: Lorimer 1971)

30 Transfer pricing is said to occur when a subsidiary pays its parent inflated prices for production goods, management services, etc, or when it charges the parent deflated prices for resource products or semi-manufactures. The intent, and effect, are to allow the multinational enterprise to take its profits in the country of its choice, whether to avoid taxation, or to repatriate profits, or for other purposes.

   Inefficient sourcing occurs when domestic suppliers are passed over in favour of foreign suppliers – either as a matter of policy or because the subsidiary is unaware of what is available on the domestic market.

   Parent controls on production and marketing decisions of subsidiaries are generally aimed at partitioning world markets to the benefit of the enterprise as a whole, though possibly to the detriment of the subsidiary.

31 Dales, *The Protective Tariff*, I, 110, 118

32 *Ibid.*, 117-22

33 *Ibid.*, 122

CHAPTER NINE: ECONOMIC POLICY

1 Canada, Royal Commission on the Economic Union and Development Prospects for Canada (Macdonald Commission), *Report*, 3 vols. (Ottawa: Minister of Supply and Services 1985)
2 *Ibid.*, I, 51
3 *Ibid.*, 60
4 *Ibid.*, II, 199, 262, 263, 616-19, 259, 381
5 *Ibid.*, I, 63
6 Jean Chrétien, *Securing the Canadian Economic Union in the Constitution*, Discussion paper published by the Government of Canada (Ottawa: Minister of Supply and Services 1980). The contents of this paper are discussed in chapter 1, above.

    John Whalley, 'Induced Distortions of Interprovincial Activity: An Overview of Issues,' in M.J. Trebilcock, J.R.S. Prichard, T.J. Courchene, and J. Whalley, *Federalism and the Canadian Economic Union* (Toronto: University of Toronto Press for the Ontario Economic Council 1983), 161-200; also Macdonald Commission, *Report*, III, 134 (a quotation is reproduced in chapter 6, note 8, above). The estimates in question do not take into account the dynamic effects of internal barriers, presumably because they are difficult or impossible to model. One suspects that, as with estimates of the costs of Quebec's possible separation from Canada, respect for methodological rigour has led economists to neglect the essence of the subject.

    Cf Sylvia Ostry, commenting on this subject as chairman of the Economic Council of Canada: 'An uneasiness that I, personally, have always felt about economic analysis of the issues at stake [the costs of Quebec's possible secession from Canada], by *anyone* – including the Economic Council – is that some of the relevant economic facts cannot be uncovered by the current tools of economic analysis .... My point is that there are *dynamic factors whose impact is both potentially large and in practice unknowable*'; Workshop on the Political Economy of Confederation, *Proceedings*, 8-10 November 1978, Institute of Intergovernmental Relations and Economic Council of Canada (Ottawa: Minister of Supply and Services 1979), xxviii.

    On the decision of the Judicial Committee of the Imperial Privy Council in the Labour Conventions Case, 1937, see Peter W. Hogg, *Constitutional Law of Canada*, 2nd edition (Toronto: Carswell 1985), 245-56.
7 Macdonald Commission, *Report*, III, 154-5
8 *Ibid.*, 563
9 *Ibid.*, 149, 150, 149
10 *Ibid.*, 198-220 (especially 215), 199, 215 (emphasis mine)
11 *Ibid.*, 217-18, 218, 219
12 *Ibid.*, 219-20
13 *Ibid.*, 220
14 John Richards and Larry Pratt, *Prairie Capitalism: Power and Influence in the New West* (Toronto: McClelland and Stewart 1979)
15 In Saskatchewan, earlier attempts to develop a manufacturing industry not based on resource production, in order to diversify the agrarian economy, had failed. The Co-operative Commonwealth Federation (CCF) government elected in 1944 neglected

important locational factors and launched enterprises unsupported by adequate managerial skills. But when mineral production – potash and uranium – made diversification of the farm economy practical, Saskatchewan, like Alberta, began successfully to develop indigenously controlled capitalist, or state capitalist, enterprise.

    Quotation: Richards and Pratt, *Prairie Capitalism*, 247

16 Kari Levitt writes: 'Political fragmentation along regional lines serves the interests of the multinational corporations ... The provinces ... reinforce the continentalism of big business by dismembering the federal structure of Canada.' See her *Silent Surrender: The Multinational Corporation in Canada* (Toronto: Macmillan 1970), 145-6. See also Garth Stevenson, *Unfulfilled Union: Canadian Federalism and National Unity*, revised edition (Toronto: Gage 1982), 228-31 and passim.

    Richards and Pratt, Prairie Capitalism, viii, 9

17 Richards and Pratt, *Prairie Capitalism*, 12. H.V. Nelles, *The Politics of Development: Forests, Mines, and Hydro-Electric Power in Ontario, 1849-1941* (Toronto: Macmillan 1974). Bruce Pollard, 'Newfoundland: Resisting Dependency,' in Peter M. Leslie ed, *Canada: The State of the Federation* 1985 (Kingston, Ontario: Institute of Intergovernmental Relations 1985), 83-117

18 Albert Breton, 'The Economics of Nationalism,' *Journal of Political Economy*, 72 (1964), 376-86

19 Richards and Pratt, *Prairie Capitalism*, 328

20 *Ibid.*, 328

21 Macdonald Commission, *Report*, III, 149

22 *Ibid.*, 186. Dales' views on this matter are summarized in chapter 8 above.

23 Macdonald Commission, *Report*, III, 562. Canada, Task Force on Industrial and Regional Benefits from Major Canadian Projects, *Major Canadian Projects, Major Canadian Opportunities* ([Ottawa: Department of Industry, Trade, and Commerce] 1981). Macdonald Commission, *Report*, II, 88

24 Macdonald Commission, *Report*, II, 182-4. Richard G. Harris, *Trade, Industrial Policy and International Competition*, volume 13 of the research studies for the Royal Commission on the Economic Union and Development Prospects for Canada (Toronto: University of Toronto Press 1985), 12-15

25 Harris, *Trade*, 11 (cf also 140), 112 (cf also 134, 151), 120-1, 151 (cf also 91: 'At present, the chance for complete free trade seems slight. Industrial subsidies and contingent protection are increasingly prevalent throughout the world. What is the optimal policy of a small open economy in these circumstances?')

26 *Ibid.*, 111. The elements proposed by Harris for an industrial policy for Canada are set out in *ibid.*, 125-43.

27 This list of the goals of economic policy includes the three welfare-increasing objectives identified in chapter 8 as forming a rationale for economic integration and adds a 'fudged' egalitarianism. The distributive justice criterion is included out of deference to Harris, who lists it together with the other three as 'the four basic economic goals of benevolent-minded policy makers' (*ibid.*, 113). Strictly speaking, though, a preferred distribution of income is not an economic objective in the sense that it contributes to aggregate welfare, since – as was pointed out in chapter 8 –

comparisons of alternative packages of goods according to a welfare criterion can be made only assuming a given distribution of income.

28 *Ibid.*, 69

29 A good survey of these issues is contained in the Gray report, *Foreign Direct Investment in Canada* (Ottawa: Information Canada 1972).

30 'Tax expenditures' are revenues forgone when rates are lowered or exemptions offered in a tax system in order to accomplish some relatively specific public purpose. Tax write-offs to encourage research and development, or exploration and development for natural resources, are examples; so is exemption of certain capital gains in the personal income tax, if it is presumed that the exemption will increase investment. Tax expenditures are difficult to estimate because the definition is rather fuzzy and because the sums involved never appear in the public accounts. Still, the term does draw attention to the fact that governments may achieve broadly comparable purposes through spending programs or through selective tax reductions; and the net effect on a government's budgetary position may be the same.

31 For a description, see chapter 5, above.

Index